DOOM TOWNS

THE PEOPLE AND LANDSCAPES OF ATOMIC TESTING

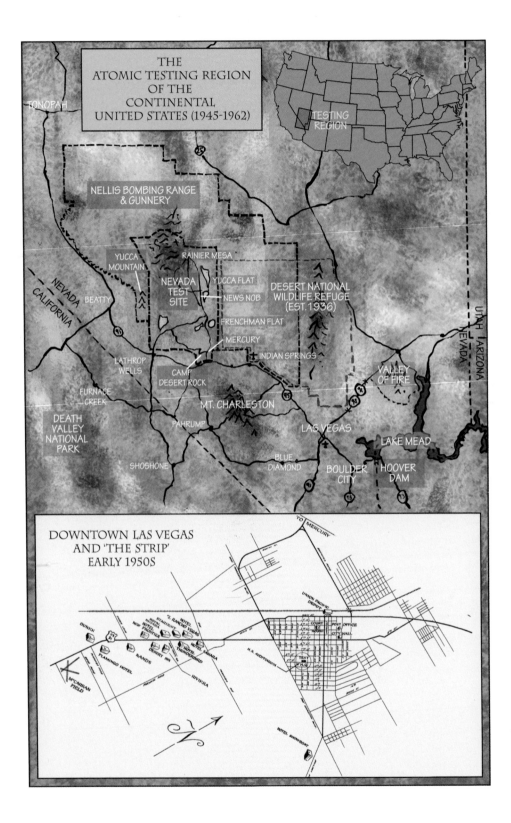

THE
ATOMIC TESTING REGION
OF THE
CONTINENTAL
UNITED STATES (1945-1962)

TESTING REGION

TONOPAH

NELLIS BOMBING RANGE
& GUNNERY

YUCCA
MOUNTAIN

RAINIER MESA

NEVADA
TEST
SITE

YUCCA FLAT

NEWS NOB

DESERT NATIONAL
WILDLIFE REFUGE
(EST. 1936)

NEVADA
CALIFORNIA

BEATTY

FRENCHMAN FLAT

MERCURY

INDIAN SPRINGS

UTAH | ARIZONA
NEVADA

LATHROP
WELLS

CAMP
DESERT ROCK

VALLEY
OF FIRE

FURNACE
CREEK

MT. CHARLESTON

DEATH
VALLEY
NATIONAL
PARK

PAHRUMP

LAS VEGAS

LAKE MEAD

SHOSHONE

BLUE
DIAMOND

BOULDER
CITY

HOOVER
DAM

DOWNTOWN LAS VEGAS
AND 'THE STRIP'
EARLY 1950S

TO MERCURY

UNION PACIFIC
DEPOT

HOTEL
EL RANCHO VEGAS

STARDUST
NEW FRONTIER
HOTEL

HOTEL
SAHARA

HOTEL
THUNDERBIRD

COURT
HOUSE

POST OFFICE
CITY HALL

DUNES

FLAMINGO HOTEL

SANDS

DESERT INN

H.S. AUDITORIUM

RIVIERA

MCCARRAN
FIELD

HOTEL SHOWBOAT

N

DOOM TOWNS

THE PEOPLE AND LANDSCAPES OF ATOMIC TESTING
A GRAPHIC HISTORY

ANDREW G. KIRK

New York   Oxford

OXFORD UNIVERSITY PRESS

Oxford University Press is a department of the University of Oxford.
It furthers the University's objective of excellence in research,
scholarship, and education by publishing worldwide.
Oxford is a registered trade mark of Oxford University Press
in the UK and certain other countries.

Published in the United States of America by
Oxford University Press
198 Madison Avenue, New York, NY 10016,
United States of America.

Library of Congress Cataloging-in-Publication Data

Names: Kirk, Andrew G., 1964- author.
Title: Doom towns : the people and landscapes of atomic testing / Andrew G. Kirk.
Description: New York : Oxford University Press, 2016. | Includes
   bibliographical references.
Identifiers: LCCN 2016015266 | ISBN 9780199375905
Subjects: LCSH: Nuclear weapons—Testing—Environmental aspects—United
   States. | United States—Military policy—Environmental aspects.
Classification: LCC U264 .K59 2016 | DDC 363.17/990973—dc23 LC record available
at https://lccn.loc.gov/2016015266

9 8 7 6 5 4 3 2 1
Printed by R.R. Donnelley, United States of America

To Lisa, Harrison, and Quinn
&
Clare, Isaac, and Dorothy

To teacher Virginia Scharff
&
in memory of Timothy Moy and Ferenc Morton Szasz

And to my father, Glenn Garrett Kirk, for faith and patience

CONTENTS

MAPS AND FIGURES

INTRODUCTION

THE ANATOMY OF AN ATOMIC TEST SITE

The time is now. You board your Nevada Nuclear Test Site (NTS) Department of Energy (DOE) tour bus just outside the entrance to the National Atomic Testing Museum in Las Vegas, Nevada. As you depart, you cross the famous Las Vegas Strip before leaving town heading north on Highway 95 once known as the "widow maker" because of the high number of fatal crashes involving sleepy workers in the dark of the desert. To the west is the spectacular escarpment of the Keystone Thrust and Red Rock National Conservation Area. On your right you can see the starkly beautiful Sheep Mountains and Nellis Air Force Base, once known as the Nevada Proving Ground. A few minutes later you pass the exit for the Desert National Wildlife Refuge (DNWR) and shortly after the entrance to Kyle Canyon and Mount Charleston looming high to your left. Eight months out of the year the 11,916-foot summit of Mount Charleston is covered with snow. Most years snow will linger in the north-facing couloirs throughout the summer with temperature differences between the valleys and the summits varying as much as sixty degrees on any given day. Dense pine forests are clearly visible throughout the Spring Mountain range as you continue north. If you turn up to Mount Charleston and drive from Kyle Canyon over to Lee Canyon, you pass an overlook where Las Vegans and reporters such as Donald English camped with thermoses of hot coffee in the cold dawn and gazed 8,000 feet down into the NTS to watch mushroom clouds rise into the atmosphere.

Farther north you pass the east entrance to the DNWR. For those who take that turn the stark, seemingly dead Sheep Mountains reveal themselves as surprisingly alive. In the desert as you gain altitude and get closer to mountains a richness of plant and animal life comes into focus. Dense groves of towering pine, quaking aspen, fields of smooth red-barked manzanita and hillsides covered with red barrel cactus are common. This,

FIG. 1 Binion's Horseshoe Club postcard with view of atomic blast captured from Mount Charleston, c. 1954. *Source:* Collection of author.

you'd think, is where I would have lived if I were an American Indian from this region hundreds of years ago—and you'd be right, because they were here and knew all of these hidden rich places for centuries and in some cases thousands of years before they were found and claimed by others. On the DOE bus you won't see these things because you are in a hurry and you can't appreciate this environment at seventy-five miles an hour. You've got to travel another forty miles up the road to take the Mercury exit and enter the security gates and officially begin your NTS tour.

As you arrive at the gates you may glimpse on your left, the Peace Camp where protesters gathered for three decades but it's harder to see than the obvious atomic village of Mercury that sits down to the right in the valley below you. And that valley is big. In fact, *big* is the word of the day. Everything about the NTS and what happened there is big, and even though you have a whole day you are barely going to scratch the surface. There is so much you won't see and so much big history behind what you will do. This book is an effort to offer a sense of that complicated history and explore some of the lingering questions surrounding the era of atomic testing, such as, how were places chosen as atomic test sites? What were the consequences of those choices for the places and people who lived there? Who lived and worked in these extraordinary experimental landscapes once they were established? What was it like?

The NTS occupies a massive swath of mountains and valleys in southern Nevada established as a bombing range in 1941. Much of the bombing range bordered the remarkable DNWR, created in 1936 in what was then

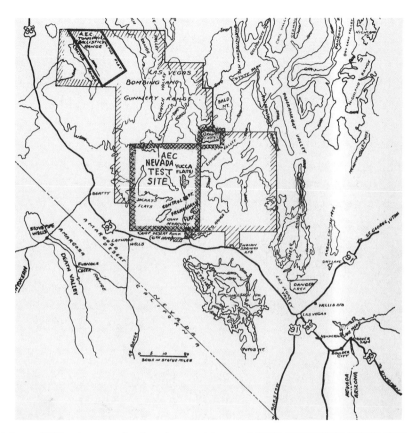

FIG. 2 Hand-drawn NTS region map distributed to participants of OPERATION PLUMBBOB 1957.
Source: William Geagley Collection on Nuclear Safety, UNLV Special Collections, MS-00792.

one of the least disturbed bighorn sheep ranges in the Southwest. The largest wildlife refuge in the lower forty-eight states at 1.6 million acres (over 2,300 square miles), the refuge is famous for its dazzling assortment of plants and creatures. In the 1960s, Los Alamos National Laboratory archaeologist Frederick Worman completed a series of studies of the nature and culture of the NTS. Working with guidelines established by the Act for the Preservation of American Antiquities (1906), Worman recorded sites and artifacts, catalogued flora and fauna, and mapped the human and natural history of the nuclear proving ground. The lab published his resulting NTS "guidebook" in 1965.[1]

---

[1]   Frederick Worman, *Anatomy of the Nevada Test Site* (Berkeley: University of California–Los Alamos Scientific Laboratory, 1965); Frederick Worman, *Archeological Investigations at the U.S. Atomic Energy Commission's Nevada Test Site and Nuclear Rocket Development Station* (Berkeley: University of California–Los Alamos Scientific Laboratory, 1969); Matthew Coolidge, *The Nevada Test Site: A Guide to America's Nuclear Proving Ground* (Los Angeles: Center for Land Use Interpretation, 1996).

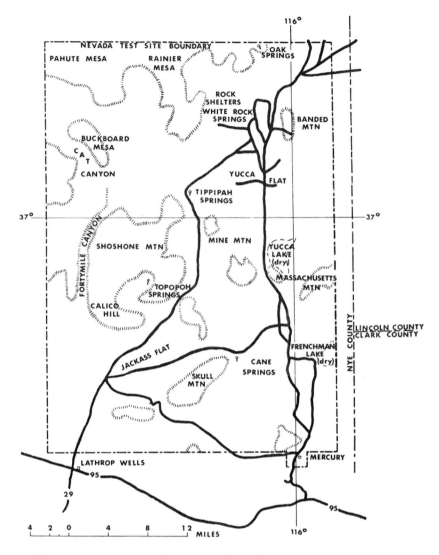

FIG. 3 Frederick Worman's 1965 map of the Nevada Test Site highlights natural and cultural features.
Source: Frederick Worman, *Anatomy of the Nevada Test Site* (Berkeley: University of California–Los Alamos Scientific Laboratory, 1965)

Anatomy of the Nevada Test Site concisely explains the geology, climatology, and biology of the testing region. The booklet includes not only illustrations of typical plants and animals but also careful descriptions of the Mojave and Great Basin environment for readers unlikely to ever to visit. "To view the blooming desert during a wet period," Worman wrote, "is to see it at its most magnificent moment. One looks out upon a myriad of flowers designed to move the amateur taxonomist to complete ecstasy which may be followed by complete despair when an attempt is made to classify them all." Extensive lists of species follow. Hundreds of birds, snakes, insects, rodents, and charismatic megafauna like big horn sheep, antelope, wild horses and burros, and mountain lion are catalogued. The region was home to the "Methuselah trees," ancient bristlecone pine trees. Among the oldest living things on Earth, some over 4,000 years old, these weather-beaten sentinels stand watch on the flanks of the high mountains surrounding the NTS. The NTS as Worman described it in 1965 at the close of the era of atmospheric atomic testing was teeming with a diversity of life and scenic beauty despite hosting over 100 above-ground nuclear explosions.

From nature, *Anatomy* turned to culture discussing the indigenous peoples, primarily Piute and Western Shoshone Indians, who lived and traveled throughout the region they called Newe Sogobia for centuries. Worman's descriptions of these regional peoples are not as thorough as his catalogue of nature. He celebrates their ability to live with the harsh demands of the Mojave and Great Basin deserts but they appear, as historian Ned Blackhawk explains of most similar accounts, only as "apparitions of humanity's distant beginnings."[2] Archeological evidence at Tippipah, White Rock, and Cain Springs suggested a persistent human presence at the NTS, as did accounts of finds by the explorers and settlers that traversed the area in the 1800s on their way to the California gold fields. Much of the evidence of human habitation of the NTS explained in *Anatomy* came from the period after the 1863 Treaty of Ruby Valley acknowledged the primacy of Western Shoshone and Southern Paiute peoples in the region but opened the door to expanded exploration and appropriation of their lands. Miners, Mormons, and ranchers lived throughout the area by the turn of the century. Worman's little booklets leave much of the history of the region untold, but even so they clearly reveal a startling, simple fact: the place that hosted the United States atomic testing program was a rich and complicated environment home to a remarkable assortment of life and a diverse group of human inhabitants who valued this landscape and knew it as home.

Touring the NTS today some areas look remarkably unchanged while others are distinctly different from the days when Worman hiked through and excavated in the early 1960s. Some of the dry desert lakebeds or *playas* are now pocked with hundreds of subsidence craters from over 800 underground tests conducted between the 1960s and early 1990s. The Sedan Crater, created as an experiment to see whether atomic bombs could be used for large-scale land excavation during PROJECT PLOWSHARE,

---

[2] Ned Blackhawk, *Violence Over the Land: Indians and Empires in the Early American West* (Cambridge, MA: Harvard University Press, 2006), 278.

FIG. 4 Stairway leading down under the desert to an underground testing complex, c. 1980. *Source:* National Atomic Testing Museum Photo Collections.

dominates this view. Visitors on the official DOE tour can stop at the rim of this quarter-mile-wide and deep crater, now listed on the National Register of Historic Places, and learn about "Atoms for Peace." Faded "RADIATION AREA" signs hanging from barbed wire mark nearby areas that remain closed to visitors for the foreseeable future. How dangerous is it to visit these places today?

Throughout the NTS, "hot spots" of lingering radiation do not permit safe passage to humans or animals even for short periods. For the few who get to go below ground, the well-preserved ruins of the second phase of atomic testing lie hidden in a labyrinth of tunnels and chambers. Down there are huge cavities that will remain highly radioactive for millennia. In each tunnel system thousands of feet of "line-of-sight pipes," used to watch and record the blasts, and millisecond-closing ten-ton vault-like containment doors to shield instruments from explosions lead to heavily sealed chambers hollowed out of solid rock by nuclear blasts. You might wonder, what does it look like inside these chambers? Will the containment systems that seal them last for the required 20,000 years or so it will take for the radioactive isotopes to fully decay? Along the sides of some of these tunnels, subterranean offices and workrooms covered with thick layers of dust

FIG. 5 (a) Ken Case, the "Atomic Cowboy," c. 1955. Source: DOE NNSA/NSO. (b) Historic American Engineering Record view of Japanese village, type B structure, facing east. Source: Library of Congress Prints and Photographs Division

are still fully furnished and frozen in time. Newspapers and coffee cups sit where they were left on abandoned desks or workstations. These seemingly hastily abandoned workplaces speak to the series of abrupt moratoriums that eventually ended nuclear testing in 1992. For the workers who built these places, the tunnels are reminders of good jobs lost, while others would see these extraordinarily vast and expensive subterranean work-scapes as evidence of waste and dangerous misjudgment.

As your tour continues through the day, you will start to appreciate the size of the NTS and wonder what it must have been like to drive these distances day after day to get to work. You may see the seven-story white test tower of Operation ICECAP standing alone in the desert perched over a 2,000-foot vertical shaft drilled straight down with a remarkable degree of precision. Cold air drifts up from the depths of the earth at the remains of this British atomic test cancelled just hours after the signing of the current nuclear test ban in 1992. Not far away are the weathered remains of a mock-Japanese village consisting of wooden buildings once fitted with rice paper windows sitting beneath the 1,527-foot-tall Bare Reactor Experiment Nevada (BREN) tower where an open nuclear reactor rained radiation down on the buildings as part of experiments to recreate the effects of radiation on civilian targets like those in Hiroshima. Most startling to those who don't know the history of testing are a row of typical American suburban houses sitting alone in vast quiet forests of Joshua trees and desert plants that have reclaimed this most disturbing experiment. Their paint is long gone due to winter winds and summer sun. Kangaroo rat nests litter their dusty corners. Steps in the hallways lead down to cool,

FIG. 6 Subsidence craters across NTS playa. *Source:* DOE NNSA/NSO.

dark basements where remains of simple home-bomb-shelter prototypes are still visible.

These haunting relics of the "Doom Towns" built in the 1950s for civil defense tests stand as clear reminders of who was in the line of atomic fire during the Cold War. Continuing your tour, you will see artifacts and structures from a farming and ranching operation. The fences, corrals, and shelters are the remains of a thirty-six-acre Environmental Protection Agency (EPA) farm that operated from 1964 to 1981 to study the effects of radiation on farm animals and agricultural products. Moving on toward the conclusion of your tour, you will encounter a very large recently secured modern facility, the entrance to the Yucca Mountain High-Level Nuclear Waste Repository. Yucca Mountain was the focus of more than two decades of intense protest and debate about the proper ways and possible places to store the remains of half a century of nuclear testing and atomic energy development. The controversy surrounding this currently dormant multi-billion-dollar facility speaks to the ongoing debates about how to manage the legacies of atomic history, a problem that will remain for distant future generations to grapple with regardless of Yucca Mountain's fate. The cultural, political, legal, and environmental inheritances of atomic testing are as complicated as the science and technologies that were tested.

THE MAKING OF DOOM TOWNS

The brief era of atmospheric atomic testing, 1946–1963, happened in the very recent past. Many of the hundreds of thousands who participated or protested are still alive and remember this history. All who lived through this period of history knew the possibility of atomic warfare as the central issue of their time. The government agencies in charge of testing released photos and films of test events by the thousands to the public and in the 1950s, invited tens of thousands to come watch in person while millions witnessed at home via the new media of television. Despite, and at times because of, this extensive official coverage, critical details of this globally significant history were shrouded in secrecy and misperception.

Researchers and students working to reveal the once-hidden histories of the atomic age face significant challenges. First, there are now millions of pages of declassified documents and sources available. Ranging from policy papers to documents related to the most complex scientific analysis, these sources are housed in byzantine government archives. Teasing specific stories out of such a vast primary archive is difficult and time consuming even for professional researchers. Many of these documents are still covered with slashes of black ink hiding once-classified sentences or whole pages from view, forcing researchers to literally read between the lines for information. A second challenge is the Cold War culture of secrecy. Atomic scientists, workers, witnesses, soldiers, and even janitors and maids were officially sworn to secrecy during the testing era. Patriotism, stoicism, and pride kept thousands of civilian testing protagonists not officially bound by secrecy equally quiet for decades. Thus the remarkable human history of life and labor in the atomic testing zones is not well known outside the communities where it all happened. Many of the participants in this history died without ever revealing their roles story or sharing their insights. Ensuring that at least some of the participants were able to share their memories and perspectives was the goal of a major oral history project launched by my university in the spring of 2004.

The Nevada Test Site Oral History Project (NTSOP) was funded by the U.S. Department of Energy and later the U.S. Department of Education. The project was designed to explore the lived experience of the U.S. continental nuclear testing region but eventually grew to include people from the Pacific test sites and with further support from the U.S. State Department, people who lived in the Soviet "Polygon" test site region near Semipalatinsk, Kazakhstan. Projects like this—collaborations between academics, institutional partners, and government sponsors—fall under the broad category of *public* or *applied* history. Unlike traditional academic historians, public historians often work in groups on projects

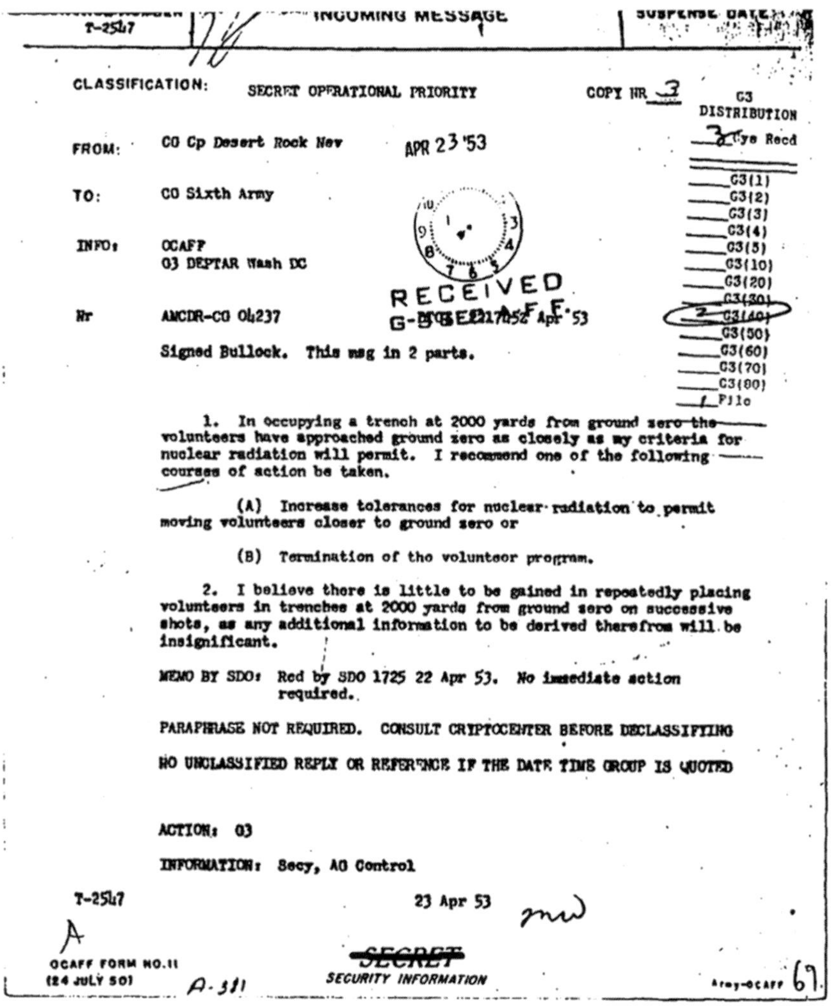

T-2547 INCOMING MESSAGE SUSPENSE DATE

CLASSIFICATION: SECRET OPERATIONAL PRIORITY COPY NR 3

G3 DISTRIBUTION

FROM: CO Cp Desert Rock Nev APR 23 '53

TO: CO Sixth Army

INFO: OCAFF
G3 DEPTAR Wash DC

RECEIVED

Nr AMCDR-CO 04237

Signed Bullock. This msg in 2 parts.

Cys Recd: G3(1), G3(2), G3(3), G3(4), G3(5), G3(10), G3(20), G3(30), G3(40), G3(50), G3(60), G3(70), G3(80), File

1. In occupying a trench at 2000 yards from ground zero the volunteers have approached ground zero as closely as my criteria for nuclear radiation will permit. I recommend one of the following courses of action be taken.

(A) Increase tolerances for nuclear radiation to permit moving volunteers closer to ground zero or

(B) Termination of the volunteer program.

2. I believe there is little to be gained in repeatedly placing volunteers in trenches at 2000 yards from ground zero on successive shots, as any additional information to be derived therefrom will be insignificant.

MEMO BY SDO: Rcd by SDO 1725 22 Apr 53. No immediate action required.

PARAPHRASE NOT REQUIRED. CONSULT CRYPTOCENTER BEFORE DECLASSIFYING

NO UNCLASSIFIED REPLY OR REFERENCE IF THE DATE TIME GROUP IS QUOTED

ACTION: G3

INFORMATION: Secy, AG Control

T-2547 23 Apr 53

OCAFF FORM NO.11 (24 JULY 50)

SECRET
SECURITY INFORMATION

FIG. 7 Example of a classified document from a report on the Camp Desert Rock volunteer program and the usefulness of testing on troops. *Source:* DOE NNSA/NSO NV0751015.

outside their universities in collaboration with the communities they study. They apply all the same high standards of academic scholarship and rigorous critical analysis of sources but also share their intellectual authority with the individuals and communities with whom they engage. Public historians also strive to make the results of their work available to a wide audience. The oral history project was designed to create an archive for scholars, students, and researchers but also to be of practical use to the wider community of testing participants whose lives were defined in some way by this complicated history. This graphic history is public history, designed to bring research insights to a broad audience, spark interest in an important subject, and open a door to a world of research possibilities for those who wish to learn more.

When this project began I had studied the history of atomic testing and knew much about the Nevada Test Site in particular, having visited on a memorable tour with some noted atomic historians when I was a graduate student at the University of New Mexico. I had also toured the Trinity Site in New Mexico, open only sixteen hours per year, and most of the other sites associated with atomic testing across the American West. But there was much I didn't know. I wasn't an expert on the science and technology of testing by any means, so with my graduate students and colleagues on the oral history project I studied the vast secondary literature of atomic history.

Early on we realized that despite a wealth of excellent scholarship on the subject, there were critical perspectives that remained hidden. The complex wonder that is the Mojave and Great Basin Desert region, for example, was rarely mentioned as anything other than a mostly empty stage for history. The hundreds of thousands of ordinary people who were neither protesters nor organizers of tests appeared usually only as statistics rather than three-dimensional people and historical actors with agency. Both of these opportunities to expand the story a little were of particular appeal to me as I had come to know both the desert and the people who lived in it as complicated subjects for study hard to reduce to just an empty stage or faceless statistic. Both the people and the place defied common expectations and stereotypes and deserved another look.

My collaborators on the oral history project, environmental sociologist Robert Futrell and noted atomic historian and oral history expert Mary Palevsky, also knew much of the history of atomic testing but shared the goal of searching for new ways to reveal the more ordinary and everyday experiences of those who had lived this history and intimately understood the environments where it happened. Mary Palevsky brought a unique perspective to our effort as a scholar of atomic history, a leading expert on the theory and method of oral history, and a daughter of two prominent atomic scientists. As a child, Palevsky encountered some of the leading figures of atomic history. Later, as an adult, she struggled to understand why her parents and their brilliant scientific community were willing to use their talents in service of the atomic military complex. She launched an oral history research project to search for answers. The result is her captivating oral history, *Atomic Fragments: A Daughter's Questions* (2000).[3]

---

[3] Mary Palevsky, *Atomic Fragments: A Daughter's Questions* (Berkeley: University of California Press, 2000); Matt Wray, "A Blast from the Past: Preserving and Interpreting the Atomic Age: The Atomic Testing Museum, The Nevada Test Site Oral History Project, The Nevada Testing Archive," *American Quarterly* 58, no. 2 (June 2006): 467–483; Nevada Test Site Oral History Project, http://digital.library.unlv.edu/ntsohp/.

FIG. 8 (a) Guard with gun on NTS boundary, 1953. Original caption reads, "The NV Proving Grounds is the most carefully guarded area of its size in the U.S." *Source:* DOE NNSA/NSO UK-53-113. (b) Burn box. Original caption reads, "All discarded papers are carefully torn into tiny pieces and put into this locked box. At the end of the day, the guards take the box into the incinerator and burn the contents. No printed matter is left in waste paper boxes, 1953." *Source:* DOE NNSA/NSO UK-53-111.

Oral history is a method of collecting historical information through recorded interviews conducted by an interviewer/researcher with an interviewee/narrator who possesses firsthand knowledge of historically significant events. The goal is to create an interview or archive of interviews that add new insights to the existing historical record. Oral history recordings and transcripts are primary sources and do not represent the final, verified, or complete narrative of the events under discussion. Rather, oral history is a spoken remembrance or dialogue, reflecting the narrator's specific questions and concerns. Oral history interviews document each interviewee's personal engagement in historical events. They are unique records, reflecting the particular meaning the interviewee draws from her/his individual life experience. Oral history alone rarely tells a complete history, but these sources offer glimpses into the emotions, motives, and thought processes of historical actors—information that is often missing from the more impersonal official documents that one might find in an archive.

As the three of us worked together to design and launch our oral history project, we wondered about the limitations of histories of secret and intentionally hidden experiences. In the case of atomic testing, the majority of people who lived and worked in and around the Nevada Test Site had signed oaths of secrecy and knew they were subject to arrest if they revealed information even to their immediate family members. Armed guards with shoot-to-kill orders patrolled the vast testing landscape, and the tense cultural climate during the atmospheric testing era ensured that confidentiality directives and threats were taken seriously. Secrecy often stifled open debate but also fostered a strong sense of shared purpose and camaraderie among most of those who spent time working at the NTS or the Pacific testing sites. Their insider knowledge of the central issue of their era, their shared experience of harshly beautiful, remote, and misunderstood environments, and their long hours and often dangerous working conditions created a strong sense of community. They thought of themselves then and now as veterans of the Cold War. Protesters and other opponents of testing obviously had a very different view of this period. We wanted to collect some of these diverse stories and share them with students, researchers, testing veterans, protesters, and the families of the participants and citizens of the testing regions. We also hoped to correct some common assumptions about regional-testing protagonists as either hapless victims or mindless supporters who simply carried out orders without thinking about what they were doing. Drawing inspiration from oral historian Allisandro Portelli's studies *The Order Has Been Carried Out* and *The Death of Luigi Trastulli*, among others, we wanted let some of these historical actors explain their own motives and understandings of why they protested or participated. Protesters, testers, downwinders, reporters, atomic military veterans, scientists, and technicians of all ranks were invited to offer their perceptions of atomic history and preserve their version of this history for future generations.

Over a period of five years, we assembled a team of talented multidisciplinary graduate students to design oral history protocols and collect these interviews. Working under the direction of Palevsky, the graduate students designed what they called a "community of voices." This consisted of eight categories of narrators: labor and support, protest and peace groups, retirees, diverse experiences, scientists and engineers, NTS administration, women and the NTS, and the military. As a digital history project from

FIG. 9 Kristian Purcell's sketch of Mary Palevsky conducting an August 2005 oral history of Shoshone spiritual leader and atomic testing protester Corbin Harney.

inception, the completed collections of interviews would live online with open access. The portal to the subject areas was brilliantly designed by our lead graduate student, Leisl Childers, to offer a nonlinear entry. The site was then brought to life and put online by our remarkable colleagues in the Lied Library, headed by digital collections director Cory Lampert. Lampert determined the metadata structure, site design, and navigation and made our ideas about open access and nonlinear navigation a reality on what became an award-winning website. On this site the story of atomic testing can be accessed through any subject or any group of narrators. This is important because we wanted to avoid a presentation of our findings that privileged one group, or one view, over another or led readers through the story in an order we chose that might inadvertently give the appearance of a hierarchy of value and importance to this contested human experience.

The result, we believed, was a primary source database of lived experience that revealed new ways to think about the history of atomic testing by experiencing voices never heard and stories never told casting the familiar big story of the science and technology of atomic testing and the Cold War in a new and more human-centered light. This archive of firsthand perspectives influenced the interpretation of atomic events in this graphic history. In some cases the interviews offered completely new ways to explain events and revealed actors previously unknown and details not in the written record. The perspectives of the oral interviewees also shaped the big story of policy. All of the narrators explained their personal stories within

FIG. 10 Dale Cox, *Mountains Seen through Test Tunnel Gates*, oil on canvas, date unknown. Source: National Atomic Testing Museum Art Collections.

this broader context and pointed to the aspects of government policy, scientific practice, and military planning that affected work on the ground and life in the region. So even the parts of the graphic history related to big policy processes and familiar historical actors reflect insights from the oral history project.

ORAL HISTORY AND GRAPHIC HISTORY

Since the publication of Art Spiegelman's landmark Pulitzer Prize–winning graphic interpretation of the Holocaust *MAUS* (1991), graphic history has gained wider acceptance as a method for presenting historical research. Many of the best graphic histories are, like *MAUS*, graphic translations of oral history. Oral history is usually transcribed into printed text so that one may read the interviews and reference specific passages easily. Researchers working on contemporary subjects often use oral history transcripts to supplement traditional sources. Since *MAUS*, authors and illustrators have also used oral history to interpret interviews through the medium of graphic sequential narratives. Emmanuel Guibert's *Alan's War* (2000), for example, beautifully demonstrated this method. Guibert used a sequential graphic format to bring his oral histories of American G.I. Alan Cope to life with a richness of detail and nuance that would have

FIG. 11 Certificate from second test series at the NTS, Buster-Jangle, in 1951. Notice the symbols along the sides that speak to rudimentary early conditions at the site. *Source:* National Atomic Testing Museum Certificates Collections.

been hard to match with text alone. Later Guibert collaborated with photojournalist Didier Lefevre and designer Frederick Lemercier to document Lefevre's experiences working with Médecins Sans Frontières (Doctors without Borders) in Afghanistan in the 1980s. Their book *The Photographer* used both oral history and documentary photographs to reveal the experiences of ordinary people caught up in extraordinary events. Filled with nuanced portraits of human experience and sophisticated understandings of historical events, these books and others like them convinced me that graphic history could be used to bring some of the perspectives of our atomic oral history project to life, adding something new to the already rich literature on atomic testing. When I explained my interests in representing atomic history in some kind of visual or graphic form to Oxford University Press editor Brian Wheel, he handed me a copy of Trevor Getz's *Abina and the Important Men*, hot off the presses. This book, along with the Oxford's subsequent graphic histories, *Mendoza the Jew* and *Inhuman Traffick*, showed exactly how graphic history works to great effect and with a high standard of scholarly rigor and research-based insight.

During the collaboration on the Nevada Test Site Oral History Project, I was fascinated by the extent to which the people who lived through and worked on atomic testing used art to record their experiences and

FIG. 12 (a) Historic image from RANGER, 1951: a photograph of the generator building, shot under high-tension wires. *Source:* Documentary photograph by W. Ogle Courtesy of Los Alamos National Laboratory, CIC-9, M-2-11. (b) Kristian Purcell's draft of same scene that appears in chapter 4.

document their labor and life. Unable to explain their work in any other way due to the restrictions of Cold War secrecy, they turned to a wide variety of forms of visual representation as a means to preserve their unique experiences. Atomic folk art created by those who lived, labored, and protested throughout the testing region captured cultural and environmental insights not found in other representations of the testing zones during the era of testing or since. This art took many forms, from formal oil paintings and carefully composed photography to model making, cartoons, drawings, sculpture, and even stained glass. Miners, engineers, and laborers who built the infrastructure of atomic testing in the desert learned the flora and fauna, geology, climate and landscape above and below ground and captured it in their art. Following military tradition, certificates, patches, stickers, and other insignia created by participants were circulated at the NTS and the Pacific Proving Grounds to personnel involved in tests. These officially sanctioned folk art souvenirs served the dual purpose of fostering a sense of exclusive community and esprit de corps while also supporting a closed culture of secrecy and silence.

The art and artifacts of the testing community led me to contemporary artists exploring the history and legacies of atomic testing in their own work. I found the paintings of British artist Kristian Purcell, who used the extensive DOE historic photo archives as the basis of his art particularly interesting. More than most of the contemporary atomic artists, Purcell focused on the people in the historic images rather than the technology or the ubiquitous mushroom clouds of atomic shots. His paintings and drawings were based on photographs but were more than reproductions: they

DOOM TOWNS
CHAPTER 4: RANGER (GRAPHIC SHEETS 41-51)

GRAPHIC SHEET NUMBER	CELL	IMAGE	TEXT	TEXT TYPE
47	1	Dorothy Grier standing with testing devices during her first months in Nevada. (Grier, Interview, 13-14. Frederick Reines, "Discussion of Radiological Hazards Associated with A Continental Test Site for Atomic Bombs, 1 August, 1950, and CONTINENTAL TEST SITE REPORT, Los Alamos National Laboratory Research Library, LAMS-1173. Environment, RANGER Operation - 1951 - Ranger construction towards Zero Point. Los Alamos National Laboratory, CIC-9, EK-M-00-10-2-3)	"One of the most interesting meetings was in August 1950, in Los Alamos during which conducting continental tests in Nevada was discussed. The things I remember most about that meeting are first, of course, the importance of all the participants, and then the talk about the prevailing winds and a meteorologist patiently explaining to someone that a northwesterly wind was from the northwest."	Bubbles
	2	Inset: Dorothy explaining her experiences during oral history interview. (Interview with Dorothy Grier, January 3, 2005, Mary Palevsky, Nevada Test Site Oral History Project, University of Nevada Las Vegas, Special Collections.)	"These were some of the most exciting and fulfilling times of my life. I worked with brilliant, stimulating people."	Oral History Box
	3	Grier at desk with co-workers the lone women in group of men (Grier Papers, NATM, O 2004.126 Box DA33)	"I went out for RANGER in January of 1951. We stayed at the Control Point, which was near Frenchman Flat. When a shot was over we'd go back to Las Vegas and stay at the Hotel Last Frontier. Las Vegas in those days had just begun to grow. I found it completely fascinating, of course."	Bubbles
	4	Last Frontier 1951 casino scene—as described (Grier, 12-15, GLADWIN HILL "ATOMIC BOOM TOWN IN THE DESERT, *The New York Times* February 11, 1951 p.158)	"When we came from the site, we'd have been up all night, we'd go sleepily through the casino to our hotel rooms, it was so amazing. Our *per diem* was six dollars a day for a hotel room (nice ones too!) and food, remember, that was 1951."	Bubbles
	5	Back out at the test site close up of Dorothy wearing dark goggles backlit by blast as she described. (RANGER Operation - 1951 - Photograph of detonation; specific test not identified. (Los Alamos National Laboratory, CIC-9, EK-M-00-10-8-10) Then out in the field looking at landscape for follow up analysis as described.	"The shots. First comes this awesome, indescribable sight, and later you feel the shock wave. And your heart starts beating again." "After the shots, we could go out into the area to see the results if radiation levels were all right."	Bubbles
	6	Desert environment with weather shown (Interview with Dorothy Grier, January 3, 2005, La Jolla, California. NTSOP, pp. 10-14.)	"Often we sat and waited for the weather to clear. There were always weather briefings right up to the decision."	Bubbles
	7	Grier's RANGER certificate (DOROTHY GRIER (WHITCOMB) RANGER CERTIFICATE NATM O 2004.126.008 box DA33)		

FIG. 13 Sample graphic sheet page.

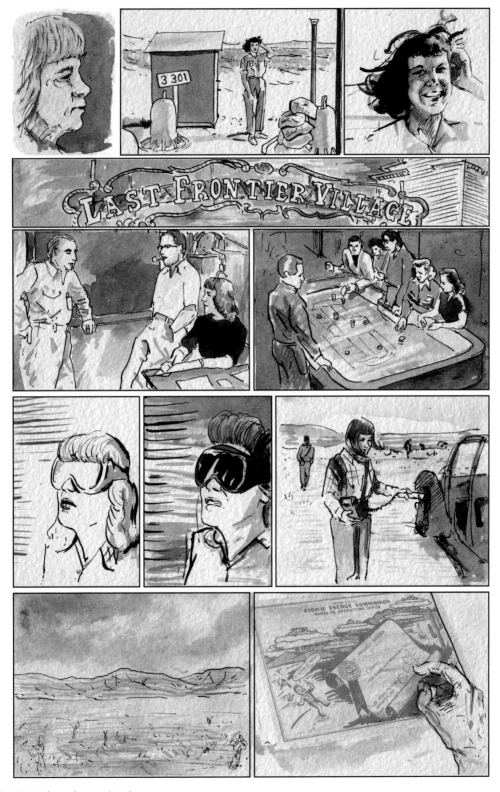

FIG. 14 Draft art for graphic sheet page.

captured a sense of emotion, context, complexity, and contingency, the same subtle qualities historians hope to convey when they interpret past events. I contacted Purcell and asked whether I could use some of his studies of atomic testing witnesses and participants in a series of public lectures. After Brian Wheel showed me *Abina*, I asked Kristian whether he would be interested in continuing our collaboration with this book, and he agreed as long as he could work primarily from actual historical images and rely as little as possible on conjecture about how things might have looked. This philosophy perfectly matched the spirit of the oral history project, and so we began.

The oral history project was collaborative from inception to completion, but this new graphic history required an even closer partnership between artist and historian to select the oral testimony, documents, and historic images that might best be used to reveal the arc of atomic testing history from the Manhattan Project prelude to the limited test ban of 1963 that ended the brief but dramatic atmospheric-testing era. To do this, I created a script for each page, explaining to Kristian the historical information, context, sources, and images linked directly to the particular subject covered in the page. The scripts looked like this:

From the beginning, Kristian used his own extensive knowledge of the historic images of the National Nuclear Security Administration (NNSA)/ DOE photo archives to expand the range of visual references for people and events. He traveled to the United States, where together we combed the previously untapped photo collections of the National Atomic Testing Museum and worked in the extraordinary NNSA/DOE archives with photos and materials not available online. As we progressed through the process Kristian patiently responded to my requests to represent subtle ideas or themes, or somehow draw concepts like *contingency*, the notion that historic events were not preordained but happened because of a variety of conditions and that other outcomes were always possible. The finer points may not be obvious to readers, but if you look closely you will see what he was able to achieve. We were lucky that atomic testing was extensively documented, showing these subtle aspects of the story while providing clear evidence of specific actions and processes. Kristian had hundreds of examples of what people wore, what they used to accomplish their work, and what they studied to learn more about radiation or how the atomic "devices" were designed and tested. Despite this rich photo archive, there was much we needed to know that was not shown. I searched through the primary documents for descriptions that would aid Kristian's graphic efforts and through the oral history archives for sections of interviews explaining the reactions, feelings, emotions, tastes, smells, sounds, and sights of events. The resulting draft graphic page from the script shown in Fig. 13 is depicted in Fig. 14.

Once we had developed this method, I needed to make some decisions about how much of this extraordinarily complicated history we should attempt to include in this all too brief introduction. Although the Manhattan Project is well documented in popular, scholarly sources and a fantastic recent graphic novel, I knew that most readers would not have encountered the part of that story relating to the site selection for testing that resulted in the Trinity event. The selection of the Trinity site was important because it set the precedent for the environmental and cultural assessment protocols that followed.

In the study of history, where you begin and where you end means a lot. If you start late or stop short, critical details remain hidden from the reader. More than just leaving blank spots in the history, the start and finish of a history shapes the interpretation. This is true in print or other forms of historical interpretation. For example, in the 1990s, an effort to place the *Enola Gay*, the beautifully restored Boeing B-29 Superfortress that dropped the bomb on Hiroshima, in the halls of the Smithsonian Museum in Washington, D.C., caused controversy in part because of the arc of the narrative.[4] At the Smithsonian, curators drafted an atomic history around the story of the *Enola Gay*. They chose to tell the story starting with the war effort and ending with the effects of the atom bombs on the Japanese targets and people who lived there. When the exhibit was made public, some appreciated the fuller version of the story that went beyond the immediate end of the war. Others were enraged that our national museum was showing the graphic and disturbing effects of atomic weapons on enemy civilians. What American child could see this, they wondered, and remain proud of their nation? Would this expanded history taint our memories of WWII widely known as the "Good War"? The exhibit was closed before most got a chance to decide for themselves. This intense, recent debate about how to interpret atomic history shows why this topic still matters today. Even after seventy years there is no consensus on how best to understand this controversial subject. The roots of the debate over atomic history that raged in the 1990s began in earnest during the summer of 1957, during OPERATION PLUMBBOB, when global questions about the necessity, ethics, and effects of nuclear testing reached a dramatic crisis point.

So, keeping the politics of beginnings and endings in mind, the graphic history relates the entire arc of the history of global atmospheric nuclear testing, from 1945 through the signing of the Limited Test Ban Treaty of 1963 that ended atmospheric nuclear testing and then briefly showing the

---

[4] Edward T. Linenthal and Tom Engelhardt, *History Wars: The Enola Gay and Other Battles for the American Past* (New York: Henry Holt & Co., 1996).

legal battles and protest that resulted in the release of the official Atomic Energy Commission (AEC)/DOE archives to the public in the 1980s. While I worked to carefully explain crucial elements of the science and technology of testing, this is a book primarily about people. The graphic history shows some of the lesser-known historical actors who experienced nuclear testing firsthand and the places and peoples of the testing landscapes. For those inspired to learn more about the science and technology the bibliography will point you to a wealth of excellent sources.

Insightful comments from Brian Wheel throughout the creation of this book and an essential set of comments from eight anonymous reviewers helped refine the graphic narrative and point out weaknesses that could be resolved through image or text. These outside perspectives enabled me to revise the draft with confidence and move toward the final version of the graphic history. One of the great challenges was limiting the story to its most essential parts, and the experts pointed to ways to do this while maintaining the integrity of the historical narrative for students and general readers. Graphic history, I quickly learned, is a brutally concise format. Each panel is precious real estate with room for very limited text that must not come at the expense of the art that is the essence of this form of storytelling. Each amazing page of art I received from Kristian reminded me that his art would be the key to success, that a picture could indeed replace a thousand words, and that I needed to restrain my historian's desire to explain in detail with text. The strict limitations imposed by the sharp lines of the panel boxes became most clear while sorting the amazing source material for use in the scripts. Each individual panel in this book is based on at least a dozen excellent and important primary sources, dozens of historic images, and as many as twenty separate oral interviews that touched on the topic at hand. Add to that excellent secondary sources for every topic and every page and you start to see the wealth of source material available to those who study this subject, and the scope of the challenge to limit our coverage. As I worked to refine the scripts, I compiled a very select list of several hundred primary sources that I considered indispensable for understanding the people and environments of testing. There are examples of these in the primary documents section of the book. They are only the tip of the iceberg but are at least representative of the materials you can access on your own.

History in all forms is a subjective translation of sources into narrative. Even in the most lengthy and complete traditional history books the author has carefully selected which aspects of the story to reveal and which to leave out. Historians make these decisions about sorting and limiting in everything they do. I worked hard to be objective, fair, and accurate in my choice of sources, inclusions and exclusions, and resulting interpretations.

Each panel in the graphic history is supported with the same precise citation methods one would use to provide evidence in support of the prose of a more traditional narrative paragraph. The dialogue comes most often verbatim from protagonists discovered in the oral history archive or primary documents. The vast majority of Kristian's graphic interpretations are based on actual historic photos, documents, maps, and other primary sources. Some liberties were required to tie it all together, but these creative decisions were made carefully and based on existing sources.

Most who study the history of the NTS encounter the stories of *New York Times* reporter Gladwin Hill. He was sent to Nevada by the *Times* in 1951 to act as a witness and to share his experiences with the wide audience of this most-significant American newspaper. Hill was western bureau chief of the *Times* and lead atomic reporter throughout the entire atmospheric testing era. His evolving views on the Mojave and Great Basin deserts, the regional residents, and the uncertain process of atomic testing mirrored broader national trends. His articles ranged from cheery encouragements to atomic tourism to more thoughtful discussions of the need for continued testing, the rightness of the choice of place, and the effects of testing on people and environments. During his time as atomic witness Hill became a savvy observer of place and environment. In the last years of atomic testing and then after the test ban, he turned his attention to emerging national environmental issues and became the *Times's* first environmental reporter, inventing the environmental beat, or "e-beat," at the beginning of the "green revolution" of the 1960s and '70s.[5] He left an extensive record of his activities, including personal journals recording his encounters with the people and nature of the Great Basin now housed at University of California, Los Angeles (UCLA) Charles E. Young Research Library. He was the obvious choice for a narrator who could help ground a history characterized by a multiplicity of viewpoints and perspectives. In reality he was not present at all of the moments where we placed him, but his narration comes directly from his own writings and collections or from other historical sources from the time.

William Geagley looms large in the section on OPERATION PLUMBBOB. Bill was an ordinary citizen civil defense representative from Lansing, Michigan, when he was chosen to travel to Nevada and witness the PLUMBBOB series. He appears in such detail in the graphic section because he meticulously recorded his time in Nevada, keeping every scrap

---

[5]   For Hill's role in the green revolution, see Adam Rome, *The Genius of Earth Day: How a 1970 Teach-In Unexpectedly Made the First Green Generation* (New York: Hill & Wang, 2013), 228–229.

of paper, receipt, and document related to his experiences, along with careful notes of what he saw and did. When I first opened his papers, a small, thin, transparent plastic wrapper drifted out of an old envelope. It was his carefully folded fork wrapper from the Capital Airlines flight that took him from Michigan to Nevada in 1957. He was absolutely thorough in his collecting and thus made a good representative for the thousands of other unknown regular people who participated in the history of testing.

Kristian took my ideas about Gladwin as narrator and Geagley as everyman and brought them to life through his art. Our collaboration on the making of this book was as enjoyable as anything I've done in my career. There were many other people who generously supported this continuation of the alliance of scholarly interest and public history experimentation that began with the oral history project. First and foremost, I thank the hundreds of atomic testing protagonists who shared their personal lives and perspectives with us during the oral history project. It takes courage to make your personal life story part of history and to share your experiences with unknown future generations. Thanks to DOE archivist Martha DeMarre, who helped with historic images; Su Kim Chung, who assisted with University of Nevada, Las Vegas (UNLV) Special Collections; and Karen Green, who opened the National Atomic Testing Museum (NATM) collections to us for weeks.

Mary Palevsky, Robert Futrell, and oral history project graduate-students-turned-colleagues Mary Wammack and Leisl Childers listened for years to my ideas about the "art of testing" and offered critical insights throughout the process of turning some of those ideas into this graphic history. Mary Palevsky was my employee, but I was her student in all things related to oral and atomic history. It was an honor to travel with her on part of her life-long quest to understand the nuclear world and the people who made it. Likewise, Mary Wammack was one of our excellent students but came to our program with a deep understanding of atomic issues after a career working on atomic legal cases and taught us at least as much as we taught her.

I am grateful to Oxford editor Brian Wheel for his early interest in this project and support throughout the very interesting process of graphic-history making and to everyone on the Oxford team who helped make this book. Thanks to Michael Schaller and the *American Horizons* author team for comments on Cold War context section and support for this project. Historian Ari Kelman, co-author with Jonathan Fetter-Vorm of the amazing *Battle Lines: A Graphic History of the Civil War*, shared his insights on graphic history and offered important encouragement for both the method and my efforts to present atomic testing history in this form. David Tannenhaus, the chair of my department, supported a sabbatical leave and offered strong backing for turning public history research into a creative publication for a wide audience. UNLV colleague and U.S. Congresswoman Dina Titus blazed the trail in atomic history in Nevada and deserves thanks for all she's done for the people who live throughout the testing region. This project might not have happened if historian Aaron Sheehan-Dean had not sent me his step-grandfather William Geagley's remarkably intact and complete PLUMBBOB witness collection. That dusty box was a treasure; thank you, Aaron, for sharing this piece of your family's history.

In 2012, the U.S. State Department MCCA Grant Program linked the National Atomic Testing Museum (NATM), UNLV, and the Karagandy Ecological Museum in Karagandy, Kazakhstan, for an exchange of researchers and students from the Soviet and U.S. atomic test site regions. At the NATM, Alan Palmer organized and funded our effort to visit the Polygon and our travels throughout the Kazakh testing zone. Medical anthropologist Magdalena Stawkowski joined us as field director for the Kazakh portion of the trip along with geographer Robert Kopack. Their combined knowledge of the region and extensive fieldwork with villagers was essential to this successful effort. Together we took a group of twelve multidisciplinary students and researchers to the Soviet Polygon to meet and interview villagers who lived and continue to live with the legacies of the Soviet nuclear testing program. Two of my colleagues at UNLV, Paul Werth and Robert Futrell, were critical partners who embraced this unique public history opportunity. Thanks also to my colleagues in atomic history, Bo Jacobs and Mick Broderick, for sharing insights from their research and extensive travels in Kazakhstan and to atomic sites around the world.

I owe a special and profound thank you to my peerless mentor, historian Virginia Scharff for inviting me to give the twenty-fifth annual Calvin Horn Lecture at the University of New Mexico in 2011. That remarkable homecoming, along with Virginia's enthusiasm for *Doom Towns* and insights about alternative forms of history, encouraged me to pursue this unique book. Similar lectures at Washington State University and then a National Endowment for the Humanities workshop, *Atomic West, Atomic World*, organized by historians Jeff Sanders and Robert McCoy, greatly aided the creation of the graphic history and offered a chance to vet the process to a wonderful group of teachers, students, and scholars. Thanks also to historian Ryan Edgington, who invited me to the College of Wooster to share this research with another group of students and faculty at one more key moment. Environmental historians Cindy Ott, Neil Maher, Phoebe Young, and Peggy Shaffer provided critical feedback on aspects of the research in this book and forums for more traditional academic publication of research results. The Black Mountain Institute at UNLV provided a fellowship in support of this project, and the University Forum Lectures and Department of History funded Kristian's Purcell's travels through the U.S. atomic bioregion and his time in the photo archives of the DOE and NATM.

This book is dedicated to Virginia Scharff and the memory of two other historians who also inspired me to study science and technology and, specifically, things atomic. The late Frank Szasz wrote the now-classic history of the Trinity test, *The Day the Sun Rose Twice*, and in 1995 arranged my first tour of the NTS. I didn't know it at the time, but that tour was the start of a long fascination with the hidden history of atomic testing, its unknown participants, and underappreciated environments. The late Tim Moy shared his contagious enthusiasm for the history of science and technology with a generation of very lucky students. Sitting in Tim's office surrounded by models of real and imagined technological wonders would make anyone want to spend time learning more about how our collective push to build new things has shaped our history for better and worse.

ABOUT THE AUTHOR

Andrew Kirk (Ph.D., University of New Mexico) is Professor of Environmental History and Public History Program Director in the Department of History at the University of Nevada Las Vegas. He is author of books and articles on environmental history, environmental culture, and the U.S. West and co-author of Oxford's *American Horizons: U.S. History in a Global Context*. He served as the Co-Principal Investigator on the award-winning Nevada Test Site Oral History Project.

ABOUT THE ILLUSTRATOR

Kristian Purcell is an artist and illustrator based in Bedford, United Kingdom.

CAST OF CHARACTERS

Dean Acheson: U.S. secretary of state

Irene Allen: Lead plaintiff in *Allen v. United States of America*; mother and advocate for downwind children from Hurricane, Utah

Kenneth Bainbridge: American physicist and Trinity test director responsible for the first atomic testing site selection

Norris Bradbury: American physicist and second director of Los Alamos Laboratory after Robert Oppenheimer

David Bradley: American physician and medical researcher during Operation Crossroads who chronicled atomic testing in his best-selling book *No Place to Hide*

Marcell Eugene Bridges: Downwind advocate

Dr. Glyn G. Caldwell: Center of Disease Control radiation health researcher who studied the soldiers and civilian participants of Shot Smoky during OPERATION PLUMBBOB

Winston Churchill: Prime minister of England

Walter Cronkite: Pioneering American television reporter

Duke Daly: Lawrence Livermore Laboratory employee and early test participant

Dr. Charles Dunham: Director of the Atomic Energy Commission (AEC) Division of Biology and Medicine

Albert Einstein: German immigrant physicist

Dwight D. Eisenhower: Thirty-fourth U.S. president

Don English: Las Vegas News Bureau photographer who captured many of the most iconic images of the atmospheric testing era

Helen Fallini: Rancher and AEC radiation monitoring program critic

Enrico Fermi: Italian immigrant and Manhattan Project physicist

Otto Frisch: Austrian-British physicist

Klaus Fuches: Theoretical physicist and atomic spy

William C. Geagley: Agricultural scientist and Michigan civil defense PLUMBBOB witness

Alvin C. Graves: Head of J Test Division at Los Alamos Laboratories

Dorothy Jean (Whitcomb) Grier: Secretary and Los Alamos Scientific Laboratory Operation Ranger participant

Leslie Groves: Military commander for Manhattan Project

Corbin Harney: Western Shoshone spiritual leader and protester

Gladwin Hill: Chief of the western bureau of the *New York Times* (1946–1968); after reporting on WWII, the lead atomic reporter and then first national environmental correspondent for the *Times* (1969)

Vernon Jones: Electrical technician at Edgerton, Germeshausen, and Grier (EG&G)

Juda: Leader of Bikini islanders during Operation Crossroads and named plaintiff in the *Juda v. United States* (1981) atomic compensation lawsuit

George F. Kennan: U.S. Soviet expert and author of the X and Long Telegrams that explained the concept of containment

Igor Kurchatov: Soviet nuclear physicist and director of Soviet atomic bomb program

Martha Bordoli Laird: Downwind advocate

Dorothea Lange: American photographer who, with photographer Ansel Adams, chronicled the downwind towns and people in 1953

Willard F. Libby: Nobel Prize–winning American chemist and AEC commissioner

David Lilienthal: American attorney and coauthor of the Acheson-Lilienthal Report

Robert Mackenzie: Curtiss Marine and veteran of Operation Castle-Bravo

Maria Martinez: Member of the San Ildefonso Pueblo and world-renowned potter

George Maynard: Atomic veteran and member of the U.S. Armed Forces Special Weapons Project

James McCormack: AEC military director

Brien McMahon: American attorney and U.S. senator (Connecticut)

Marie McMillian: NTS contract employee, wife of Duke Daly, civil rights activist, and teacher

Robert Oppenheimer: American physicist, scientific director of the Manhattan Project, first director of Los Alamos Laboratory, and chairman of the General Advisory Committee to the Atomic Energy Commission (AEC)

Rudolf Peierls: British physicist

Val Peterson: Federal Civil Defense Administration chief

Bertrand Russell: British philosopher and antinuclear testing activist

Morse Salisbury: AEC director of information services

Albert Schweitzer: German theologian, humanitarian, and antinuclear activist

Louis Slotin: Canadian physicist and chemist

Joseph Stalin: Leader of the Soviet Union

Lewis Strauss: AEC chair from 1953 to 1958 and architect of U.S. atmospheric testing program

Olzhas Suleimenov: UN ambassador, Kazakh poet, and international antinuclear testing advocate who founded Nevada-Semipalatinsk in 1989, linking indigenous protest in Kazakhstan and Nevada

Leo Szilard: Hungarian physicist who collaborated with Enrico Fermi on the first nuclear reactor

Edward Teller: Hungarian-born American theoretical physicist known as the "father of the hydrogen bomb"

Harry S. Truman: Thirty-third U.S. president, he ordered the use of the atomic bombs on Hiroshima and Nagasaki and approved atomic testing regime that followed

Navor Tito Valdez: Core driller at Reynolds Electrical and Engineering Company, uranium miner, and downwinder

Henry Wallace: U.S. vice president under Harry S. Truman and chronicler of early atomic debates

Herbert York: Physicist, first director of the Lawrence Livermore Laboratory, arms control negotiator, and director of research and engineering at the U.S. Department of Defense

DOOM TOWNS

THE PEOPLE AND LANDSCAPES OF ATOMIC TESTING

THE GRAPHIC HISTORY

CHAPTER 1
TRINITY

REMAINS OF THE PEACE CAMP ARE ON YOUR LEFT…

…THAT, OF COURSE, IS MERCURY DOWN IN THE VALLEY…

…MOST OF THESE STRUCTURES WE'RE DRIVING THROUGH NOW ARE WHAT REMAIN OF THE "CIVIL EFFECTS TESTS"…

…TAKE A LOOK AT THAT STEEL GIRDER UP THERE ON THE MOCKUP OF A BRIDGE, BENT LIKE A TWIG FROM THE BLAST.

Mercury 1 MILE NO SERVICES

NEVADA TEST SITE

RADIATION HAZARD
TOUCHING OR REMOVING SCRAP OBJECTS IS PROHIBITED

The letter was part of an international effort of the scientific community to warn of the potential use of the tiny atom to create weapons of mass destruction beyond any previously imagined.

This new future started on August 2, 1939, as the war in Europe was about to begin...

...famed scientist Albert Einstein wrote a letter to President Roosevelt explaining critical developments in atomic physics.

Two years later F.D.R., convinced that the Germans were working to create an atomic super-weapon, authorized a joint U.S. and British effort to beat them to the punch.

The "Manhattan Project" became the most expensive and sophisticated science project in history.

Lead scientist Robert Oppenheimer and military commander Leslie Groves were assigned the seemingly impossible task of revealing the innermost workings of the universe and harnessing the immense power that lay hidden within the nucleus of the atom.

Working in total secrecy, they brought together the most brilliant minds from around the world.

Many of the scientists were Jews who fled the Nazis as they rose to power. They had no doubt that Hitler would use the atom if his scientists discovered its secrets first.

Secret Manhattan Project laboratories were set up in New York, Chicago, England, Washington State, and Tennessee.

These labs were hidden under the bleachers at the University of Chicago and woven into the fabric of bustling places, often hidden in plain sight.

But Oppenheimer and Groves knew that they needed a bigger centralized location to gather large numbers of scientists and support staff together for the big push to create the weapon.

They chose a remote location deep in the heart of the Sangre de Cristo Mountains of New Mexico to build their secret atomic city.

Between 1942 and the spring of 1945, the scientists and more than 125,000 anonymous laborers and technicians worked around the clock to build an atomic bomb.

These women, for example, operated control panels at the Oak Ridge, Tennessee, uranium-enriching "Calutron" facility.

They were never told what their work was for, only how to adjust the controls to keep certain readings set on the dials in front of them.

Their experience was typical of workers involved in the Manhattan Project.

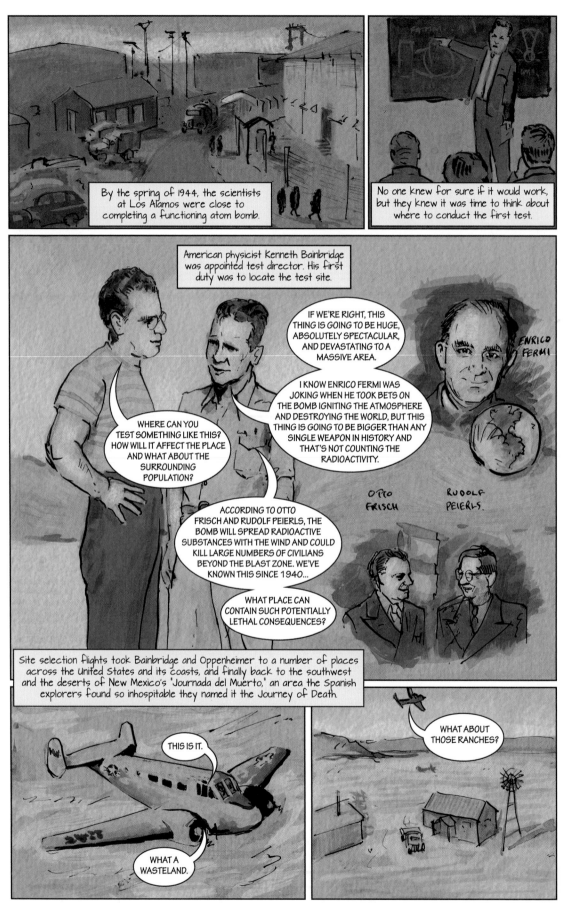

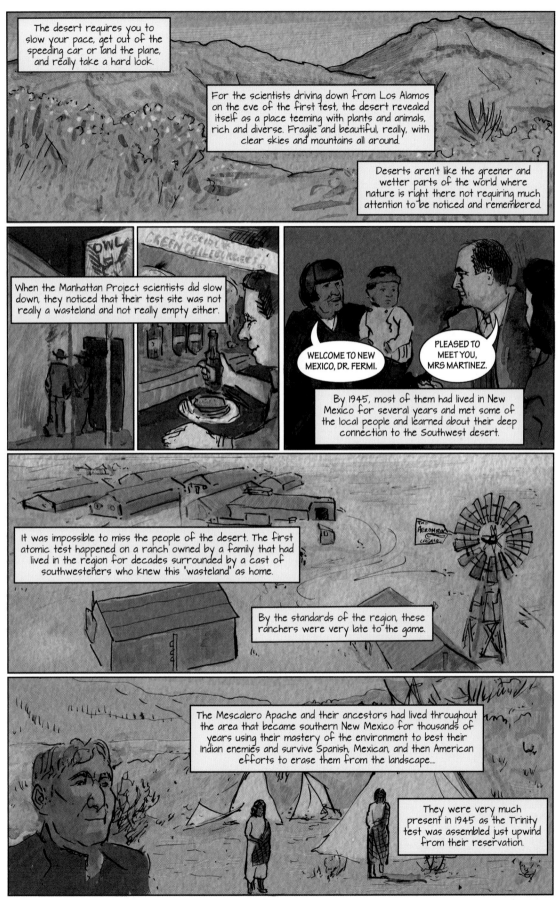

The desert requires you to slow your pace, get out of the speeding car or land the plane, and really take a hard look.

For the scientists driving down from Los Alamos on the eve of the first test, the desert revealed itself as a place teeming with plants and animals, rich and diverse. Fragile and beautiful, really, with clear skies and mountains all around.

Deserts aren't like the greener and wetter parts of the world where nature is right there not requiring much attention to be noticed and remembered.

When the Manhattan Project scientists did slow down, they noticed that their test site was not really a wasteland and not really empty either.

WELCOME TO NEW MEXICO, DR. FERMI.

PLEASED TO MEET YOU, MRS MARTINEZ.

By 1945, most of them had lived in New Mexico for several years and met some of the local people and learned about their deep connection to the Southwest desert.

It was impossible to miss the people of the desert. The first atomic test happened on a ranch owned by a family that had lived in the region for decades surrounded by a cast of southwesterners who knew this "wasteland" as home.

By the standards of the region, these ranchers were very late to the game.

The Mescalero Apache and their ancestors had lived throughout the area that became southern New Mexico for thousands of years using their mastery of the environment to best their Indian enemies and survive Spanish, Mexican, and then American efforts to erase them from the landscape....

They were very much present in 1945 as the Trinity test was assembled just upwind from their reservation.

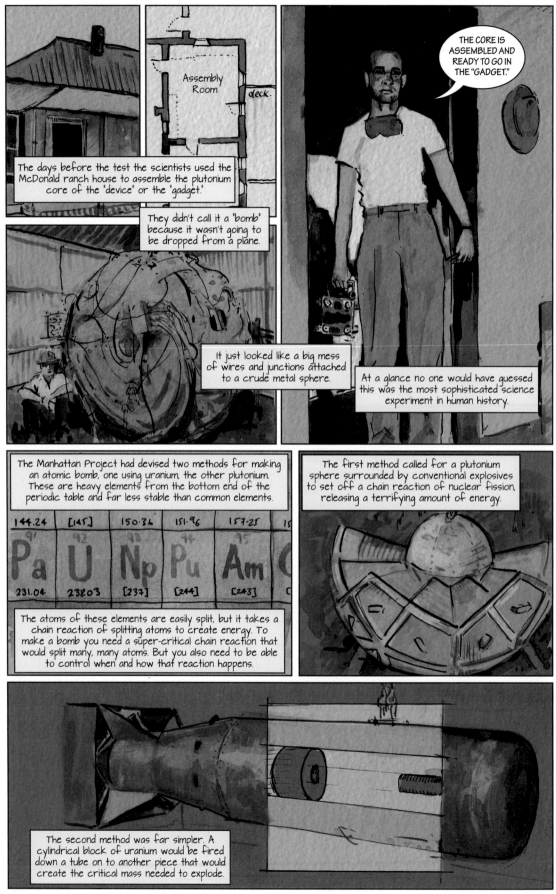

The days before the test the scientists used the McDonald ranch house to assemble the plutonium core of the "device" or the "gadget."

Assembly Room

deck.

THE CORE IS ASSEMBLED AND READY TO GO IN THE "GADGET."

They didn't call it a "bomb" because it wasn't going to be dropped from a plane.

It just looked like a big mess of wires and junctions attached to a crude metal sphere.

At a glance no one would have guessed this was the most sophisticated science experiment in human history.

The Manhattan Project had devised two methods for making an atomic bomb, one using uranium, the other plutonium. These are heavy elements from the bottom end of the periodic table and far less stable than common elements.

144.24	[145]	150.36	151.96	157.25	15
91 Pa	92 U	93 Np	94 Pu	95 Am	C
231.04	238.03	[237]	[244]	[243]	

The atoms of these elements are easily split, but it takes a chain reaction of splitting atoms to create energy. To make a bomb you need a super-critical chain reaction that would split many, many atoms. But you also need to be able to control when and how that reaction happens.

The first method called for a plutonium sphere surrounded by conventional explosives to set off a chain reaction of nuclear fission, releasing a terrifying amount of energy.

The second method was far simpler. A cylindrical block of uranium would be fired down a tube on to another piece that would create the critical mass needed to explode.

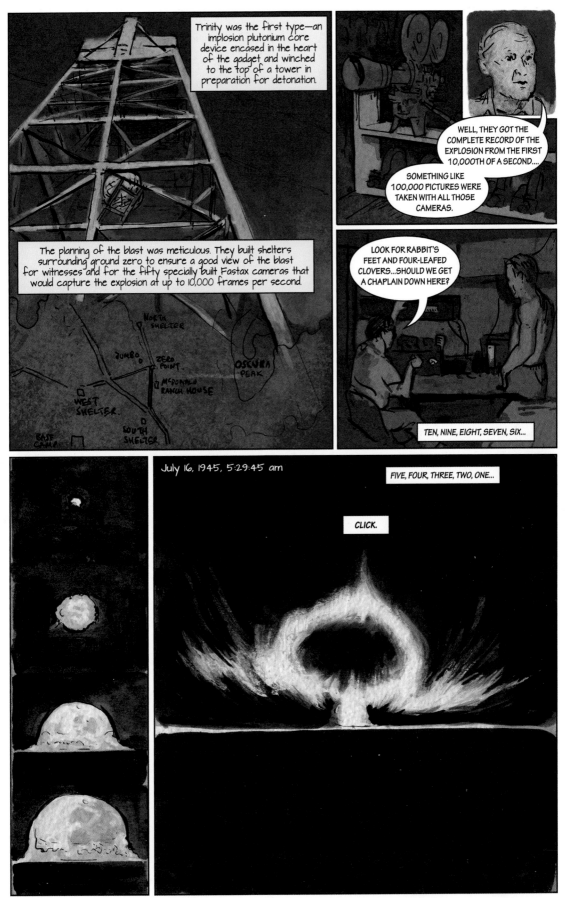

Approximately 200 tons of sand and soil were vaporized, instantly spreading billions of silica particles into the wind.

Eighty acres of desert sand melted into a vast sheet of green glass the scientists called "Trinitite."

Three hundred and sixty radioactive isotopes were created and many adhered to the silica in the air. Some isotopes had a very short "half-life" and decayed in minutes.

CHICAGO

TRINITY

Others, like strontium-90, had long half-lives, and circled the globe, showing up in cows' milk as far away as Chicago.

Some of the plutonium, very deadly stuff, survived the blast.

Scattered across a mile-wide circle of the desert, it could stay dangerous to living things for up to 24,000 years.

The flash and blast were seen and felt for hundreds of miles.

Germany had formally surrendered on May 8, 1945...

NAZIS QUIT WAR
VE DAY TODAY

...Even as the German guns finally fell silent, it was clear that the peace would be complicated and contested.

WE HAVE A NEW WEAPON OF UNUSUAL DESTRUCTIVE FORCE.

GLAD TO HEAR IT.

While citizens and soldiers rejoiced, political and military leaders remained deeply concerned by news of deteriorating relations with Stalin.

Soviet Influence

West Germany

The Soviets occupied Berlin and controlled a vast territory stretching from the Black Sea in Romania to Poland's Baltic shores. They also controlled a large swath of eastern Germany past Berlin and up the Elbe River.

It was becoming increasingly clear that a new conflict was brewing even as the war in Europe drew to a close.

16

Dear Dick: August 9, 1945

I read your telegram of August seventh with
a lot of interest.

I know that Japan is a terribly cruel and
uncivilized nation in warfare but I can't
bring myself to believe that, because they
are beasts, we should ourselves act in the
same manner.

For myself, I certainly regret the necessity
of wiping out whole populations because of
the "pigheadedness" of the leaders of a nation
and, for your information, I am not going to
do it unless it is absolutely necessary. It
is my opinion that after the Russians enter
into war the Japanese will very shortly fold
up.

My object is to save as many American lives
as possible but I also have a humane feeling
for the women and children in Japan.

Sincerely yours,

HARRY S. TRUMAN

NAGASAKI
TARGET AREA

Truman had been president for only a little more than
three months when faced with the decision to use
atomic weapons on human targets. He believed it was
necessary but understood exactly what he was doing.

WE HAVE SPENT MORE THAN TWO BILLION
DOLLARS ON THE GREATEST SCIENTIFIC
GAMBLE IN HISTORY AND WE HAVE WON.

HAVING FOUND THE BOMB, WE HAVE
USED IT—IT IS AN AWFUL RESPONSIBILITY
WHICH HAS COME TO US.

WE THANK GOD IT HAS COME TO US,
INSTEAD OF OUR ENEMIES; AND WE
PRAY THAT HE MAY GUIDE US TO USE
IT IN HIS WAYS AND IN HIS PURPOSES.

WHAT
IS IT?

THE JAPS
SURRENDERED!

THANK GOD
FOR THAT!

The soldiers bound for the Japanese mainland weren't alone
in celebrating the bombing of Hiroshima and Nagasaki.

WAR ENDS

WAR

For millions across the Pacific and back in the
United States, the bombs seemed more humane than
a continuation of the hideous combat on the ground.

18

I was the first reporter to fly over Berlin after the final bombing raids. It was just like Truman said—a "ghost city."

HIROSHIMA—EXTENT OF FIRE DAMAGE

Tokyo was almost as bad after Curtis LeMay ordered the city carpet-bombed with incendiaries the weeks before.

Those firebombs on that wooden city burned by the square mile and killed tens of thousands of civilians. The worst single bombing in history. Some said when we burned Tokyo we crossed the Rubicon. The U.S. rules of war had changed forever.

Its buildings, people, economy were in ruins. But Hiroshima and Nagasaki were different. They were obliterated instantly and almost completely.

Together the atomic bombs killed more than the incendiaries in Tokyo.

The Hiroshima and Nagasaki victims were vaporized, burned or killed by impact.

DAILY EXPRESS

THE ATOMIC PLAGUE

'I write this as a warning to the world'

THE PICTURE THAT DOES NOT TELL THE WHOLE STORY

DOCTORS FALL AS THEY WORK

Poison gas fear: All wear masks

But the ghosts of these blasts—the radiation—lingered on and kept killing those who dodged the bombs for weeks, months, years after. The evidence of radiation sickness was everywhere and easy to see and map.

Survivors of the bomb, the hibakusha—Japanese for 'explosion-affected people'—would be studied for generations as doctors and others looked for the long-term effects of radiation exposure.

I WONDER IF THE DEAD WEREN'T LUCKIER THAN THE SURVIVORS.

Toward the end of the war, it was assumed the atomic bomb would be used on Tokyo to finish the job. But the military leaders didn't think so. The Manhattan Project was a science experiment of the highest order, and the testing phase needed to be as controlled and precise as possible to ascertain the exact effects of the new weapon.

Groves and Oppenheimer's 'Target Committee' had picked a list of lesser known cities because they were 'pristine,' places untouched by bombing.

Many of the scientists had agreed that the bomb should not be used against human targets under any circumstances.

PACIFIC.

It had to break the will of the Japanese to continue fighting and send a message to the world. That is why they dropped the A-bombs on actual targets.

They had witnessed Trinity and thought you might just blow one up out in the ocean and that would be enough to show its power. But the military, Oppenheimer, and eventually Truman disagreed. It had to be a real demonstration of this new weapon's power.

CHAPTER 2
CROSSROADS

In the weeks following the end of the war, debates about the future of atomic bombs dominated radio and newspapers. There were several key questions that emerged and no consensus.

IN WHAT WAYS WOULD ATOMIC WEAPONS CHANGE WAR IN THE FUTURE?

WHAT WOULD SUCH A BOMB DO TO A BATTLESHIP? OR AN ENTIRE FLEET?

SHOULD WE SHARE THE SECRETS OF THE MANHATTAN PROJECT WITH OUR ALLIES? THE SOVIETS?

WHO SHOULD CONTROL THE BOMB? THE MILITARY OR A NEW CIVILIAN AUTHORITY?

Greatest Story Of the Age

We Enter a New — The Atomic Age

Atomic Bomb Op en New Era!

THE ATOMIC BOMB!

Hopes for a new era of international cooperation were not entirely unfounded. The charter of the United Nations had been signed by world leaders in San Francisco in June 1945, establishing an international council to maintain security and peace.

The New York Times News Room

On one hand you had the atomic scientists like Oppenheimer, certified geniuses and "heroes of the war," who were arguing that we needed international control of atomic energy.

On the other hand there were the military leaders and their supporters who were scrambling for command of A-bombs and fighting among themselves just as they always had when new technology changed the rules of war.

WE NEED TO ACT DECISIVELY TO DISPROVE THESE RUMORS AND DEMONSTRATE THE STRATEGIC IMPORTANCE OF THE NAVY IN THE NEW ERA.

THE PAPERS PAINT THE ARMY AIR FORCE AS THE FUTURE OF THE MILITARY AND ASSUME THE NAVY IS OBSOLETE IN AN ATOMIC WAR.

WE'VE CAPTURED WHAT'S LEFT OF THE JAPANESE NAVY.

Senator Brien McMahon called for new atomic tests.

IN ORDER TO TEST THE DESTRUCTIVE POWERS OF THE ATOMIC BOMB AGAINST NAVAL VESSELS, I WOULD LIKE TO SEE THESE JAPANESE SHIPS TAKEN TO SEA AND AN ATOMIC BOMB DROPPED ON THEM. I CAN THINK OF NO BETTER USE FOR THEM!

THE PRESIDENT SAID THAT THE RELEASE OF ATOMIC ENERGY WAS A NEW FORCE TOO REVOLUTIONARY TO CONSIDER IN THE FRAMEWORK OF OLD IDEAS...

I COULDN'T AGREE MORE AND HOPE THIS MEANS HE IS WILLING TO JOIN OUR EFFORTS TO PLAN FOR INTERNATIONAL CONTROL OF ATOMIC ENERGY.

I WONDER IF HE KNOWS HOW TRUE THIS REALLY IS...

...THE FISSION OF ONE URANIUM ATOM RELEASES 200 MILLION TIMES AS MUCH AS THE ENERGY RELEASED BY ATOMS IN SIMPLE CHEMICAL BURNING.

TWO HUNDRED MILLION TIMES IS INDEED A REVOLUTIONARY CHANGE THAT FEW POLITICIANS OR MILITARY LEADERS SEEM TO UNDERSTAND. IN SHORT ORDER THE RUSSIANS WILL HAVE THE BOMB, AND OTHERS WILL FOLLOW.

THESE NEW BOMBS WILL NEVER AGAIN, AS IN JAPAN, COME IN ONES OR TWOS, BUT, COME IN HUNDREDS, EVEN IN THOUSANDS. THIS NEW POWER WILL CHANGE THE WORLD.

INDIVIDUAL NATION STATES CANNOT CONTROL A FORCE OF THIS SCALE. WE MUST ACHIEVE SUPRANATIONAL SECURITY, LEST WE SET THE STAGE FOR THE DESTRUCTION OF HUMANITY.

IF THIS HAPPENS, THERE WILL BE NO DEFENSE. NATURAL BARRIERS WILL CEASE TO MATTER AND EVEN TINY STATES OR CITIES COULD HOLD VASTLY LARGER ENEMIES AT BAY.

I HAVE NO DOUBT ABOUT ONE POINT—WE SHALL BE ABLE TO SOLVE THE PROBLEM WHEN IT WILL BE CLEARLY EVIDENT TO ALL THAT THERE IS NO OTHER, NO CHEAPER WAY OUT OF THE PRESENT SITUATION. THERE WILL BE ONE WORLD OR NONE.

In November 1945, atomic scientists from the Manhattan Project labs in Chicago, Los Alamos, and Oak Ridge, Tennessee, founded a new national organization, the Federation of Atomic Scientists.

By early 1946, the scientists organized a campaign supporting civilian control of atomic energy.

They gained powerful allies in the U.S. Senate, where the chair of the Senate Committee on Atomic Energy, Brien McMahon, gave them a voice in the U.S. Capital.

...PHYSICIST LEO SZILARD WILL NOW PRESENT BEFORE CONGRESS....

Political support for the scientists' goal of civilian control of the atom resulted in the passage of the Atomic Energy Act of 1946.

This landmark legislation created the Atomic Energy Commission (AEC), seemingly achieving one of the scientists' central goals.

But the newly formed civilian AEC had a powerful military committee built into its structure and a strong mandate to use the agency to support national security above all else.

Following the creation of the AEC, 515 scientists signed a manifesto calling for global cooperation suited to the new realities of the atomic age. Their message was simple and stark...

TODAY WE DEDICATE THIS DOOMSDAY CLOCK AND SET IT TO 7 MINUTES TO MIDNIGHT TO SYMBOLIZE HOW CLOSE HUMANITY HAS MOVED TO ENGINEERING ITS OWN EXTINCTION.

Still, plans to test three more atomic bombs on the captured remains of the Japanese fleet in the Pacific continued....

27

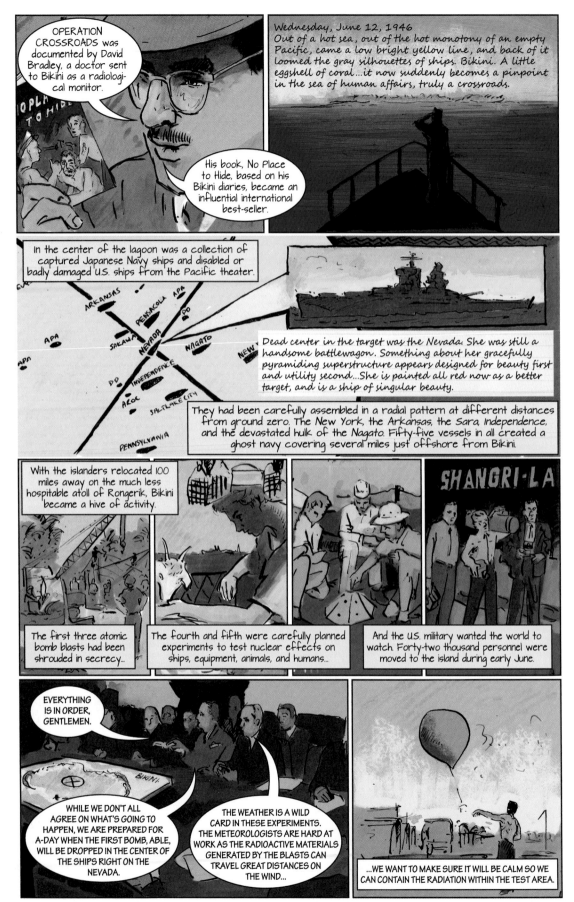

OPERATION CROSSROADS was documented by David Bradley, a doctor sent to Bikini as a radiological monitor.

His book, No Place to Hide, based on his Bikini diaries, became an influential international best-seller.

Wednesday, June 12, 1946
Out of a hot sea, out of the hot monotony of an empty Pacific, came a low bright yellow line, and back of it loomed the gray silhouettes of ships. Bikini. A little eggshell of coral...it now suddenly becomes a pinpoint in the sea of human affairs, truly a crossroads.

In the center of the lagoon was a collection of captured Japanese Navy ships and disabled or badly damaged U.S. ships from the Pacific theater.

Dead center in the target was the Nevada. She was still a handsome battlewagon. Something about her gracefully pyramiding superstructure appears designed for beauty first and utility second...She is painted all red now as a better target, and is a ship of singular beauty.

They had been carefully assembled in a radial pattern at different distances from ground zero. The New York, the Arkansas, the Sara, Independence, and the devastated hulk of the Nagato. Fifty-five vessels in all created a ghost navy covering several miles just offshore from Bikini.

With the islanders relocated 100 miles away on the much less hospitable atoll of Rongerik, Bikini became a hive of activity.

The first three atomic bomb blasts had been shrouded in secrecy...

The fourth and fifth were carefully planned experiments to test nuclear effects on ships, equipment, animals, and humans...

And the U.S. military wanted the world to watch. Forty-two thousand personnel were moved to the island during early June.

EVERYTHING IS IN ORDER, GENTLEMEN.

WHILE WE DON'T ALL AGREE ON WHAT'S GOING TO HAPPEN, WE ARE PREPARED FOR A-DAY WHEN THE FIRST BOMB, ABLE, WILL BE DROPPED IN THE CENTER OF THE SHIPS RIGHT ON THE NEVADA.

THE WEATHER IS A WILD CARD IN THESE EXPERIMENTS. THE METEOROLOGISTS ARE HARD AT WORK AS THE RADIOACTIVE MATERIALS GENERATED BY THE BLASTS CAN TRAVEL GREAT DISTANCES ON THE WIND...

...WE WANT TO MAKE SURE IT WILL BE CALM SO WE CAN CONTAIN THE RADIATION WITHIN THE TEST AREA.

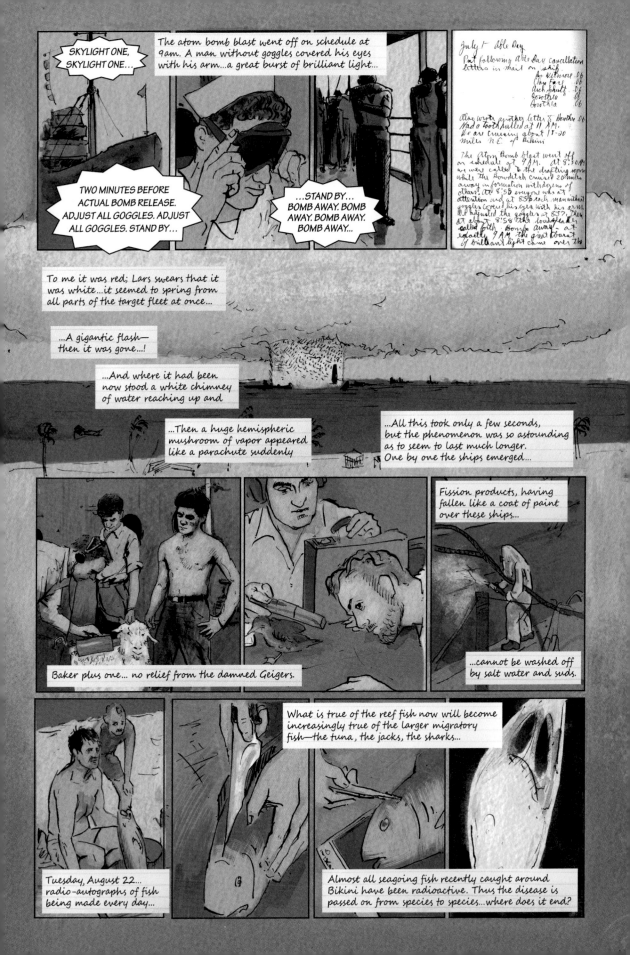

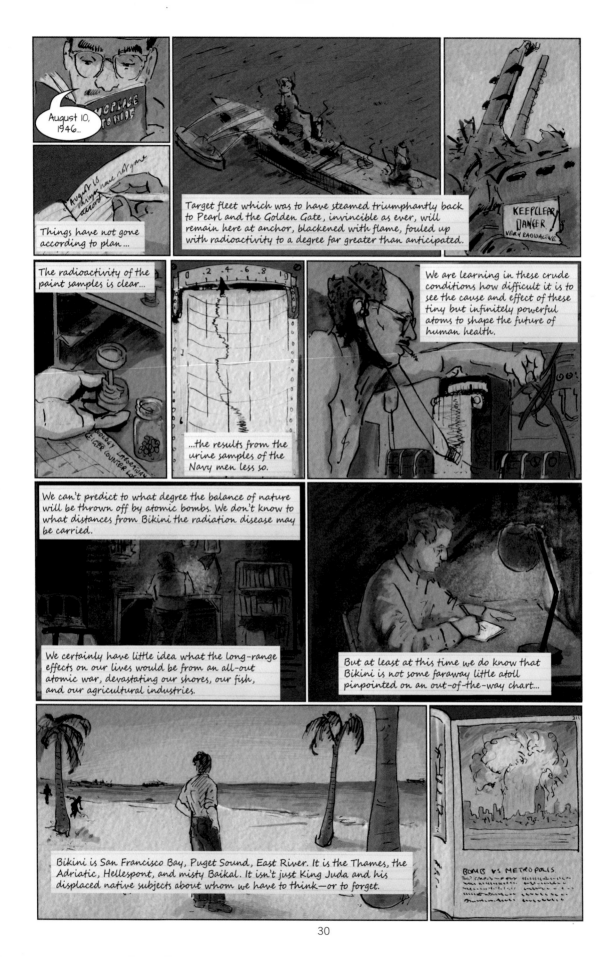

Bradley's careful firsthand observations about radioactive fallout captured the real terror of the atomic age.

That the unintended consequences of our actions would ripple out through environments and bodies changing the very nature of life on Earth.

Radiation—invisible, tasteless, odorless, deadly—was the "shadow of the colossus which looms behind tomorrow."

Beyond the obvious evidence of radiation sickness witnessed at Hiroshima and Nagasaki...

...those planning for future testing had access to data from secret medical experiments conducted at asylums and hospitals across the United States.

At Hanford, Washington, they tested the effects of radiation on pigs, sheep, fish, and stray dogs.

Starting in April 1945, patients suffering from a variety of conditions were unknowingly injected with plutonium and other radioactive substances.

These studies revealed critical facts about the effects of radiation on human health.

Radiation is sequestered in bodies through a process called bioaccumulation.

In the early 1930s, 33 mental patients at an Elgin, Illinois, asylum were fed radium-226. All subsequently died of cancers.

SECRET

RADIOLOGICAL DATA 1930 -1945

Radiation consumed or encountered through environmental exposure becomes concentrated in certain areas depending on the source. Plutonium and strontium collect in the bones and iodine collects in the thyroid gland.

As early as 1945, researchers knew that it could be exceedingly difficult to determine cause and effect in radiation exposure, even when doses were high.

Radiation was insidiously random in effect, and no two studies seemed identical in reaction.

At very high doses every animal died quickly.

At high doses they died at different rates.

Medium doses caused a variety of health effects.

Low doses might not cause any immediate effects but could cause genetic mutations.

So even an "acceptable" dose could have disastrous implications in the future.

31

In 1946, President Truman needed to respond to the issues of atomic safety while formulating a clear policy addressing the balance of power in the atomic age. There were many tensions at play at both national and international levels.

The military and scientists were fighting over command and control of atomic energy.

The Soviets were unwilling to accept a U.S. atomic monopoly.

ACTION COPY
EP

DEPARTMENT OF STATE
INCOMING TELEGRAM

TOP SECRET

0035

The answer for the foreign policy plan Truman needed came from Soviet expert George F. Kennan.

unclassified

retary of State
Washington,

In February '46, he sent an 8,000-word analysis of the postwar Soviet Union to the Treasury from his post in Moscow. This highly influential communication became known as "The Long Telegram."

In it Kennan argued that Soviet communism was "impervious to the logic of reason," inherently expansionist, and controllable only through "long-term, patient but firm and vigilant containment."

On March 12, 1947, Truman explained the theory of containment to the U.S. Congress.

ENIWETOK ISLAND

Meanwhile in the Pacific...

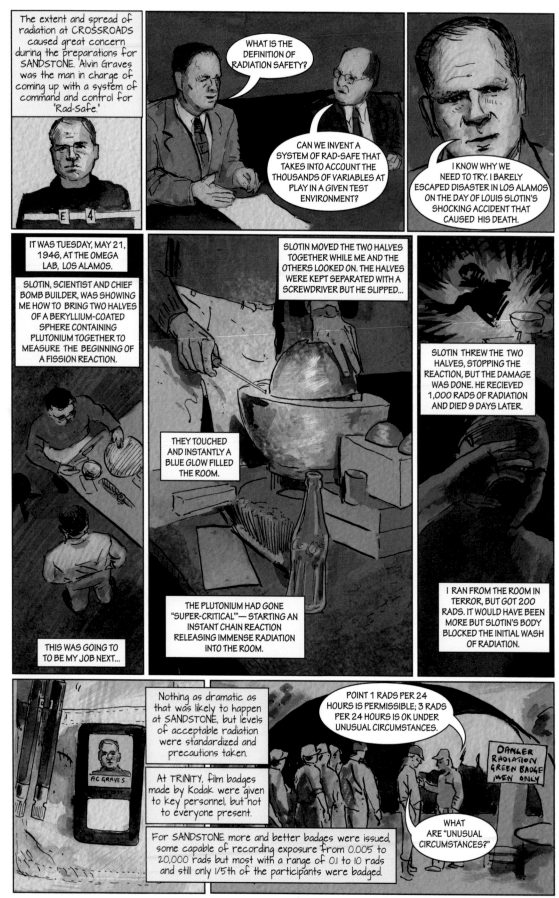

The extent and spread of radiation at CROSSROADS caused great concern during the preparations for SANDSTONE. Alvin Graves was the man in charge of coming up with a system of command and control for "Rad-Safe."

WHAT IS THE DEFINITION OF RADIATION SAFETY?

CAN WE INVENT A SYSTEM OF RAD-SAFE THAT TAKES INTO ACCOUNT THE THOUSANDS OF VARIABLES AT PLAY IN A GIVEN TEST ENVIRONMENT?

I KNOW WHY WE NEED TO TRY. I BARELY ESCAPED DISASTER IN LOS ALAMOS ON THE DAY OF LOUIS SLOTIN'S SHOCKING ACCIDENT THAT CAUSED HIS DEATH.

IT WAS TUESDAY, MAY 21, 1946, AT THE OMEGA LAB, LOS ALAMOS.

SLOTIN, SCIENTIST AND CHIEF BOMB BUILDER, WAS SHOWING ME HOW TO BRING TWO HALVES OF A BERYLLIUM-COATED SPHERE CONTAINING PLUTONIUM TOGETHER TO MEASURE THE BEGINNING OF A FISSION REACTION.

THIS WAS GOING TO TO BE MY JOB NEXT...

SLOTIN MOVED THE TWO HALVES TOGETHER WHILE ME AND THE OTHERS LOOKED ON. THE HALVES WERE KEPT SEPARATED WITH A SCREWDRIVER BUT HE SLIPPED...

THEY TOUCHED AND INSTANTLY A BLUE GLOW FILLED THE ROOM.

THE PLUTONIUM HAD GONE "SUPER-CRITICAL"— STARTING AN INSTANT CHAIN REACTION RELEASING IMMENSE RADIATION INTO THE ROOM.

SLOTIN THREW THE TWO HALVES, STOPPING THE REACTION, BUT THE DAMAGE WAS DONE. HE RECIEVED 1,000 RADS OF RADIATION AND DIED 9 DAYS LATER.

I RAN FROM THE ROOM IN TERROR, BUT GOT 200 RADS. IT WOULD HAVE BEEN MORE BUT SLOTIN'S BODY BLOCKED THE INITIAL WASH OF RADIATION.

Nothing as dramatic as that was likely to happen at SANDSTONE, but levels of acceptable radiation were standardized and precautions taken.

At TRINITY, film badges made by Kodak were given to key personnel, but not to everyone present.

For SANDSTONE more and better badges were issued, some capable of recording exposure from 0.005 to 20,000 rads but most with a range of 0.1 to 10 rads and still only 1/5th of the participants were badged.

AC GRAVES

POINT 1 RADS PER 24 HOURS IS PERMISSIBLE; 3 RADS PER 24 HOURS IS OK UNDER UNUSUAL CIRCUMSTANCES.

DANGER RADIATION GREEN BADGE MEN ONLY

WHAT ARE "UNUSUAL CIRCUMSTANCES?"

CHAPTER 3
NUTMEG

Summer 1949. Deep in the Kazak steppe, an area that will be known as "The Polygon."

USSR

KAZAKHSTAN

CHINA

SEVENTY KILOMETERS SOUTH IS WHERE WE WILL CONSTRUCT THE TEST SITE.

THE RESEARCH CAMP IS HERE, TO THE NORTHWEST OF THE SETTLEMENT SEMIPALATINSK-21, ON THE RIVER IRTYSH.

TELL ME ABOUT YOUR MEMORIES OF THE LANDSCAPE THERE...

...AND MIRAGES OF MYSTERIOUS MOUNTAINS AND LAKES.

THE STEPPES WERE COVERED IN FEATHER-GRASS AND WORMWOOD...

...A SMALL FLOCK OF BLACK STARLINGS, AND SOMETIMES A HAWK IN THE SKY...

THE PEOPLE OF THIS REGION ARE MOSTLY HORSEMEN AND HERDERS, DESCENDENTS OF THE NOMADS OF THE STEPPES.

DURING THE PERIOD OF FORCED STATE FARMS, A QUARTER OF THE POPULATION STARVED. THE KARLAG GULAG WAS A PLACE OF DEATH AND MISERY FOR HUNDREDS OF THOUSANDS.

'GULAG' DEATH CAMPS

POLYGON TEST SITE

KAZAKHSTAN

38

The Soviets knew few specifics about the effects of nuclear weapons from either the bombings in Japan or the U.S. tests. They constructed elaborate stage sets populated with animals, soldiers, and equipment.

TOMORROW AT 6 AM...

...WE SEE IF WE LIVE IN GLORY AS HEROES OF SOCIALIST LABOR....

...OR DIE AS FAILURES.

40

43

WELCOME TO LOS ALAMOS. THE PURPOSE OF THIS MEETING IS TO CONSIDER, FROM THE POINT OF VIEW OF RADIOLOGICAL HAZARD, WHETHER OR NOT IT IS ACCEPTABLE TO CONDUCT TESTS OF ATOMIC WEAPONS AT THE CONTINENTAL SITE...

...LET ME STRESS THE EXTREME UNCERTAINTY OF THE ELEMENTS WE HAVE TO GO ON, AND THAT WE DID OUR BEST WITH THESE...

...THE GROUP IS ATTEMPTING TO AGREE ON PHYSICAL FACTS.

ASSUME A CERTAIN DENSITY OF POPULATION, EXCLUDING THE CITIES AND TAKING ONLY THE RURAL POPULATION. LET US CONSIDER THE ZONE OF 100 MILES FROM GROUND ZERO WILL BE GUARDED, HEAVILY MONITORED, EVACUATED, ETC.

THE ZONE OF INTEREST, THEN, IS THE ONE BETWEEN 100 AND 300 MILES IN RADIUS, AN AREA ROUGHLY 4 X 104 MI2. NOW, 1% OF THIS AREA WILL BE EXPOSED TO DOSES RANGING FROM ~10 TO ~50 R, SO THAT 400 MI2 WILL ACTUALLY BE EXPOSED TO THIS DOSE.

FOR A RURAL POPULATION, THE MATHEMATICAL EXPECTANCY WILL BE SOME AVERAGE NUMBER OF PEOPLE EXPOSED TO DOSES OF THIS ORDER OF MAGNITUDE.

IN CITIES, OF COURSE, THE EXPECTANCY WILL HAVE LESS MEANING SINCE THERE ARE MUCH WIDER FLUCTUATIONS. THE PROBABILITY OF 1% IS ASSUMED FOR BOTH CASES—THIS IS THE SIZE OF THE RISK...

AFTER DOROTHEA LANGE

WHAT DOES HE MEAN BY "SIZE OF THE RISK"?

THE NUMBER OF PEOPLE IN THE TEST ZONE LIKELY TO RECEIVE A HIGHER THAN RECOMMENDED DOSE OF RADS.

...I'M SORRY TO BRING UP PSYCHOLOGICAL IMPLICATIONS...

...BUT IF CONDITIONS ARE SUCH THAT 10 R WILL BE RECEIVED, PEOPLE SHOULD BE WARNED TO STAY INDOORS, TAKE SHOWERS, ETC.

GENTLEMEN, I REFUSE TO HAVE MY NAME ON THIS REPORT...

46

48

CHAPTER 4
RANGER

TREATY WITH THE WESTERN SHOSHONI, 1863.

Treaty of Peace and Friendship made at Ruby Valley, in the Territory of Nevada, this first day of October, A. D. one thousand eight hundred and sixty-three, between the United States of America, represented by the undersigned commissioners, and the Western Bands of the Shoshonee Nation of Indians, represented by their Chiefs and Principal Men and Warriors, as follows:

...THEY SAID THIS PLACE WAS UNINHABITED, BUT JUST LOOKING AROUND IT SEEMS LIKE THERE MUST HAVE BEEN PEOPLE LIVING HERE FOR A LONG, LONG TIME...

...THEY TOLD ME THIS PLACE WAS "LIFELESS," BUT EVERYWHERE I LOOK I SEE ANIMALS. I HEARD ONE OF THE GUYS WORKING ON THE MOUNTAIN SAW A PANTHER.

Immediately after the announcement that the Nevada site was chosen, work began on PROJECT RANGER.

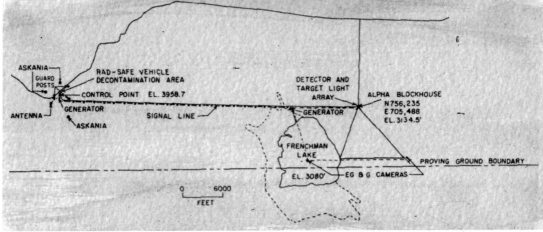

ASKANIA
GUARD POSTS
RAD-SAFE VEHICLE DECONTAMINATION AREA
CONTROL POINT EL. 3958.7
ANTENNA
GENERATOR
ASKANIA
SIGNAL LINE
DETECTOR AND TARGET LIGHT ARRAY
GENERATOR
ALPHA BLOCKHOUSE
N 756,235
E 705,488
EL. 3134.5'
FRENCHMAN LAKE
EL. 3080'
PROVING GROUND BOUNDARY
EG & G CAMERAS
0   6000
FEET

For the first Nevada tests, cars were placed across the desert to see the effect of a blast on civilian vehicles and occupants.

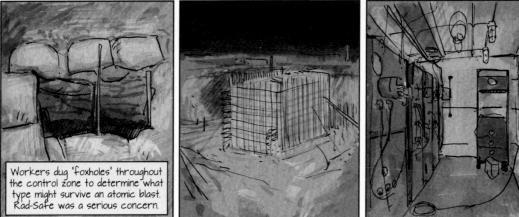

Workers dug "foxholes" throughout the control zone to determine what type might survive an atomic blast. Rad-Safe was a serious concern.

Las Vegas, Nevada, is one of the most amiably raffish communities in the nation.

The sunshine seems to be permanent. Breakfast is served 24 hours a day.

Even the filling stations have their batteries of slot machines.

Just what the nuclear scientists and the military men are up to is what every Las Vegan wonders.

It is assumed that the experiments are concerned with such problems as the production of a lighter-weight bomb, with bombs in the form of guided missiles...

...with whether an atomic blast produces sufficient heat to "trigger" the infinitely more destructive hydrogen bomb.

The Las Vegans don't know the answers, of course. All they can do is "live with the bomb," tolerating it as they might any other perplexing visitor.

All in all, Las Vegas can be described as pleased with its new acquisition. There has been an influx of visitors, and the town's publicity man has had the local hairdresser create an "atomic" coiffure.

On a more solemn note, the local paper said, "Now we have become part of the most important work carried on by our country today."

THERE WAS A KINDA FLASH LIT UP THE WINDOW—A REAL BIG FLASH IT WAS.

WITH IT COMES A BANG—BINGO! JUST LIKE THAT.

I THOUGHT TWO CARS MUST HAVE HIT INTO ONE ANOTHER ON THE ROAD OUTSIDE.

THIS WHITE FLASH STARTED ON THE GROUND AND SORT OF SWOOSHED UP INTO THE AIR.

I RECKONED THERE WASN'T MUCH I COULD DO ABOUT IT. SO I JUST SAT DOWN AND ATE MY BREAKFAST.

DURING THE RANGER SERIES, MANY OF YOU HAVE ASKED WHY NUCLEAR WEAPONS AND DEVICES ARE FIELD TESTED.

IN A WORLD IN WHICH FREE PEOPLE HAVE NO NUCLEAR MONOPOLY, THE UNITED STATES MUST KEEP ITS ATOMIC STRENGTH AT PEAK LEVEL.

THAT IS THE BASIC REASON FOR THESE TESTS IN NEVADA.

MAIL

THEN, THERE ARE AT LEAST NINE DEVELOPMENTAL PURPOSES SERVED BY FULL-SCALE NUCLEAR TESTS.

ONLY FOR THE FIRST PURPOSE, A PROOF TEST, WOULD THE DETONATION NECESSARILY BE OF A WEAPON AS SUCH...

...IN MOST CIRCUMSTANCES, AN EXPERIMENTAL DEVICE IS DESIGNED...

...IN EITHER CASE TESTING IMPROVES THE STOCKPILE POSITION.

a. To proof test a weapon for desired military characteristics before it enters the national stockpile.

b. To provide a firm basis for undertaking the extensive engineering and fabrication effort which must be expanded to carry a "breadboard" model to a version satisfactory for stockpile purposes.

c. To demonstrate the adequacy, inadequacy or limitations of current theoretical approaches.

d. To explore phenomena which can vitally affect the efficiency and performance of weapons but which are not susceptible to prior theoretical analysis of sufficient certainty.

e. To provide a basis of choice among existing theoretical methods of weapon improvement so as to concentrate effort along lines of greatest practical significance.

f. To determine the validity of entirely new and untried principles proposed for applications to improve performance.

g. To provide entirely new information pertinent and valuable to weapon development and arising simply as a by-product of scientific observation of full-scale detonations.

h. To gain time in very urgent development programs by substituting tests for a portion of a possible but lengthy program of laboratory calculations and experiments.

i. To provide as a by-product basic scientific information to add to the stockpile of such knowledge.

Over the next year things really picked up. In the Pacific on Eniwetok the "boosted item," an experiment to use fission to spark fusion, was successfully detonated.

The Soviets completed another test series in Kazakhstan and seemed to be catching up quickly.

In Nevada the proving ground was buzzing with activity.

Security was tighter. Every time you came through the gates to the site, you had to show your official ID—no matter how many times you came and went.

The folks living around the test site were told in no uncertain terms that if they tried to enter without permission they would be shot on sight, no questions asked.

Stories of Russian spies in New Mexico made the threat of espionage seem real. There was no doubt that the Cold War was a WAR out at Mercury!

That sense was heightened when 5,000 soldiers from the III Corps arrived to take part in Camp Desert Rock I as part of Operation Buster-Jangle in the fall of '51.

We all knew there was something different about BUSTER-JANGLE.

There were lots of new kinds of experiments and the scale was much bigger.

Most intriguing was Camp Desert Rock, which was both a place—third biggest town in Nevada in 1951—and an operation to test the effect of atomic blasts on American G.I.s.

Desert Rock troops set up foxholes and trenches all across the desert in the control point zone radiating out from 'Ground Zero,' or 'GZ,' as they called it.

They drove all kinds of vehicles and tanks into position.

There were helicopters, planes of all description, and basically the setup for a major battle.

During the blasts of BUSTER-JANGLE, the military men tested out the effect of atomic bombs on their equipment, but they were really there to test the effect on the men themselves.

I don't mean they wanted to do them physical harm—they tried hard to avoid physical injury, which is pretty tough when you're asking G.I.s to run straight into the immediate aftermath of an atomic blast!...

...No, the real experiment at Desert Rock was on the soldiers' minds.

Military leaders were worried that the sheer otherworldly horror of an atomic blast could scramble the brain of your average soldier, render him helpless before he even got any effect from the blast or radiation.

SOMETIMES WE WENT LIKE FORTY OR FIFTY HOURS WITH NO SLEEP.

WE DIDN'T REALLY KNOW A LOT ABOUT THE HAZARDS OF RADIATION...WE DROVE 140 MILES BACK AND FORTH EACH DAY...OR WE STAYED OUT

THE SHOTS WERE SCARY...

...I MEAN THEY WERE BEAUTIFUL TO LOOK AT BUT VERY SCARY TO THINK WHAT WOULD HAPPEN IF THEY EVER HAD TO USE IT.

BUT IT WAS INTERESTING, AND IF YOU NEEDED A BREAK IN MERCURY, THERE WAS A BOWLING ALLEY, MOVIE THEATER, A LIBRARY...

...EVEN A FANCY WESTERN STEAK HOUSE WITH SOME OF THE BEST FOOD IN THE STATE.

THE VARIETY AND EXTENT OF THE TESTS WAS INTERESTING TOO.

THERE WERE AIR DROPS WITH TROOPS RIGHT THERE WITHIN THE THREE-MILE RADIUS OF THE BULLSEYE.

THERE WERE TOWER SHOTS.

FOR THESE THEY BUILT THESE HUGE STEEL FRAME TOWERS 500 FEET TALL WITH LONG GUIDE WIRES HOLDING THEM

THE DEVICE WOULD BE SECURED AT THE TOP.

WHAT STRUCK ME WAS THE BLINKING LIGHT WAY UP ON THAT TOWER.

WHEN YOU WERE IN A TRENCH PEEKING UP AT THAT FLASHING RED LIGHT IN THE DARK QUIET OF THE DESERT...

...AND THEN THE ECHO OF THE COUNTDOWN THROUGH THOSE HUGE LOUDSPEAKERS.

COUNTING DOWN THE SECONDS WAS REALLY EERIE...

THE TIME SEEMED TO DRAG ON FOREVER...

...THEN...

...BOOM!...

...RIGHT DOWN INTO YOUR SKELETON.

THEN WE SCRAMBLED UP AND WALKED QUICKLY TOWARD GROUND ZERO.

OF COURSE WE KNEW WE GOT SOME RADS. THEY TOLD US WE WOULD.

FEELING THAT SOUND IN YOUR BONES MADE YOU PRAY HARD WE WOULD NEVER USE IT ON PEOPLE AGAIN.

THEY CHECKED US WITH GEIGER COUNTERS, WHICH WERE CLICKING LIKE CRAZY...

CLICK! CLICK! CLICK!

THEN THEY HAD A GUY WHO SWEPT US OFF WITH A BROOM, JUST A REGULAR OLD KITCHEN BROOM THAT WAS NEW AND LOOKED LIKE IT CAME RIGHT OFF THE RACK AT SEARS ROEBUCK!

FUNNY THAT WAS WHAT THEY HAD TO USE FOR CLEANING US UP AFTER BLOWING UP A BOMB WORTH MILLIONS OF DOLLARS MADE BY A WHOLE TEAM OF NOBEL PRIZE-WINNING SCIENTISTS.

WHEN WE GOT BACK TO OUR HOME BASE AT FORT CAMPBELL, KENTUCKY...

...WE ALL HAD TO TAKE A POLYGRAPH WHILE A TEAM OF DOCTORS TOOK NOTES.

61

OPERATION IVY, NOVEMBER 1952
ENEWETOK ATOLL

ELUGELAB
ISLAND

1952 was an important year for testing, finishing in the Pacific with MIKE, the first full-scale H-bomb experiment.

MIKE looked crude, but was, according to Oppenheimer, "technically sweet."

Standing 20 feet tall on end, with a diameter of almost 7 feet, and weighing 82 tons, MIKE was not a deliverable bomb.

...But it worked.

Yielding 10.4 megatons, the blast was massive, with the cloud soaring above 100,000 feet.

CONTROL POINT, COME IN... ELUGELAB IS GONE! THE WHOLE ISLAND IS JUST GONE!

I HAVE A SENSE OF FOREBODING WHENEVER I THINK OF MIKE. IT MARKED A REAL CHANGE IN HISTORY...

...A MOMENT WHEN THE COURSE OF THE WORLD SUDDENLY SHIFTED, FROM A PATH IT HAD BEEN ON TO A MORE DANGEROUS ONE...

CHAPTER 5
DOOM TOWN

November 4, 1952. Four days after the successful detonation of MIKE, Dwight D. Eisenhower becomes the 34th president of the United States.

MISTER PRESIDENT, DOCUMENTS RELATED TO THE MOST RECENT TEST SERIES IN THE PACIFIC FROM CHAIRMAN DEAN.

The island of the atoll that was used for the shot—Elugelab—is missing, and in its place there is now an underwater crater of some 1,500 yards in diameter.

COMPLETE DESTRUCTION IS THE NEGATION OF PEACE.

IN THE NAME OF THE PRESIDENT, I CALL UPON EVERY AMERICAN TO SPEED CIVIL DEFENSE PROGRAMS IN THE IMMEDIATE, URGENT INTEREST OF OUR NATIONAL SECURITY.

It was still cold and windy when reporters started arriving at the test site in March of 1953.

There were thousands of people out there working on a wide range of experiments.

Driving around the desert over hundreds of square miles, I could hardly believe the extent of it only 3 years after they first set the place up.

We drove past a huge set of "Collimators" that were used March 24, 1953, for the first time in continental nuclear tests. This system replaced a pretty crude and expensive cable system for recording gamma rays or neutrons.

Inside the control point command center a corp of smart young guys from the best universities were busy working out the trajectories of drops and blasts.

The rays move from a portion of the detonation on the far tower through the line-of-sight holes in successive towers to an underground recording station, covering approximately 4,000 feet of transmission. I was told this was all to get a better sense of the radiation effect and fallout from a test.

It all felt like a level up from the hasty rough and tumble of RANGER.

Between March and June we watched a whole series of tests that demonstrated just how far the atomic weapons program had progressed. I was struck in particular by the GRABLE event.

For this test they constructed an atomic shell small enough to be fired by a 280-mm cannon.

I'm sure I was not alone in thinking that there was something truly spooky about the idea that atomic bombs had gone from these giant experimental-looking things, so big a plane could barely lift one, to something so small you could shoot it out of a cannon. The bomb was physically little but yielded 15 kilotons.

During Upshot-Knothole there was another extensive set of Desert Rock troop exercises.

This time, though, some of the brass had to participate on the front line because of complaints about "human guinea pigs" from the test the previous year.

The most interesting and disturbing series that summer was OPERATION DOORSTEP and the so-called Doom Town built for that show.

OPERATION DOORSTEP was the first opportunity for the Federal Civil Defense Administration (FCDA) to participate in a major test demonstration program...

...Including an "open shot" with more than 600 dignitaries watching from bleachers and the biggest corps of photographers and reporters ever assembled.

There were two parts to the civil effects test in the summer of '53 and over the next several years.

First, to test the immediate effect of atomic blasts on civilian infrastructure.

Second, to study the radiation effects through nearby and off-site fallout. To document the "intensity patterns, particle size, and radiostrontium deposition," as the scientists say.

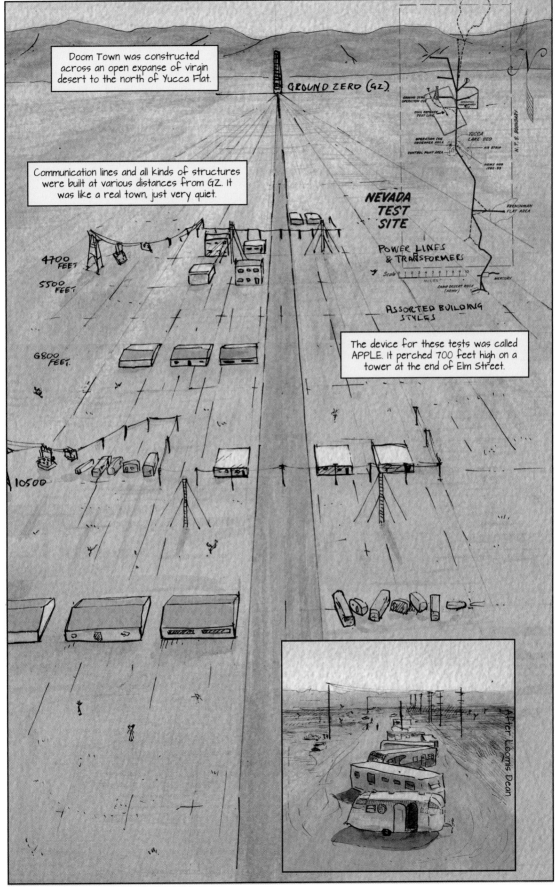

Doom Town was constructed across an open expanse of virgin desert to the north of Yucca Flat.

GROUND ZERO (GZ)

Communication lines and all kinds of structures were built at various distances from GZ. It was like a real town, just very quiet.

4700 FEET

5500 FEET

6800 FEET.

10500

NEVADA TEST SITE

POWER LINES & TRANSFORMERS

ASSORTED BUILDING STYLES

The device for these tests was called APPLE. It perched 700 feet high on a tower at the end of Elm Street.

After Loomis Dean

67

The focal point of this experiment was two typical colonial two-story houses standing in for the average American home.

The houses were built at 3,500 and 7,500 feet from the bomb tower. They were identical except for different exterior finishes.

Out in the desert around the houses, workers parked a variety of civilian passenger cars...

...And in them they placed fully dressed mannequins.

These strange tourists were proxies for citizens used to determine the amount of exposure to radiation and physical protection that might be afforded those hiding in their car during attack.

One simple question concerned the effect of an atomic blast on the motor...

...Would it still work so that you might drive to safety?

Each house had a full basement with a different kind of rudimentary bomb shelter where the family was supposed to hide during attack.

The FCDA said they wanted to impress upon Americans the "seriousness of nuclear weapons" and the necessity for civil defense.

WE ARE TAKING YOUR PLACE IN NEVADA'S ATOMIC TESTS MARCH 17

Men, women, children, and even baby mannequins were acquired from the L.A. Darling Company and trucked in from Las Vegas along with full sets of clothes donated by the local J.C. Penney Co.

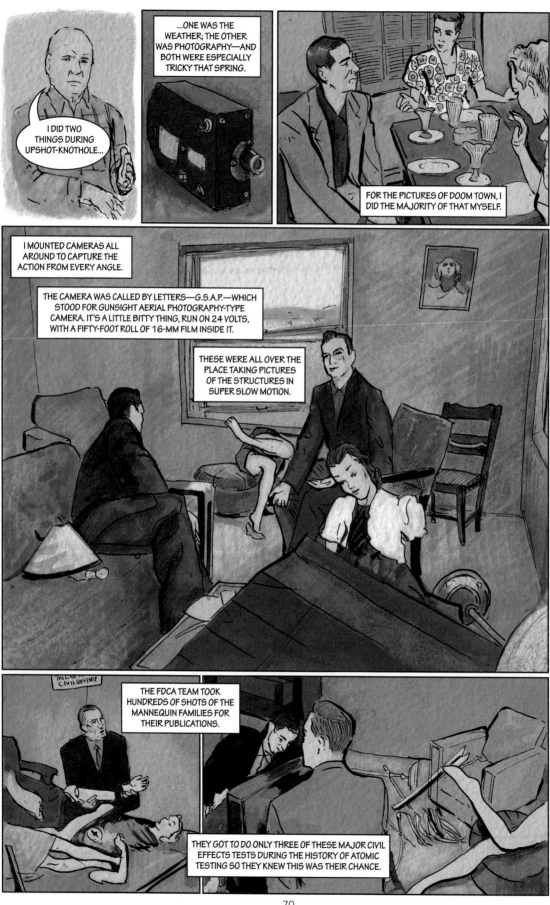

I DID TWO THINGS DURING UPSHOT-KNOTHOLE...

...ONE WAS THE WEATHER; THE OTHER WAS PHOTOGRAPHY—AND BOTH WERE ESPECIALLY TRICKY THAT SPRING.

FOR THE PICTURES OF DOOM TOWN, I DID THE MAJORITY OF THAT MYSELF.

I MOUNTED CAMERAS ALL AROUND TO CAPTURE THE ACTION FROM EVERY ANGLE.

THE CAMERA WAS CALLED BY LETTERS—G.S.A.P.—WHICH STOOD FOR GUNSIGHT AERIAL PHOTOGRAPHY-TYPE CAMERA. IT'S A LITTLE BITTY THING, RUN ON 24 VOLTS, WITH A FIFTY-FOOT ROLL OF 16-MM FILM INSIDE IT.

THESE WERE ALL OVER THE PLACE TAKING PICTURES OF THE STRUCTURES IN SUPER SLOW MOTION.

THE FDCA TEAM TOOK HUNDREDS OF SHOTS OF THE MANNEQUIN FAMILIES FOR THEIR PUBLICATIONS.

THEY GOT TO DO ONLY THREE OF THESE MAJOR CIVIL EFFECTS TESTS DURING THE HISTORY OF ATOMIC TESTING SO THEY KNEW THIS WAS THEIR CHANCE.

THE CAMERAS WERE STILL GOING THROUGHOUT.

I'LL TELL YOU WHAT HAPPENED...

AS SOON AS THE LIGHT WENT OFF FROM THE BOMB, IT WOULD TRIGGER THE CAMERA.

...THAT ALL HAPPENED IN A COUPLE OF SECONDS, THEN YOU COULD TURN AROUND...

...IT WAS ETHEREAL.

I REMEMBER THE YUCCA PLANTS, ALL THE DESERT PLANTS, CAUGHT FIRE FOR MILES AROUND, AND IT WAS GHOSTLIKE BECAUSE IT LOOKED LIKE A CITY THAT HAD BEEN INCINERATED.

THEN A FEW SECONDS LATER, *BAMMM!!!*, THE SHOCK WAVE HIT, SO YOU GOT THAT.

GENTLEMEN, NEXT UP IS **ENCORE,** THE MOST EXTENSIVE SERIES OF EXPERIMENTS TO DATE DURING ONE TEST.

Don English's images lightened the mood, but most of ENCORE was dead serious.

The Army set up a complete hospital to test the extent of destruction to health services.

The Desert Rock soldiers, more than 13,000 total, conducted full-scale mock battles in the aftermath of the shot.

The Army and U.S. Forest Service placed 145 ponderosa pine trees with an average height of 51 feet, in a grove out in the playa 6,500 feet from GZ.

Taken from the slopes of Mt. Charleston, they were cemented into the desert floor.

The footage of that little forest blown apart was some of the most famous ever shot.

There were five more wooden houses set up to show still more about how our homes would be destroyed during attack.

To evaluate the protection against skin burns in an atomic blast, the Army prepared 55 shaved pigs dressed in uniforms and placed at varying distances from GZ.

The pigs were used because their flesh is very similar to human flesh. The joke was that the desert smelled like bacon.

Of course, Rad-Safe was important with all those reporters around, but it didn't all go as planned...

LOCAL TRAJECTORIES

THE EARLY REPORTS REVEAL EXCEPTIONALLY HIGH READINGS FROM THE SIMON EVENT.

WE NEED ALL HANDS HELPING WITH TRACKING DATA AND RAD-SAFE TEAMS WORKING OVERTIME ON BADGES AND ON-SITE READINGS.

THIRTY-NINE INDIVIDUALS EXCEEDED 3.9 RADS—THAT'S QUITE UNEXPECTED.

WE'RE SEEING A PATTERN HERE...

...OFF-SITE MONITORS ARE GETTING AS HIGH AS 0.46 R RIGHT ON THE DAMN HIGHWAY NEAR GLENDALE, NEVADA. WE NEED ROAD BLOCKS NOW. CALL THE LOCAL AND STATE POLICE. WE NEED CARS CHECKED.

WHAT DO WE DO IF THEY'RE HIGH?

OFFER THEM A FREE CAR WASH AND TELL THEM "NOT TO WORRY. SIMPLY A PRECAUTION."

WHAT'S HAPPENING HERE?

AEC BUSINESS.

YOUR VEHICLE HAS BEEN CONTAMINATED FROM A TEST OVER AT THE SITE THAT TOOK OFF IN THE WIND.

NOTHING TO WORRY ABOUT. JUST A PRECAUTION. AND YOU'RE GOING TO GET A CAR WASH OUT OF THE DEAL.

NO ONE QUESTIONED OUR AUTHORITY FOR OUR ACTIONS.

WHAT WAS THEIR REACTION?

THEY APPEARED TO BE NOT OVERLY CONCERNED.

THEY MERELY WANTED TO KNOW WHAT TO DO AND HOW TO GO ABOUT IT.

ONCE THIS WAS EXPLAINED, EVERYTHING FLOWED VERY SMOOTHLY.

CHAPTER 6
FALLOUT

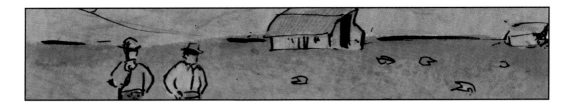

PORTRAIT OF PHOTOGRAPHERS ANSEL ADAMS AND DORTHEA LANGE, *THREE MORMON TOWNS OF SOUTHERN UTAH, 1953*

CEDAR CITY, UTAH

I AM SPEAKING TODAY IN A LANGUAGE THAT IS NEW...

...THE LANGUAGE OF ATOMIC WARFARE.

SINCE THE FIRST ATOMIC TEST IN ALAMAGORDO, WE HAVE CONDUCTED 42 ATOMIC TEST EXPLOSIONS.

TODAY, ONE AIRCRAFT CARRIER OF OUR NAVY COULD DELIVER BOMBS EXCEEDING THE EXPLOSIVE EQUIVALENT OF ALL THE BOMBS AND ROCKETS DROPPED BY GERMANY ON THE UNITED KINGDOM THROUGH ALL THE YEARS OF WWII.

AGAINST THE DARK BACKGROUND OF ATOMIC BOMBING, THE UNITED STATES DOES NOT WISH MERELY TO PRESENT STRENGTH, BUT ALSO TO PROMOTE PEACE.

THE UNITED STATES, HEEDING THE SUGGESTION OF THE GENERAL ASSEMBLY OF THE UNITED NATIONS, IS PREPARED TO MEET PRIVATELY WITH THE SOVIET UNION TO SEEK "AN ACCEPTABLE SOLUTION" TO THE ATOMIC ARMAMENTS RACE WHICH OVERSHADOWS NOT ONLY THE PEACE, BUT THE VERY LIFE, OF THE WORLD.

ATOMS FOR PEACE

THE SOVIET H-BOMB COULD NEGATE OUR SUBSTANTIAL LEAD IN DESTRUCTIVE CAPABILITY.

OBVIOUSLY, WE NEED TO ACCELERATE THE HIGH-YIELD THERMONUCLEAR WEAPONS PROGRAM AND LOW-YIELD FISSION PRODUCTS FOR TACTICAL USES.

IF WE PROCEED AS YOU SUGGEST, BY 1957 THE STOCKPILE WOULD BE THE EQUIVALENT OF SEVERAL BILLIONS OF TONS OF TNT.

THAT QUANTITY OF NUCLEAR WEAPONS COULD PERHAPS DESTROY THE ENTIRE ARABLE PORTION OF THE U.S.S.R.

SEND THE INFORMATION TO PRESIDENT EISENHOWER. THE MEMO NEEDS TO STATE CLEARLY THAT THE UPCOMING CASTLE-BRAVO THERMONUCLEAR TESTS IN THE PACIFIC AT BIKINI ARE NOW IMPERATIVE.

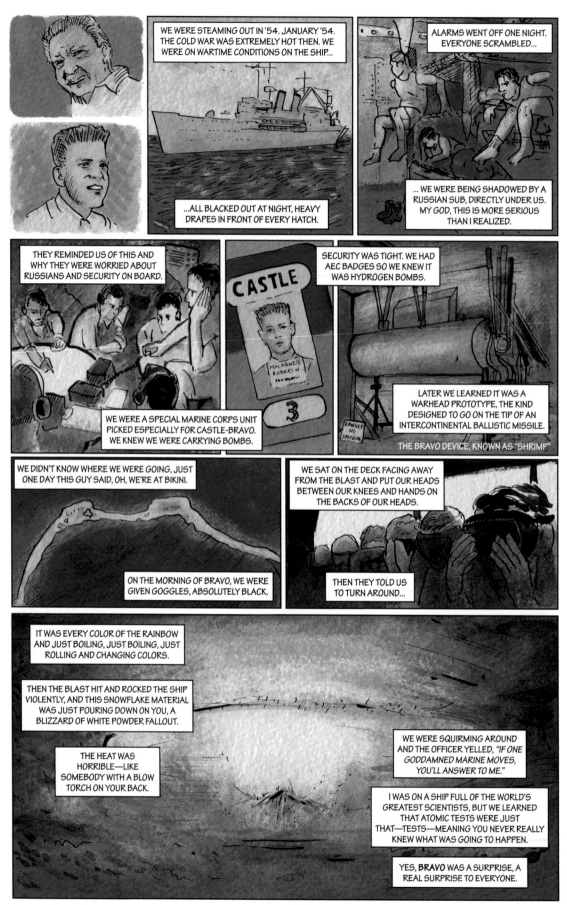

WE WERE STEAMING OUT IN '54. JANUARY '54. THE COLD WAR WAS EXTREMELY HOT THEN. WE WERE ON WARTIME CONDITIONS ON THE SHIP...

...ALL BLACKED OUT AT NIGHT, HEAVY DRAPES IN FRONT OF EVERY HATCH.

ALARMS WENT OFF ONE NIGHT. EVERYONE SCRAMBLED...

... WE WERE BEING SHADOWED BY A RUSSIAN SUB, DIRECTLY UNDER US. MY GOD, THIS IS MORE SERIOUS THAN I REALIZED.

THEY REMINDED US OF THIS AND WHY THEY WERE WORRIED ABOUT RUSSIANS AND SECURITY ON BOARD.

WE WERE A SPECIAL MARINE CORPS UNIT PICKED ESPECIALLY FOR CASTLE-BRAVO. WE KNEW WE WERE CARRYING BOMBS.

CASTLE

MACKENZIE ROGERS W

3

SECURITY WAS TIGHT. WE HAD AEC BADGES SO WE KNEW IT WAS HYDROGEN BOMBS.

DANGER NO SMOKING

LATER WE LEARNED IT WAS A WARHEAD PROTOTYPE, THE KIND DESIGNED TO GO ON THE TIP OF AN INTERCONTINENTAL BALLISTIC MISSILE.

THE BRAVO DEVICE, KNOWN AS "SHRIMP"

WE DIDN'T KNOW WHERE WE WERE GOING, JUST ONE DAY THIS GUY SAID, OH, WE'RE AT BIKINI.

ON THE MORNING OF BRAVO, WE WERE GIVEN GOGGLES, ABSOLUTELY BLACK.

WE SAT ON THE DECK FACING AWAY FROM THE BLAST AND PUT OUR HEADS BETWEEN OUR KNEES AND HANDS ON THE BACKS OF OUR HEADS.

THEN THEY TOLD US TO TURN AROUND...

IT WAS EVERY COLOR OF THE RAINBOW AND JUST BOILING, JUST BOILING, JUST ROLLING AND CHANGING COLORS.

THEN THE BLAST HIT AND ROCKED THE SHIP VIOLENTLY, AND THIS SNOWFLAKE MATERIAL WAS JUST POURING DOWN ON YOU, A BLIZZARD OF WHITE POWDER FALLOUT.

THE HEAT WAS HORRIBLE—LIKE SOMEBODY WITH A BLOW TORCH ON YOUR BACK.

WE WERE SQUIRMING AROUND AND THE OFFICER YELLED, "IF ONE GODDAMNED MARINE MOVES, YOU'LL ANSWER TO ME."

I WAS ON A SHIP FULL OF THE WORLD'S GREATEST SCIENTISTS, BUT WE LEARNED THAT ATOMIC TESTS WERE JUST THAT—TESTS—MEANING YOU NEVER REALLY KNEW WHAT WAS GOING TO HAPPEN.

YES, **BRAVO** WAS A SURPRISE, A REAL SURPRISE TO EVERYONE.

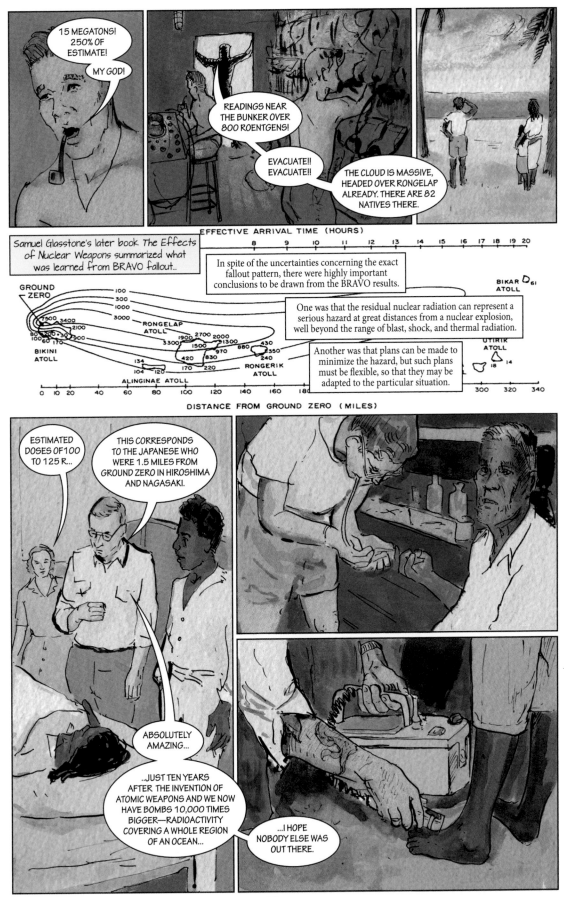

Samuel Glasstone's later book *The Effects of Nuclear Weapons* summarized what was learned from BRAVO fallout...

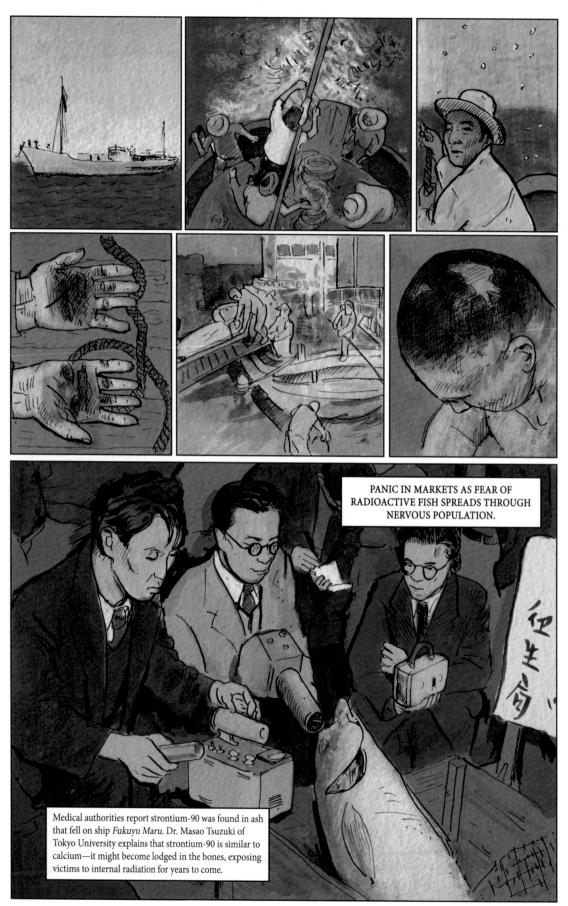

PANIC IN MARKETS AS FEAR OF
RADIOACTIVE FISH SPREADS THROUGH
NERVOUS POPULATION.

Medical authorities report strontium-90 was found in ash
that fell on ship *Fukuyu Maru*. Dr. Masao Tsuzuki of
Tokyo University explains that strontium-90 is similar to
calcium—it might become lodged in the bones, exposing
victims to internal radiation for years to come.

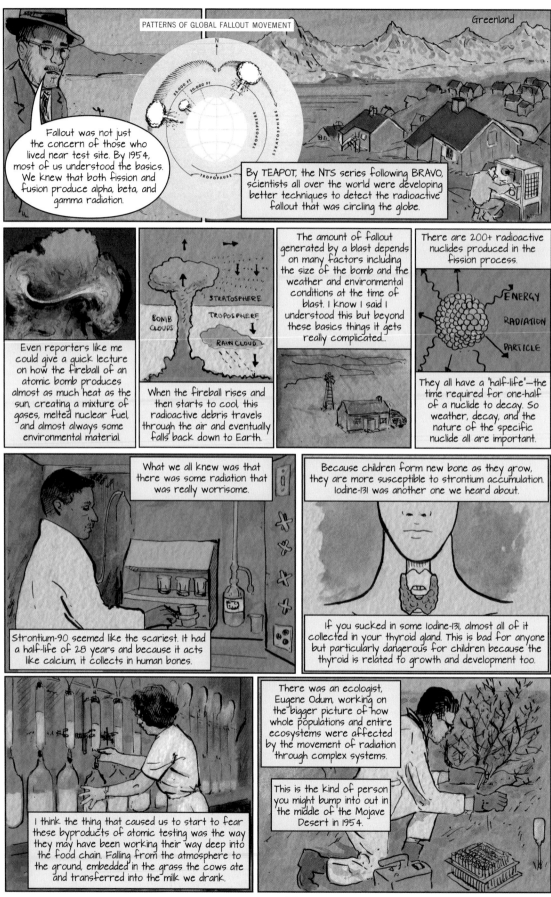

PATTERNS OF GLOBAL FALLOUT MOVEMENT

Greenland

Fallout was not just the concern of those who lived near test site. By 1954, most of us understood the basics. We knew that both fission and fusion produce alpha, beta, and gamma radiation.

By TEAPOT, the NTS series following BRAVO, scientists all over the world were developing better techniques to detect the radioactive fallout that was circling the globe.

Even reporters like me could give a quick lecture on how the fireball of an atomic bomb produces almost as much heat as the sun, creating a mixture of gases, melted nuclear fuel, and almost always some environmental material.

STRATOSPHERE
TROPOSPHERE
BOMB CLOUDS
RAIN CLOUD

When the fireball rises and then starts to cool, this radioactive debris travels through the air and eventually falls back down to Earth.

The amount of fallout generated by a blast depends on many factors including the size of the bomb and the weather and environmental conditions at the time of blast. I know I said I understood this but beyond these basics things it gets really complicated...

There are 200+ radioactive nuclides produced in the fission process.

ENERGY
RADIATION
PARTICLE

They all have a "half-life"—the time required for one-half of a nuclide to decay. So weather, decay, and the nature of the specific nuclide all are important.

What we all knew was that there was some radiation that was really worrisome.

Strontium-90 seemed like the scariest. It had a half-life of 28 years and because it acts like calcium, it collects in human bones.

Because children form new bone as they grow, they are more susceptible to strontium accumulation. Iodine-131 was another one we heard about.

If you sucked in some Iodine-131, almost all of it collected in your thyroid gland. This is bad for anyone but particularly dangerous for children because the thyroid is related to growth and development too.

I think the thing that caused us to start to fear these byproducts of atomic testing was the way they may have been working their way deep into the food chain. Falling from the atmosphere to the ground, embedded in the grass the cows ate and transferred into the milk we drank.

There was an ecologist, Eugene Odum, working on the bigger picture of how whole populations and entire ecosystems were affected by the movement of radiation through complex systems.

This is the kind of person you might bump into out in the middle of the Mojave Desert in 1954.

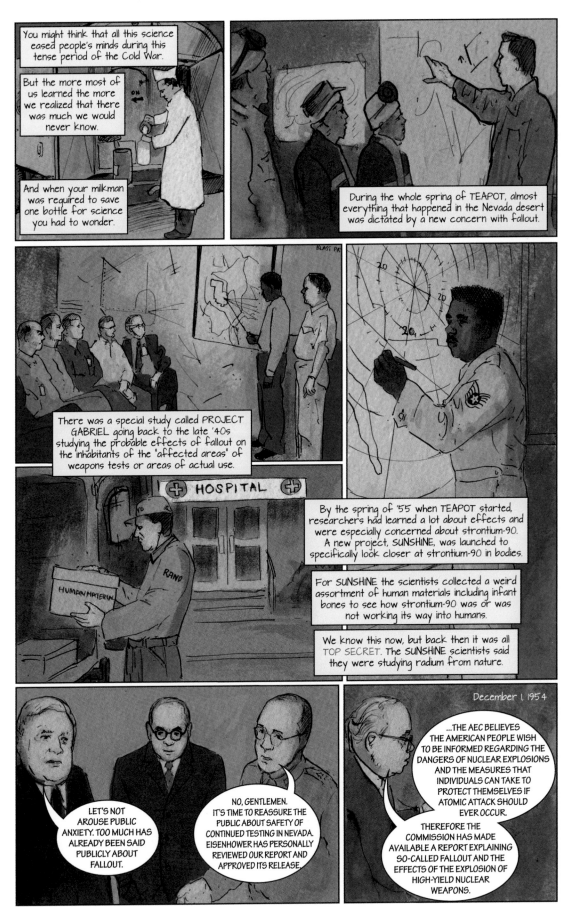

89

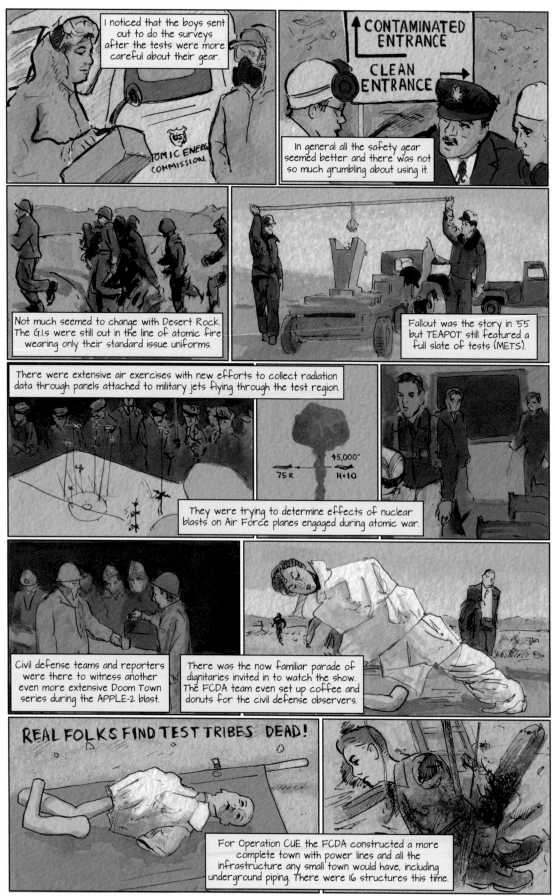

Despite growing concern about fallout, atomic tests were still an attraction in Las Vegas. Casinos held parties to watch the shots light up the early morning sky. The influx of observers and workers was a major boost to the local economy.

Public information films about atomic war were common by '55. In shorts before movies patrons far from testing saw the action provided by the FCDA and corporate sponsors.

The numbers were pretty impressive. Six-hundred civil defense observers, 300 reporters, 3,100 soldiers, 55 Patton tanks, 24 armored personnel carriers with more than 2,500 observers, workers, and others present for the TEAPOT Doom Town blast.

On the night of the 40 kt Apple-2 test, a huge storm blew across the desert with winds up to 50 mph.

LAS VEGAS REVIEW JOURNAL

VEGANS MISS BATH OF RADIATION

WIND CHANGE CAUSES FEARS

The wind direction was unusual, heading south-southwest right across Las Vegas.

That ferocious wind really spooked a lot of people and changed the tone about fallout.

TEAPOT began when there was still snow on the mountains and Joshua tree forests.

The series came to an end in May amid the bloom of desert flowers.

THE HOUSE IN THE MIDDLE

IN EVERY TOWN YOU'LL FIND RUNDOWN HOUSES...

...AND WHAT'S MORE, THAT HOUSE MAY BE DOOMED IN AN ATOMIC WAR.

TESTS WERE MADE OF ATOMIC HEAT ON MINIATURE HOUSES IN VARYING STAGES OF UPKEEP. DRY LEAVES AND LITTER SIMULATE CONDITIONS YOU'VE SEEN TOO MANY TIMES IN SLUM AREAS.

IN THE HOUSE ON THE RIGHT, AN EYESORE, OLD UNPAINTED WOOD AND TRASH IN THE YARD. THE HOUSE ON THE LEFT, DRY WOOD AND RUNDOWN CONDITION. THE PRODUCT OF YEARS OF NEGLECT, A TINDERBOX WAITING TO TURN INTO A BLAZING TORCH.

THE HOUSE IN THE MIDDLE, WELL MAINTAINED AND PAINTED WITH ORDINARY HOUSE PAINT. LET'S SEE WHAT HAPPENS.... THE LIGHT FLASH, THE HEAT WAVE, AND THEN THE BLAST WAVE!

THE HOUSE ON THE RIGHT IS THE FIRST TO IGNITE. THE TRASH SERVES AS KINDLING. THE HOUSE ON THE LEFT SMOLDERS, THEN IGNITES. IS THIS YOUR HOUSE?

PRODUCED BY THE NATIONAL CLEAN UP - PAINT UP - FIX UP BUREAU

THE HOUSE IN THE MIDDLE, CLEANED-UP, FIXED-UP, PAINTED-UP, DID NOT CATCH FIRE!

There were two more test series in the Pacific, quick on the heels of TEAPOT. WIGWAM was especially interesting. It took place in May of 1955, just 500 miles off the west coast of California out in open water.

97%

39,000'

REDWING was a series of tests aimed at weapons improvements.

The openness of REDWING was very different from the secrecy of CASTLE-BRAVO. The reason for this was obvious to anyone following U.S. politics. 1956 was an election year, and a nuclear test ban was a central issue throughout the preceding year.

On July 9, 1955, Bertrand Russell, a British philosopher, presented a manifesto against atomic weapons.

His call to the nations to "remember their humanity" was cosigned by Albert Einstein in his last public action before his death in April that year.

That same month U.S. president Dwight Eisenhower presented his "Open Skies" plan for arms control at a conference in Geneva, Switzerland. L to R: Russian premier Nikolai Bulganin, Eisenhower, French premier Edgar Faure, British prime minister Sir Anthony Eden.

Eisenhower's democratic opponent, Adlai Stevenson, supported a nuclear test ban and made it a key issue in the election.

FOR PRESIDENT
ADLAI E. STEVENSON

REDWING PRODUCED GOOD RESULTS. WITH EACH TEST SERIES WE HAVE A BETTER UNDERSTANDING OF HOW NUCLEAR WEAPONS WILL SERVE DURING ACTUAL WARFARE.

WE CAN ESTIMATE THAT A NUCLEAR ATTACK ON THE U.S.S.R. WOULD RESULT IN SEVERAL HUNDRED MILLION DEATHS.

WITH UNFAVORABLE WINDS IT COULD BE AS HIGH AS 500 MILLION DEATHS INCLUDING MILLIONS IN WESTERN EUROPE.

GENERAL SAYS H-BOMBS COULD KILL HALF-A-BILLION INCLUDING SOME OF OUR ALLIES...

STEVENSON SAYS WE MUST SPARE HUMANITY THE INCALCULABLE EFFECTS OF UNLIMITED HYDROGEN BOMB TESTING...

...POPE PIUS XII, WHO ALSO WARNS OF THE DANGERS OF TESTING, ASKS LEADERS TO SEEK COMPROMISE.

THIS AWFUL PROBLEM...

...ALL OUR DEFENSE PLANNING SEEMS TO OVERLOOK THE FACT THAT NOBODY CAN WIN A THERMONUCLEAR WAR.

WE HAVE GOT TO MOVE ON A TEST BAN OF SOME SORT OR WE ARE DOOMED.

YES SIR...

...BUT WHAT ABOUT PLUMBBOB?

CHAPTER 7
BOLTZMANN

95

I got a letter that June too, fom my pal Morse Salisbury, the director of the AEC's information services.

He was a fan of a speech I gave about the life of an atomic reporter...

...and asked me if I'd like to show up "in costume" for the next round of atomic reporting during PLUMBBOB.

BE CAREFUL.

WESTERN UNION
TELEGRAM
1207 (4-55)
W. P. MARSHALL, PRESIDENT

DOMESTIC SERVICE
Check the class of service desired; otherwise this message will be sent as a fast telegram
TELEGRAM
DAY LETTER
NIGHT LETTER

INTERNATIONAL SERVICE
Check the class of service desired; otherwise the message will be sent at the full rate
FULL RATE
LETTER TELEGRAM
SHORE-SHIP

NO. WDS-CL. OF SVC. | PD. OR COLL | CASH NO. | CHARGE TO THE ACCOUNT OF | TIME FILED
Michigan Department of Agriculture

To   Hugh D. Ivey   June 13, 19 57
Street and No.   CETO Director Program 36 Federal Civil Defense
Care of or
Apt. No.   Adm 3119192   Destination   Battle Creek, Michigan

Leave Lansing June sixteen seven thirty morning arrive Las
Vegas three forty five afternoon same date.

Even now the atmosphere at each test is supercharged with the knowledge that something new is being tried, and the suspicion that this time they may have put in too much vermouth and will touch off the end of the world.

Having seen a dozen or so tests, I knew this summer was different.

Senders's name and address (For reference)

Twenty-four shots, most ever.

Eighteen thousand DoD personnel, most ever.

Six thousand citizen civil defense community monitors invited for training.

It was quite a show they had planned for the lucky citizens who got a ticket.

SPECI

Knothole St

Mr.Geagley, you will find your accommodation in dormitory 501.

HUTMEN

QUONSET AREA

504
503
502
501

Upshot Ave

Jangle Street

A   E   L
B   F   M
C   G   N
D   H   O
P

114

112   115   110

Snapper Street

113   108   J   K   Buster
109   102

Crossroad Ave.

Ranger Ave.

Sandstone Ave.

104
103
105
106
107

116   100   127   11
125

Las Vegas and

Teapot Street

Mercury, Nevada

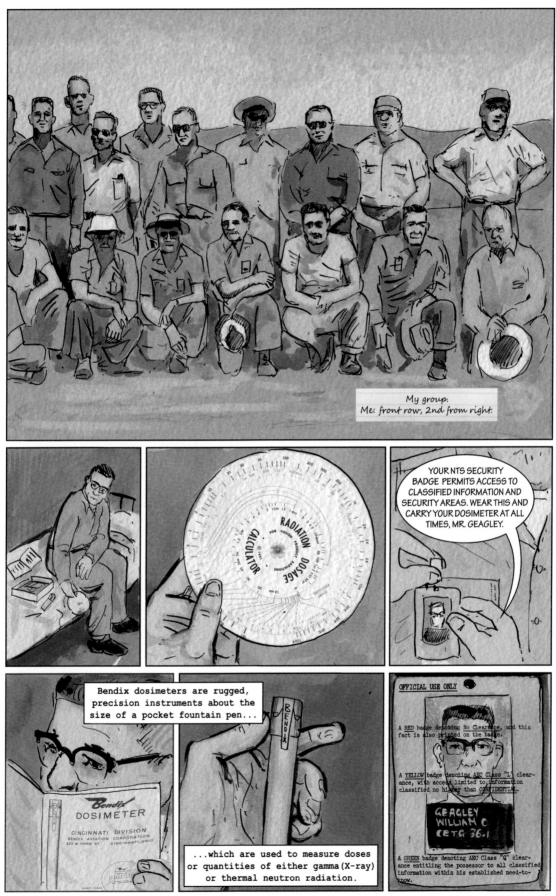

My group.
Me: front row, 2nd from right.

YOUR NTS SECURITY BADGE PERMITS ACCESS TO CLASSIFIED INFORMATION AND SECURITY AREAS. WEAR THIS AND CARRY YOUR DOSIMETER AT ALL TIMES, MR. GEAGLEY.

Bendix dosimeters are rugged, precision instruments about the size of a pocket fountain pen...

...which are used to measure doses or quantities of either gamma (X-ray) or thermal neutron radiation.

OFFICIAL USE ONLY

A RED badge denoting No Clearance, and this fact is also printed on the badge.

A YELLOW badge denoting AEC Class "L" clearance, with access limited to information classified no higher than CONFIDENTIAL.

GEAGLEY
WILLIAM C
CETG 36.1

A GREEN badge denoting AEC Class "Q" clearance entitling the possessor to all classified information within his established need-to-know.

The STOKES shot was one to remember. The balloon was raised and ready to go, with the device hanging from the bottom like a basket normally would.

BALLOON
CAB
STATION
CO-AXIAL CABLE
INFLATION PAD
STATION
BALLOON DETECTOR STATION AND GROUND ZERO
STATION
GUY CABLE & SHELTER
HOISTING CABLE TRENCH
BURIED COAXIAL CABLES
STATION
KOALA (URSLA) DETECTOR
INSTRUMENT BLOCKHOUSE
GENERATOR SHELTER
N

About four miles away was a Navy blimp anchored out in the desert to test military effects on naval equipment. When the shock wave hit it, it crashed to the ground. Navy blimp in the desert!

Traveling through little towns like Alamo, Nevada, revealed a very different side to life with the bomb.

These were the only Americans living with the reality of atomic war. They didn't need to imagine what it would be like to have a bomb dropped near your home.

They weren't all angry.

THE RAYS—HOW LONG THEY GOING TO BE HERE?

Most people I interviewed seemed calm or at least resolved.

I checked in with the doctors in the Bordoli case.

All three denied they suggested the link between testing and leukemia. But they seemed sympathetic and certainly did not dismiss the idea that fallout was a vexing problem. Several asked me, as if I knew, why can't they just tell us the truth?

When I got back to Mercury it was still business as usual. BANG! BANG! BANG!

FRANKLIN

LASSEN

WILSON

But PRISCILLA generated some interest.

It was primarily a project of the Department of Defense and was one of the largest military effects tests ever conducted...

...34 different military projects and Desert Rock exercises...

...1,700 troops for this one, many Marines.

Project 4.1—Effects of "Nuclear Detonations on a Large Biological Specimen."

That was another major round of animal experiments.

Seven hundred and nineteen pigs scattered around GZ for PRISCILLA.

Other stations with mice and dogs—dalmatians.

There was a large series of civil and structural effects tests too, with mannequins and doom structures and a series of various shelter designs.

There were hundreds of observers for PRISCILLA including an international delegation to watch the shots and learn about U.S. Rad-Safe precautions.

Along with the hundreds of the citizen CD guys who were into their second or third week of training and getting used to the drill of waking at 1 am to watch the bombs go off.

PRISCILLA was big, 37 kt, but nothing compared to what came next.

HOOD was gigantic.

At 74 kt, it was the biggest ever exploded in Nevada and almost as big as the first H-bomb.

Shot JOHN was an air-to-air missile experiment.

A 2 kt atomic rocket launched from an F-89J fighter aircraft.

US AIR FORCE

Five guys volunteered to stand directly under the blast point to show that it was safe from fallout.

This little press gimmick was not the only way this shot was meant to show how testing was still OK.

GROUND ZERO POPULATIONS

Gallup said polls were running two-to-one against testing if some kind of international moratorium could be achieved.

This little atomic missile was a tactical defense weapon that the military boys thought was key to balance the Soviets growing nuclear capabilities.

We wrote about these new developments, of course, but the technical side of weapons effects felt less interesting than the protests erupting across the world and for the first time in Nevada.

STOP ATOMIC TESTS!

UNITED STATES ATOMIC ENERGY COMMISSION LAS VEGAS FIELD OFFICE

There was a guy sitting outside the Las Vegas AEC headquarters on a hunger strike for almost two weeks. "May God Arouse you from your Lethargy," his sign said.

CHAPTER 8
SMOKY

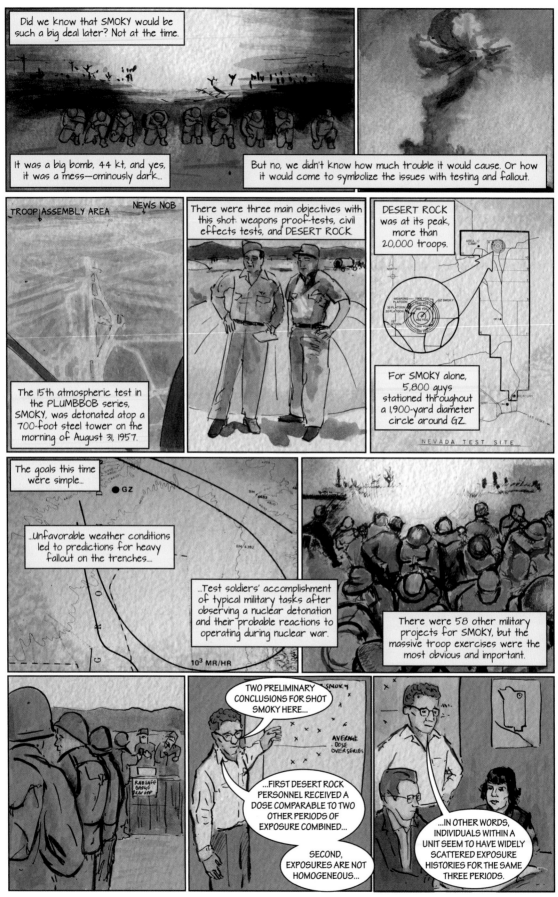

Did we know that SMOKY would be such a big deal later? Not at the time.

It was a big bomb, 44 kt, and yes, it was a mess—ominously dark...

But no, we didn't know how much trouble it would cause. Or how it would come to symbolize the issues with testing and fallout.

TROOP ASSEMBLY AREA   NEWS NOB

The 15th atmospheric test in the PLUMBBOB series, SMOKY, was detonated atop a 700-foot steel tower on the morning of August 31, 1957.

There were three main objectives with this shot: weapons proof-tests, civil effects tests, and DESERT ROCK.

DESERT ROCK was at its peak, more than 20,000 troops.

For SMOKY alone, 5,800 guys stationed throughout a 1,900-yard diameter circle around GZ.

NEVADA TEST SITE

The goals this time were simple...

● GZ

...Unfavorable weather conditions led to predictions for heavy fallout on the trenches....

...Test soldiers' accomplishment of typical military tasks after observing a nuclear detonation and their probable reactions to operating during nuclear war.

10^3 MR/HR

There were 58 other military projects for SMOKY, but the massive troop exercises were the most obvious and important.

RAD SAFE BADGE DROP OFF

TWO PRELIMINARY CONCLUSIONS FOR SHOT SMOKY HERE...

SMOKY

AVERAGE DOSE OVERSERIES

...FIRST DESERT ROCK PERSONNEL RECEIVED A DOSE COMPARABLE TO TWO OTHER PERIODS OF EXPOSURE COMBINED...

SECOND, EXPOSURES ARE NOT HOMOGENEOUS...

...IN OTHER WORDS, INDIVIDUALS WITHIN A UNIT SEEM TO HAVE WIDELY SCATTERED EXPOSURE HISTORIES FOR THE SAME THREE PERIODS.

At the time the Desert Rock exercises just seemed like a bigger version of the familiar testing protocols.

Honestly, not that exciting compared to years past.

I turned my atomic reporter speech into an article, "Watching the Bombs Go Off," for those just discovering atomic tourism.

The trainees, observers, and press were given more information about technical innovations like the 'streak camera' that could record images in one-billionth of a second.

By August we learned how the tests were proof-firing for Talos-W surface-to-air missiles; smaller, lighter warheads for Nike-B missiles and ICBM warheads; and even an atomic depth charge for submarine warfare.

For the first time, some of the action was below ground.

RAINIER was the first full-scale effort to construct a completely underground test facility...

...With the goal of containing the entire blast and all fallout in a sealed subterranean environment.

WE SURVEYED RAINER MESA FOR THE 1,700-FOOT TUNNEL DUG HORIZONTALLY, DEEP INTO THE SIDE OF THE MOUNTAIN. WHEN IT WENT OFF, BECAUSE IT WAS CONTAINED, ALL YOU REALLY FELT WAS THE EARTH TREMOR.

The AEC folks were excited about the potential for use of underground atomic blasts to release untapped reserves of oil and gas that would be liberated from the earth's grip by the power of the atom.

At RAINIER, the rock was volcanic tuff, which is a silica material.

When the bomb detonated, the heat caused the silica material to fuse, forming a huge glass-lined bubble underground.

Can you imagine an immense glass chamber deep under the desert full of radioactive gas?

That was something I really thought about during those hot August nights.

HOPE YOU'VE ENJOYED YOUR STAY HERE IN MERCURY, BILL...

I'LL NEVER FORGET IT.

YOU'RE OFFICIALLY A DESERT RAT NOW.

ITS NOT WHAT I EXPECTED. BEAUTIFUL, PEACEFUL...

PEACEFUL? ATOM BOMBS?

THE DESERT, I MEAN. THE PLACE.

I GET YA, BILL. TELL THE FOLKS BACK IN MICHIGAN WERE NOT CRAZY FOR LIVIN' HERE!

Back in 1951, when they opened this place, the governor of Nevada said that he was happy to be hosting...

...that it was "exciting that the sub-marginal land of the proving ground was furthering science and helping national defense..."

...that "We had long ago written off that terrain as wasteland and today it's blooming with atoms."

CONTROL ROOM, MERCURY

THOSE OBSERVERS ARE LEAVING JUST IN TIME.

NOT GOING TO BE AS MUCH OF A SHOW WITH THINGS MOVING UNDERGROUND. NOT AS MUCH EXCITEMENT.

But there was excitement. Even underground, it was hard to "cage the dragon," as the scientists called it. The PASCAL-A event showed that.

DOOR

This "tiny" 0.2 kt device was put 500 feet down a borehole with a big vault-type door sealing the entrance.

This was so little by the standards of the summer. The whole protocol was pretty casual.

500FT

A few guys out in the field with a little remote control unit set it off.

DEVICE

I THINK WE JUST LAUNCHED THE FIRST MAN-MADE OBJECT INTO SPACE, BROTHER.

I GUESS THE DRAGON NEEDS MORE CAGE!

Boy, were they surprised when the blast shot a burst of brilliant blue flame a thousand feet up in the air with the two-ton door flying straight into space like a rocket!

113

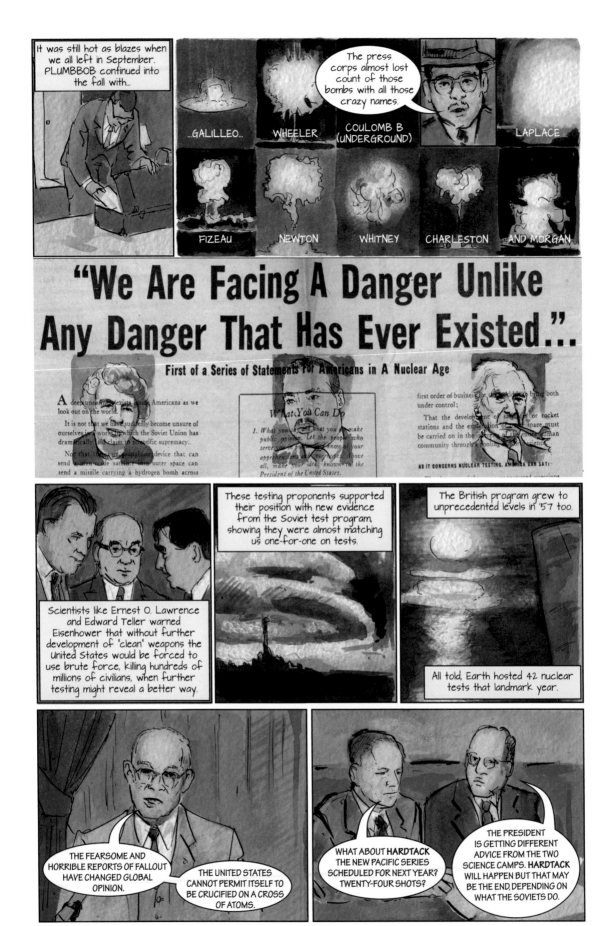

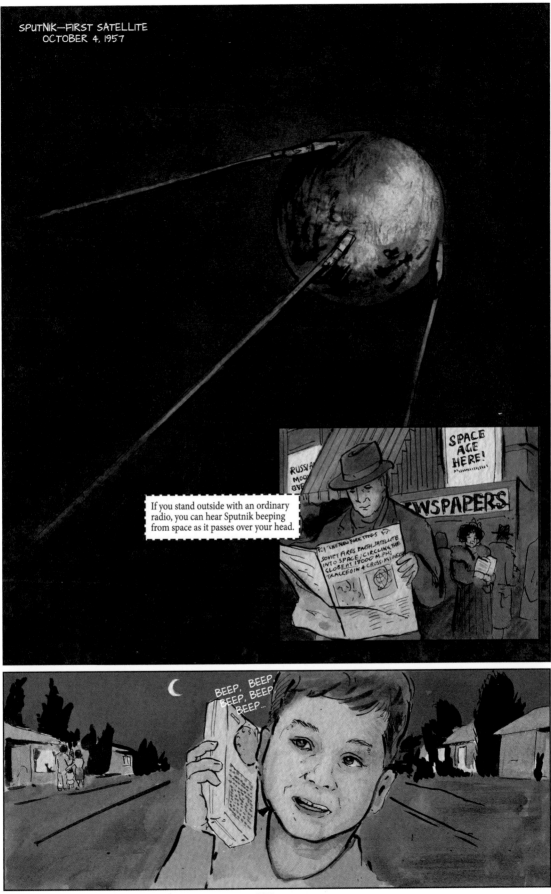

SPUTNIK—FIRST SATELLITE
OCTOBER 4, 1957

HARDTACK was every bit as dramatic as all the others. Giant mushroom clouds, missiles launching from ships, stunned observes blinded by the atomic sublime. But HARDTACK was the beginning of the end of atmospheric testing.

There were 77 U.S. atomic tests in 1958, leading up to a global moratorium on nuclear testing that came out of intense negotiations between the United States and the Soviet Union in Geneva.

TESTING MORATORIUM BEGINS OCT 31
GENEVA TALKS REACH DEAL
HOW LONG WILL THIS LAST?

Things got pretty quiet at the Nevada Test Site after the moratorium, but it didn't all come to a stop. There were interesting things going on like the testing of Freeman Dyson's nuclear rocket engines out on Jackass Flats.

FREEMAN DYSON

ONLY ONCE IN MY LIFE HAVE I EXPERIENCED ABSOLUTE SILENCE...

...THAT WAS JACKASS FLATS UNDER THE MIDDAY SUN...

...YOU ARE ALONE WITH GOD IN THAT SILENCE.

When JFK became president, he traveled to the NTS to see the nuclear rocket program. He was enthusiastic about peaceful applications of nuclear technology and space applications in particular. If Dyson's rockets worked, we could have a man on Mars.

Kennedy inherited the Geneva testing talks, which continued throughout his short presidency.

116

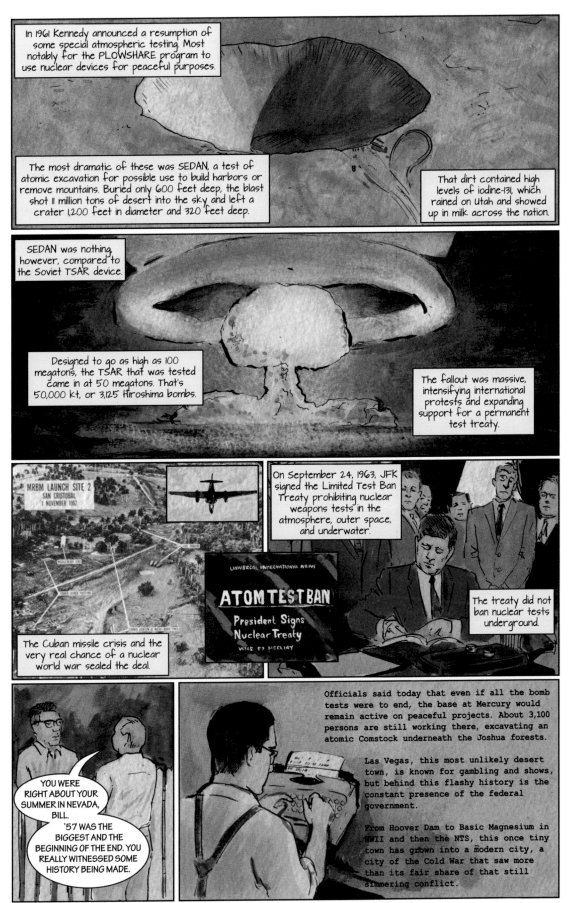

In 1961 Kennedy announced a resumption of some special atmospheric testing. Most notably for the PLOWSHARE program to use nuclear devices for peaceful purposes.

The most dramatic of these was SEDAN, a test of atomic excavation for possible use to build harbors or remove mountains. Buried only 600 feet deep, the blast shot 11 million tons of desert into the sky and left a crater 1,200 feet in diameter and 320 feet deep.

That dirt contained high levels of iodine-131, which rained on Utah and showed up in milk across the nation.

SEDAN was nothing, however, compared to the Soviet TSAR device.

Designed to go as high as 100 megatons, the TSAR that was tested came in at 50 megatons. That's 50,000 kt, or 3,125 Hiroshima bombs.

The fallout was massive, intensifying international protests and expanding support for a permanent test treaty.

MRBM LAUNCH SITE 2
SAN CRISTOBAL
1 NOVEMBER 1962

The Cuban missile crisis and the very real chance of a nuclear world war sealed the deal.

On September 24, 1963, JFK signed the Limited Test Ban Treaty prohibiting nuclear weapons tests in the atmosphere, outer space, and underwater.

UNIVERSAL INTERNATIONAL NEWS
ATOM TEST BAN
President Signs Nuclear Treaty
VOICE ED MCCLINY

The treaty did not ban nuclear tests underground.

YOU WERE RIGHT ABOUT YOUR SUMMER IN NEVADA, BILL.

'57 WAS THE BIGGEST AND THE BEGINNING OF THE END. YOU REALLY WITNESSED SOME HISTORY BEING MADE.

Officials said today that even if all the bomb tests were to end, the base at Mercury would remain active on peaceful projects. About 3,100 persons are still working there, excavating an atomic Comstock underneath the Joshua forests.

Las Vegas, this most unlikely desert town, is known for gambling and shows, but behind this flashy history is the constant presence of the federal government.

From Hoover Dam to Basic Magnesium in WWII and then the NTS, this once tiny town has grown into a modern city, a city of the Cold War that saw more than its fair share of that still simmering conflict.

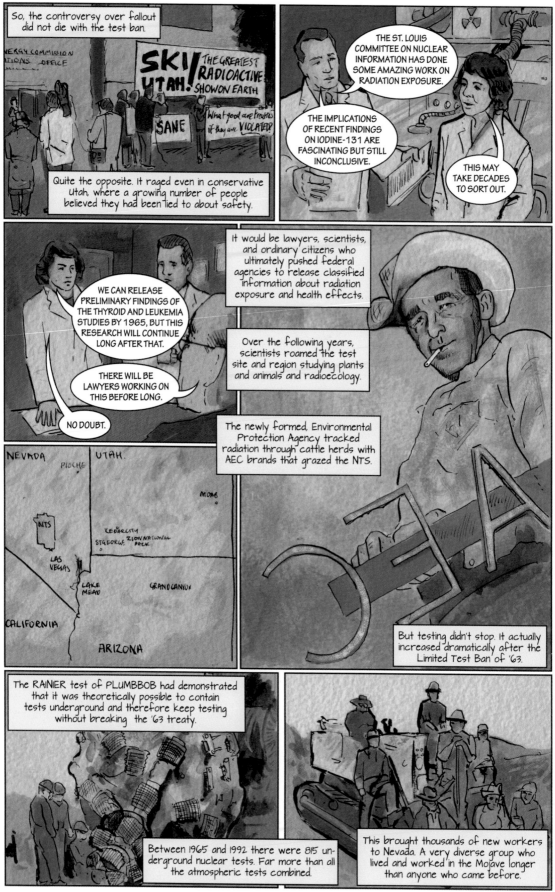

So, the controversy over fallout did not die with the test ban.

SKI UTAH! THE GREATEST RADIOACTIVE SHOW ON EARTH

SANE

What good are treaties if they are VIOLATED?

Quite the opposite. It raged even in conservative Utah, where a growing number of people believed they had been lied to about safety.

THE ST. LOUIS COMMITTEE ON NUCLEAR INFORMATION HAS DONE SOME AMAZING WORK ON RADIATION EXPOSURE.

THE IMPLICATIONS OF RECENT FINDINGS ON IODINE-131 ARE FASCINATING BUT STILL INCONCLUSIVE.

THIS MAY TAKE DECADES TO SORT OUT.

WE CAN RELEASE PRELIMINARY FINDINGS OF THE THYROID AND LEUKEMIA STUDIES BY 1965, BUT THIS RESEARCH WILL CONTINUE LONG AFTER THAT.

THERE WILL BE LAWYERS WORKING ON THIS BEFORE LONG.

NO DOUBT.

It would be lawyers, scientists, and ordinary citizens who ultimately pushed federal agencies to release classified information about radiation exposure and health effects.

Over the following years, scientists roamed the test site and region studying plants and animals and radioecology.

The newly formed, Environmental Protection Agency tracked radiation through cattle herds with AEC brands that grazed the NTS.

NEVADA UTAH
PIOCHE
MOAB
NTS
CEDAR CITY
ST GEORGE ZION NATIONAL PARK
LAS VEGAS
LAKE MEAD
GRAND CANYON
CALIFORNIA
ARIZONA

But testing didn't stop. It actually increased dramatically after the Limited Test Ban of '63.

The RAINIER test of PLUMBBOB had demonstrated that it was theoretically possible to contain tests underground and therefore keep testing without breaking the '63 treaty.

Between 1965 and 1992 there were 815 underground nuclear tests. Far more than all the atmospheric tests combined.

This brought thousands of new workers to Nevada. A very diverse group who lived and worked in the Mojave longer than anyone who came before.

118

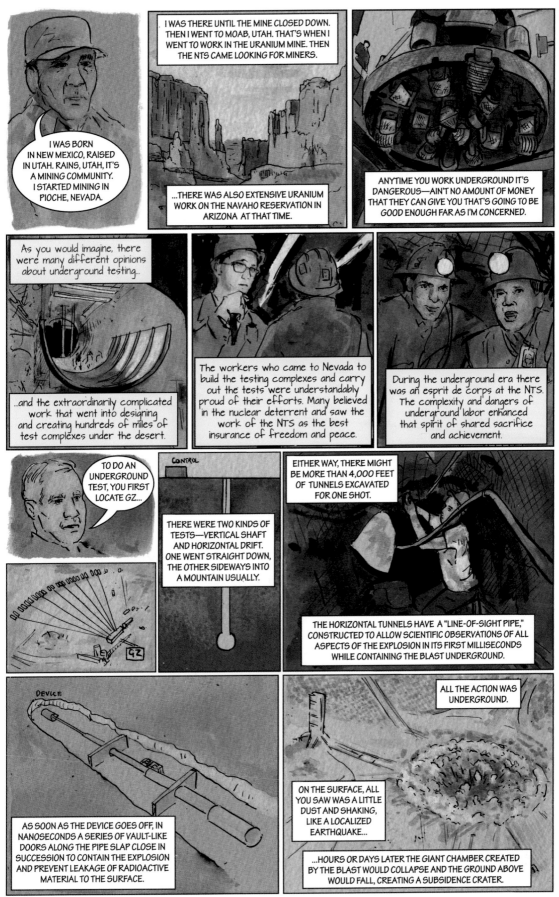

I WAS THERE UNTIL THE MINE CLOSED DOWN. THEN I WENT TO MOAB, UTAH. THAT'S WHEN I WENT TO WORK IN THE URANIUM MINE. THEN THE NTS CAME LOOKING FOR MINERS.

I WAS BORN IN NEW MEXICO, RAISED IN UTAH. RAINS, UTAH, IT'S A MINING COMMUNITY. I STARTED MINING IN PIOCHE, NEVADA.

...THERE WAS ALSO EXTENSIVE URANIUM WORK ON THE NAVAHO RESERVATION IN ARIZONA AT THAT TIME.

ANYTIME YOU WORK UNDERGROUND IT'S DANGEROUS—AIN'T NO AMOUNT OF MONEY THAT THEY CAN GIVE YOU THAT'S GOING TO BE GOOD ENOUGH FAR AS I'M CONCERNED.

As you would imagine, there were many different opinions about underground testing...

...and the extraordinarily complicated work that went into designing and creating hundreds of miles of test complexes under the desert.

The workers who came to Nevada to build the testing complexes and carry out the tests were understandably proud of their efforts. Many believed in the nuclear deterrent and saw the work of the NTS as the best insurance of freedom and peace.

During the underground era there was an esprit de corps at the NTS. The complexity and dangers of underground labor enhanced that spirit of shared sacrifice and achievement.

TO DO AN UNDERGROUND TEST, YOU FIRST LOCATE GZ...

CONTROL

THERE WERE TWO KINDS OF TESTS—VERTICAL SHAFT AND HORIZONTAL DRIFT. ONE WENT STRAIGHT DOWN, THE OTHER SIDEWAYS INTO A MOUNTAIN USUALLY.

GZ

EITHER WAY, THERE MIGHT BE MORE THAN 4,000 FEET OF TUNNELS EXCAVATED FOR ONE SHOT.

THE HORIZONTAL TUNNELS HAVE A "LINE-OF-SIGHT PIPE," CONSTRUCTED TO ALLOW SCIENTIFIC OBSERVATIONS OF ALL ASPECTS OF THE EXPLOSION IN ITS FIRST MILLISECONDS WHILE CONTAINING THE BLAST UNDERGROUND.

DEVICE

ALL THE ACTION WAS UNDERGROUND.

ON THE SURFACE, ALL YOU SAW WAS A LITTLE DUST AND SHAKING, LIKE A LOCALIZED EARTHQUAKE...

AS SOON AS THE DEVICE GOES OFF, IN NANOSECONDS A SERIES OF VAULT-LIKE DOORS ALONG THE PIPE SLAP CLOSE IN SUCCESSION TO CONTAIN THE EXPLOSION AND PREVENT LEAKAGE OF RADIOACTIVE MATERIAL TO THE SURFACE.

...HOURS OR DAYS LATER THE GIANT CHAMBER CREATED BY THE BLAST WOULD COLLAPSE AND THE GROUND ABOVE WOULD FALL, CREATING A SUBSIDENCE CRATER.

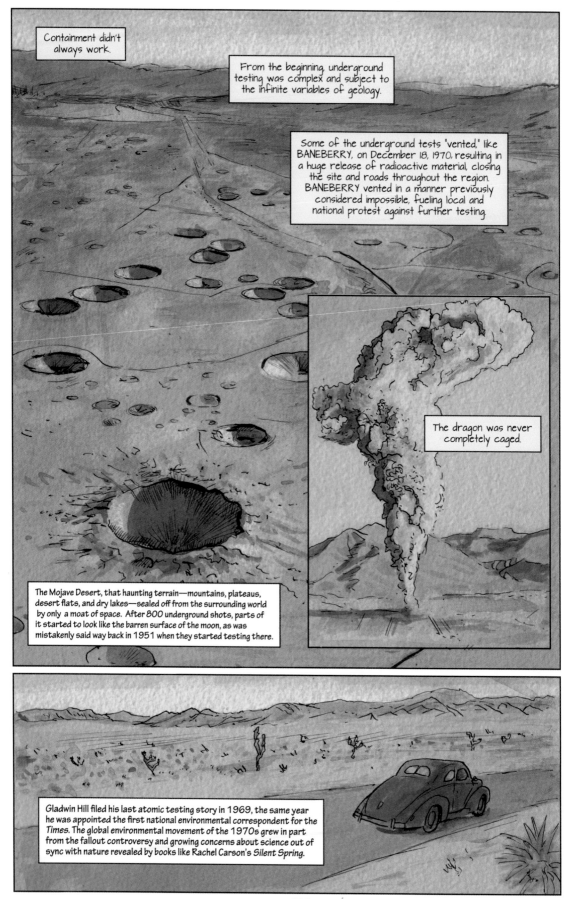

Containment didn't always work.

From the beginning, underground testing was complex and subject to the infinite variables of geology.

Some of the underground tests "vented," like BANEBERRY, on December 18, 1970, resulting in a huge release of radioactive material, closing the site and roads throughout the region. BANEBERRY vented in a manner previously considered impossible, fueling local and national protest against further testing.

The dragon was never completely caged.

The Mojave Desert, that haunting terrain—mountains, plateaus, desert flats, and dry lakes—sealed off from the surrounding world by only a moat of space. After 800 underground shots, parts of it started to look like the barren surface of the moon, as was mistakenly said way back in 1951 when they started testing there.

Gladwin Hill filed his last atomic testing story in 1969, the same year he was appointed the first national environmental correspondent for the *Times*. The global environmental movement of the 1970s grew in part from the fallout controversy and growing concerns about science out of sync with nature revealed by books like Rachel Carson's *Silent Spring*.

CHAPTER 9
SECRECY AND HISTORY

Throughout the underground testing era, the antinuclear testing protest movement grew.

Throngs Fill Manhattan to Protest Nuclear Weapons

DIVIDER, THE LAST TEST CONDUCTED AT THE NTS

In 1992, the United States conducted its 1,030th and last nuclear test. The total estimated cost of these tests was $35,100,000,000.

Shortly after that final test, the United States approved a unilateral testing moratorium announced the previous year by Russia. In 1996, President Clinton signed the Comprehensive Test Ban Treaty (CTBT).

"НЕВАДА-СЕМЕЙ"
"НЕВАДА-СЕМИПАЛАТИНСК"
"NEVADA-SEMEY"

НЕТ-ЯДЕРНЫМ

GLOBAL ANTI-NUCLEAR ALLIANCE

The indigenous residents of the testing regions played a central role in the protest movement from the 1940s through the present...

...and forged alliances like the **Nevada-Semipalatinsk Movement** to link their efforts across the globe.

In Kazakhstan, nuclear testing protests led to an independence movement in the 1980s and directly contributed to the creation of the independent modern state of Kazakhstan in 1991 after the fall of the Soviet Union.

The peoples of the testing zones shared a desire to understand precisely how their environments and health had been and would be affected by nuclear testing.

They also shared the common goal of better explaining the nature of their home places that had been chosen for testing because of widespread assumptions about wastelands.

The simple idea that some environments are inherently better than others helped justify the location and extent of atomic testing.

In deeming places wastelands, those in power directly or indirectly contributed to assumptions about the people who lived in these places.

NEVADA IS NOT A WASTELAND

All of the residents of the testing regions, regardless of their views on the rightness of testing, could agree that environmental misperception was a problem they needed to help solve.

YUCCA MOUNTAIN—SITE OF PROPOSED NUCLEAR WASTE REPOSITORY

CRATER—POLYGON, KAZAKHSTAN

CONCRETE DOME—BIKINI ATOLL

To help make the case for their cultures, they needed to better describe their environments and show how their places had meaning, intrinsic beauty, and value.

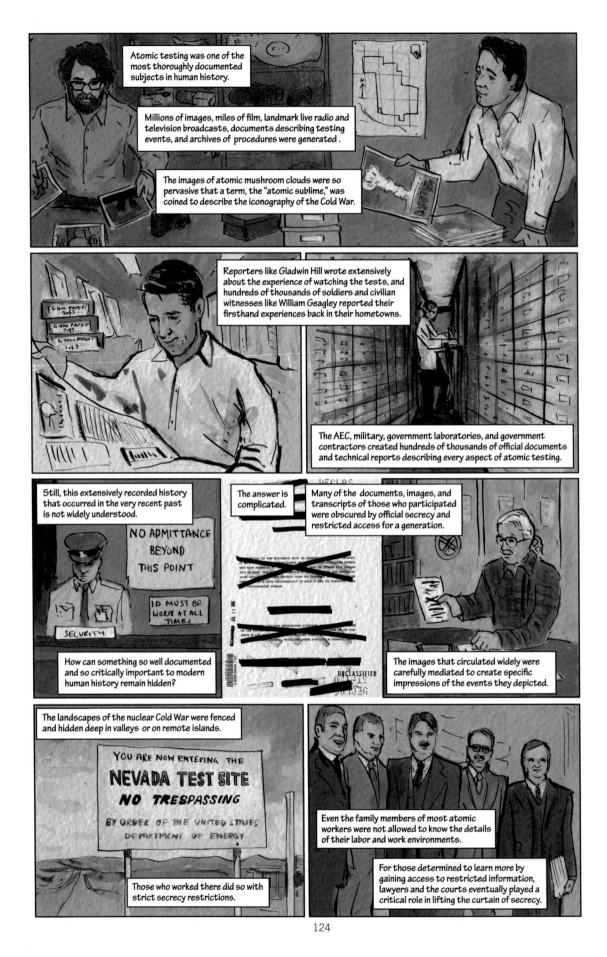

Atomic testing was one of the most thoroughly documented subjects in human history.

Millions of images, miles of film, landmark live radio and television broadcasts, documents describing testing events, and archives of procedures were generated.

The images of atomic mushroom clouds were so pervasive that a term, the "atomic sublime," was coined to describe the iconography of the Cold War.

Reporters like Gladwin Hill wrote extensively about the experience of watching the tests, and hundreds of thousands of soldiers and civilian witnesses like William Geagley reported their firsthand experiences back in their hometowns.

The AEC, military, government laboratories, and government contractors created hundreds of thousands of official documents and technical reports describing every aspect of atomic testing.

Still, this extensively recorded history that occurred in the very recent past is not widely understood.

NO ADMITTANCE BEYOND THIS POINT

ID MUST BE WORN AT ALL TIMES

SECURITY

How can something so well documented and so critically important to modern human history remain hidden?

The answer is complicated.

UNCLASSIFIED

Many of the documents, images, and transcripts of those who participated were obscured by official secrecy and restricted access for a generation.

The images that circulated widely were carefully mediated to create specific impressions of the events they depicted.

The landscapes of the nuclear Cold War were fenced and hidden deep in valleys or on remote islands.

YOU ARE NOW ENTERING THE NEVADA TEST SITE NO TRESPASSING BY ORDER OF THE UNITED STATES DEPARTMENT OF ENERGY

Those who worked there did so with strict secrecy restrictions.

Even the family members of most atomic workers were not allowed to know the details of their labor and work environments.

For those determined to learn more by gaining access to restricted information, lawyers and the courts eventually played a critical role in lifting the curtain of secrecy.

In the 1980s a series of legal cases involving atomic fallout made their way through the courts.

The case of *Irene Allen et al. v. United States* was the most dramatic.

THE EVIDENCE CLEARLY SHOWS THAT THE INFORMATION GIVEN TO DOWNWINDERS WAS WOEFULLY DEFICIENT...

...THE COURT FINDS THAT THE DEFENDANT FAILED TO ADEQUATELY WARN THE PLAINTIFFS...

...OF KNOWN OR FORESEEABLE LONG-RANGE BIOLOGICAL CONSEQUENCES FROM EXPOSURE TO FALLOUT.

IN THE LAW, AS IN SCIENCE, ONE ALWAYS FACES UNCERTAINTY....

...DISPUTE RESOLUTION DEMANDS RATIONAL DECISION, NOT PERFECT KNOWLEDGE.

During the *Allen* trial thousands of pages of documents were entered into the record in an effort to reconstruct the history of atomic testing and explain the state of atomic science at critical moments in the process when decisions about human health were made by authorities.

Trial testimony revealed information from previously classified government documents and scientific reports.

These documents showed a level of uncertainty about atomic science that was rarely reflected in AEC publications and public reports that consistently downplayed danger and emphasized command and control.

Medical studies loomed large in the fallout trials.

For atomic veterans, an extensive study by Dr. Glyn G. Caldwell of the Center for Disease Control analyzing the SMOKY shot was especially important.

1957 SMOKY NTS FILMBADGES

REPORTED LEUKEMIA CASES PERIOD

NATIONAL AVERAGE

1957 SMOKY SHOT OBSERVERS

Medical researchers like Caldwell assembled extensive data tracing atomic exposure through populations in an attempt to ascertain cause and effect. Did exposure to radiation, even in tiny amounts, cause human disease or genetic mutation?

Caldwell was also interested in civilian witnesses during PLUMBBOB.

To: Participants in Program 36,
From: Director, Program 36, CETG, Operation Plumbbob

Subject: Total Dose Recorded for Operation Plumbbob

Below is the reported total dose resulting from your participation in Program 36, Operation Plumbbob.

Name	Total Dose
William C. Geagley	0 mr

Since, in many cases, partial doses resulting from film badge measurements were punched into cards and machine tabulated to obtain the total dose, there may be an occasional error.

If you have reason to believe that an error has been made in your reported dose, please inform me, together with the reasons, so that the information can be furnished to the AEC people for inclusion in their study of this approach to dosimetry records.

William Geagley died of leukemia in 1971.

DEPARTMENT OF HEALTH, EDUCATION, AND WELFARE
PUBLIC HEALTH SERVICE
CENTER FOR DISEASE CONTROL
ATLANTA, GEORGIA 30333
TELEPHONE: (404) 633-3311

Mrs. Geagley
Cambrey Drive
Lansing, Michigan 48906

Mrs. William C. Geagley   July 19, 1977
3621 Cambrey Drive
Lansing, Michigan 48906

Dear Mrs. Geagley:

Thank you for contacting us regarding personnel involved in nuclear testing
in Nevada. The Cancer Branch, Chronic Diseases Division, Bureau of
Epidemiology, Center for Disease Control, is primarily interested in
developing a cohort of men exposed to a particular atomic device detonated
on August 31, 1957 (Smoky). If the data show these men were at increased
risk for development of malignancies, we may study other groups of men
exposed in some of the other tests for confirmation. However, until the
Smoky study is completed, we will hold all material related to other tests
for future study.

Thank you for your interest.

                                        Sincerely yours,

                                        Glyn G. Caldwell, M.D.
                                        Glyn G. Caldwell, M.D.
                                        Deputy Chief, Cancer Branch
                                        Chronic Diseases Division
                                        Bureau of Epidemiology

The Allen case and other legal actions led to the creation of a vast new historic archive maintained by the U.S. Department of Energy (the successor to the AEC) that citizens and historians can use to piece together the story of atomic testing without critical details blacked out.

The archive contains more than 140,000 recently declassified documents related to the history of nuclear testing and most of the government photographs and films made during the atmospheric era.

BALLOON SHOT DIAGRAMS, INTERESTING...

Many of these documents were digitized and made available through the DOE OpenNet system so that citizens, lawyers, students, and researchers could access some of this content online.

The sources you will find here are excellent and critically important. But they tell the story from one direction...

...top down.

These are the documents created and assembled by policymakers and leaders.

If you want to understand the complete picture of this vast and complicated history you must learn how ordinary people experienced these events.

Oral history is one method that adds voices to the official record.

In 2004 an oral history project was begun to record the lived experience of testing participants of all types.

These carefully researched and documented oral testimonies filled in gaps in our understanding of the thoughts and motives of high-ranking officials and scientists...

...while giving new voice to hundreds of more ordinary people who lived and worked in the atomic testing world but had never told their stories in the past.

This new digital archive of oral testimony is also online and open to all who wish to learn more about what it was like to live during the atomic Cold War.

This archive, not a top-down version of the story, is a community of voices that include all perspectives—from scientists to protesters, miners to workers, and engineers to administrators.

Labor and Support

Women and the NTS

Retirees and Reunions

NTS Administration

Scientists & Engineers

Diverse Experiences

For the researchers and graduate students who created the oral history archive, a sense of balance was critical.

STOP NUCLEAR TESTING NOW

The history of atomic testing can't be reduced to Cold Warriors versus Protesters.

There were around 300,000 people directly involved in this history. Many passionately believed they were doing something vitally important for history. Others were simply doing a job.

To truly understand these experiences, you must visit the contested environments of atomic testing.

The DOE offers a tour of the NTS to any American citizen. You can stand on the rim of the SEDAN crater now listed on the National Register of Historic Places.

On the DOE tour it's their version of the story with a scripted text and carefully selected stops, but it does give you a sense of the scope and natural environment of the NTS.

During the oral history project, historians were granted access to some of the vast subterranean world of testing.

The miners and workers who built it explained the test process and the complicated geology of the Mojave.

PORKY

The workers took great pride in their labor and engineering achievements, though they differed in their opinions about the policies that drove their efforts.

One thing was always clear about all the people who spent time in and around the NTS: they understood the nature of the desert and had unique insights about the relationship between history and environment.

Protesters who camped for years, the sheriffs from the nearby towns who arrested them, the miners and workers, the downwinders and ranchers—they all knew the Mojave and Great Basin as a complicated and beautiful place. The idigenous peoples of the regional had long understood this.

The same is true of the natural and cultural landscapes of atomic testing all over the world.

Traveling to these remote atomic regions of the globe, what will you find?

Are they irredeemable wastelands?

Are they empty?

What are the lasting consequences of the testing on these places and their people?

Are there obvious effects from atomic radiation?

Are answers about cause and effect revealed when you stand at these sites?

Researching this topic required arduous travel to dangerous places to see and listen to how the lived experience of the villagers of the Soviet Polygon test site in Kazakhstan compared with the Nevada-Utah experience, and the experience of the Pacific islanders.

All of these places have witnesses to this recent history still living.

Few will be able to see these places, which are very remote by design.

But there are many easier ways to experience parts of this history.

Museums and archives now display the artifacts and material culture of atomic history along with the records and oral histories.

But you should remember that despite the vast archives and hundreds of books, much of this story remains to be told.

By triangulating the sources and listening to different perspectives, you can reach your own conclusions about this controversial history of technology and secrecy, culture and nature, knowledge and uncertainty.

PART II
PRIMARY SOURCES

There are many types of sources historians use to reconstruct the past and explain change over time. In the case of atomic history there are hundreds of published *secondary sources* in the form of books and articles including Pulitzer Prize–winning histories. These sources are *secondary* because they were created after the events actually happened. A review of this vast secondary atomic literature was an important part of the creation of this book. The graphic history you just read is another example of a secondary source, a new historical interpretation of the past informed by existing secondary literature and new *primary* source research. Primary sources are documents, testimony, media coverage, photos, and other evidence created during the historic period being studied. They are the unmediated original records of historical events. Creating this new graphic narrative of atomic testing required extensive primary research, which was complicated because of the extraordinary array of these sources. Lack of sources obviously makes historic research more difficult. A wealth of sources poses another problem because it can be difficult for the uninitiated to know where to begin or where to end. How to make sense of hundreds of thousands of documents relating to the testing of atomic weapons has vexed historians, lawyers, and others studying this period of history. The motives of the actors, the culture that supported and protested this activity, and the politics and policies of testing have often been obscured by the sheer enormity of this historic record. Most of these documents were once top secret and were declassified only in the past thirty years.

As you learned in the graphic history, in the 1980s, a series of legal actions forced government agencies to provide much greater access to the once hidden official history. Most of the government documents you see below were declassified during this period. Arranged by chapter and in chronological order they were chosen because each was important for the historical interpretation in the graphic narrative. In many cases the dialogue in the narrative came verbatim from these documents. Study them carefully and they will give you a much deeper understanding of the story you just read. For every small bubble of dialogue in the graphic there are many pages, often hundreds of pages, of material every bit as interesting and sometimes shocking as what was included.

DIVING INTO THE VAST SECONDARY LITERATURE AND PRIMARY SOURCES

After reading this graphic history you may be inspired to explore the secondary literature of atomic history. Even the excellent books on this topic are too numerous to list here. To construct the graphic history I needed to focus on the most essential studies. The Manhattan Project is the most extensively documented part of this story. Richard Rhodes won a Pulitzer Prize for his monumental *The Making of the Atomic Bomb* (1986) and followed with another prize-winning history of the H-bomb, *Dark Sun* (1995). There are many other excellent sources including Ferenc Morton Szasz's classic *The Day the Sun Rose Twice: The Story of the Trinity Site Nuclear Explosion* (1984) and an excellent recent graphic history, *Trinity: A Graphic History of the First Atomic Bomb* by Jonathan Fetter-Vorm (2012).

The bombings of Hiroshima and Nagasaki inspired hundreds of secondary accounts. Most notable is one of the first, John Hersey's landmark best-seller *Hiroshima* (1946). First published as a complete issue of the magazine *The New Yorker* and then as a book, this account of the horror of the first use of atomic weapons on humans has shocked readers for three generations. J. Samuel Walker's excellent *Prompt & Utter Destruction: Truman and the Use of Atomic Bombs Against Japan* (2008) explains the critical decision to use the bombs. There are many more excellent sources. As you learned, Operation Crossroads was chronicled by David Bradley in *No Place to Hide* (1948) and later by historian Jonathan M. Weisgall in *Operation Crossroads: The Atomic Tests at Bikini Atoll* (1994). Once you move toward Operation Nutmeg and the selection of Nevada as host for a continental test site, the secondary sources move in several directions. Some are biographies of the key figures, while others are studies of atomic towns and regions. For the purposes of the graphic history I was most interested in sources focused on the environments and regionally located experiences of atomic testing. Of these, Dina Titus, *Bombs in the Backyard* (1986), Valerie Kuletz, *The Tainted Desert* (1998), Peter Bacon Hales, *Atomic Spaces* (1997), Rebecca Solnit, *Savage Dreams* (1994), Barton C. Hacker, *Elements of Controversy* (1994), and Terrence R. Fehner and F. G. Gosling, *Battlefield of the Cold War* (2006) were invaluable sources.

The art in the graphic comes primarily from the vast photographic record of atomic testing housed primarily on the DOE OpenNet. This online repository contains hundreds of thousands of historic images and videos of the atmospheric testing era and a linked network of government archives. OpenNet offers an online portal to student researchers with many of the key primary documents used in this project, as well as those not listed below. Through OpenNet you can access thousands of declassified historical documents related to all aspects of atomic testing. The black lines, scratch-outs, and poor condition of copies of these documents speak to the decades of secrecy when very few Americans had access to this kind of information. Even a cursory review of these documents compared to press releases and government publications reveals the complexity of this history and demonstrates why opinions were so divided and understandings of these events so different. The doubts and concerns of leading proponents of atomic testing are revealed in these documents, as are internal debates about scientific, political, and ethical uncertainty. Included here are also examples of documents from individuals that offer a glimpse into the experience of ordinary people like William Geagley and Gladwin Hill.

CHAPTER 1: TRINITY

DOCUMENT 1.1 LETTER FROM ALBERT EINSTEIN TO PRESIDENT FRANKLIN DELANO ROOSEVELT ABOUT THE POSSIBLE CONSTRUCTION OF NUCLEAR BOMBS. *Source:* Franklin Delano Roosevelt Library, Miscellaneous Historical Documents Collection

DOCUMENT 1.2 KENNETH BAINBRIDGE TO ALL CONCERNED WITH PROJECT TR. *Source:* DOE NNSA/NSO ALLA0000919

DOCUMENT 1.3 OPPENHEIMER AND KISTIAKOWSKY ACTIVITIES AT TRINITY. *Source:* DOE NNSA/NSO ALLA0004059

DOCUMENT 1.4 PHILIP MORRISON "IF THE BOMB GETS OUT OF HAND." *Source:* Excerpt from *One World or None*, NY, New Press, 2007

PHOTO 1.5 MCDONALD RANCH CONTROL POINT. *Source:* DOE NNSA/NSO 004039-30

CHAPTER 2: CROSSROADS

DOCUMENT 2.1 DEAR DR. SHIELDS WARREN. *Source:* DOE NNSA/NSO NV04087743

DOCUMENT 2.2 VICE ADMIRAL W. H. P. BLANDY FOREWORD TO BOMBS AT BIKINI. *Source: Bombs at Bikini: The Official Report of Operation Crossroads* (New York: Wm. H. Wise & Co., 1947)

DOCUMENT 2.3 DOSE SUMMARY FOR CROSSROADS. *Source: For the Record—A History of the Nuclear Test Personnel Review Program, 1978–1993*, Defense Nuclear Agency, DNA 001-91-C-0022, March 1996

DOCUMENT 2.4 U.S. NATIONAL MUSEUM (SMITHSONIAN) CURATOR OF ICHTHYOLOGY, LEONARD P. SCHULTZ'S DIARY FROM ABLE DAY, JULY 1, 1946. *Source:* Smithsonian Institution Archives, http://www.mnh.si.edu/onehundredyears/profiles/leonard_schultz.html, last access 08/09/16

PHOTO 2.5 CARL MYDANS'S GRAVEYARD ON BIKINI ISLAND, 1946. *Source:* Getty Images

CHAPTER 3: NUTMEG

DOCUMENT 3.1 PROJECT NUTMEG REPORT FAVORABLE WEATHER (pages 39–40). *Source:* DOE NNSA/NSO NV0411323

DOCUMENT 3.2 FREDERICK REINES, CONTINENTAL TEST SITE REPORT. *Source:* Los Alamos National Laboratory Research Library, DOE NNSA/NSO, LAMS-1173

DOCUMENT 3.3 FREDERICK C. WORMAN, ANATOMY OF THE NEVADA TEST SITE. *Source:* Los Alamos Scientific Laboratory, DOE NNSA/NSO, NV0016244, LAMS-1173

DOCUMENT 3.4 WHY NUCLEAR WEAPONS ARE TESTED, NEVADA TEST ORGANIZATION. *Source:* William Geagley Collection on Nuclear Safety, UNLV Special Collections, MS-00792

DOCUMENT 3.5 U.S. ATOMIC ENERGY COMMISSION, "AN INTERIM REPORT OF BRITISH WORK ON JOE," September 22, 1949. *Source:* Harry S. Truman Library, President's Secretary's Files, Box 199, NSC-Atomic

DOCUMENT 3.6 WARNING POSTER. *Source:* National Atomic Testing Museum, Ephemera Collections

PHOTO 3.7 ATOM BOMB—TESTS—NEVADA—1951 (front and back). *Source:* National Atomic Testing Museum Photo Collections

CHAPTER 4: RANGER

DOCUMENT 4.1 GLADWIN HILL, "ATOMIC BOOM TOWN IN THE DESERT." *Source: The New York Times,* February 11, 1951, p. 158

DOCUMENT 4.2A CAMP DESERT ROCK I: A PSYCHOLOGICAL STUDY OF TROOP REACTIONS TO AN ATOMIC EXPLOSION. *Source:* DOE NNSA/NSO NV0006252

DOCUMENT 4.2B DESERT ROCK 1: SKETCH MAP DOE NNSA. *Source:* NSO NV0767719

DOCUMENT 4.3 BUSTER-JANGLE FALLOUT PLAN. *Source:* DOE NNSA/NSO NV0404739

PHOTO 6.7 TREATMENT OF RADIATION VICTIMS AFTER BRAVO. *Source:* National Atomic Testing Museum Photo Collections

CHAPTER 7: BOLTZMANN

DOCUMENT 7.1 DEAR MR. GEAGLEY. *Source:* William Geagley Collection on Nuclear Safety, UNLV Special Collections, MS-00792

DOCUMENT 7.2 GLADWIN HILL SPEECH ON ATOMIC TEST COVERAGE. *Source:* UCLA Charles E. Young Research Library, Gladwin Hill Papers (1706), box 50

DOCUMENT 7.3 GLADWIN HILL FIELD NOTEBOOK, MAY, 1957. Text of four-page series reads in part, "Waitress, they're going to kill us off. Robert Murray aged 9: The rays—how long they going to be here?, Brown: Oh, they are out in 3–4 hours."
Source: UCLA Charles E. Young Research Library, Gladwin Hill Papers (1706), Box 50

DOCUMENT 7.4 PLUMBBOB PRE-SERIES BRIEFING, NEVADA TEST ORGANIZATION OFFICE OF TEST INFORMATION, LAS VEGAS, NV (MAY 1957). *Source:* William Geagley Collection on Nuclear Safety, UNLV Special Collections, MS-00792

DOCUMENT 7.5 AEC 141/33—RADIOLOGICAL CRITERIA FOR THE NEVADA TEST SITE. *Source:* DOE NNSA/NSO NV0408756

DOCUMENT 7.6 GLADWIN HILL "AEC MEN DEFEND TESTS IN NEVADA." *Source: The New York Times*, May 26, 1957, p. 24

DOCUMENT 7.7 LINUS PAULING TO BARRY COMMONER, JUNE 11, 1957. *Source:* Ava Helen and Linus Pauling Papers, 1873–2013, Oregon State University Special Collections, Box #5.002, Folder 2.1

PHOTO 7.8 WILLIAM C. GEAGLEY I.D. PHOTO FROM MER-CURY SECURITY ENTRY POINT, 1957. *Source:* William Geagley Collection on Nuclear Safety, UNLV Special Collections, MS-00792

CHAPTER 8: SMOKY

DOCUMENT 8.1 THE LITTLE GREEN BOOK, *ATOMIC TESTS IN NEVADA*, UNITED STATES ATOMIC ENERGY COMMIS-SION, MARCH 1957. *Source:* William Geagley Collection on Nuclear Safety, UNLV Special Collections, MS-00792

DOCUMENT 8.2 Q CLEARANCE FORM WITH EXECUTIVE ORDER NO. 10450 RESTRICTIONS. *Source:* William Geagley Collection on Nuclear Safety, UNLV Special Collections, MS-00792

DOCUMENT 1.1 LETTER FROM ALBERT EINSTEIN TO PRESIDENT FRANKLIN DELANO ROOSEVELT ABOUT THE POSSIBLE CONSTRUCTION OF NUCLEAR BOMBS SOURCE: FRANKLIN DELANO ROOSEVELT LIBRARY, MISCELLANEOUS HISTORICAL DOCUMENTS COLLECTION

Albert Einstein
Old Grove Rd.
Nassau Point
Peconic, Long Island

August 2nd, 1939

F.D. Roosevelt,
President of the United States,
White House
Washington, D.C.

Sir:

Some recent work by E.Fermi and L. Szilard, which has been communicated to me in manuscript, leads me to expect that the element uranium may be turned into a new and important source of energy in the immediate future. Certain aspects of the situation which has arisen seem to call for watchfulness and, if necessary, quick action on the part of the Administration. I believe therefore that it is my duty to bring to your attention the following facts and recommendations:

In the course of the last four months it has been made probable - through the work of Joliot in France as well as Fermi and Szilard in America - that it may become possible to set up a nuclear chain reaction in a large mass of uranium,by which vast amounts of power and large quantities of new radium-like elements would be generated. Now it appears almost certain that this could be achieved in the immediate future.

This new phenomenon would also lead to the construction of bombs, and it is conceivable - though much less certain - that extremely powerful bombs of a new type may thus be constructed. A single bomb of this type, carried by boat and exploded in a port, might very well destroy the whole port together with some of the surrounding territory. However, such bombs might very well prove to be too heavy for transportation by air.

-2-

The United States has only very poor ores of uranium in moderate quantities. There is some good ore in Canada and the former Czechoslovakia, while the most important source of uranium is Belgian Congo.

In view of this situation you may think it desirable to have some permanent contact maintained between the Administration and the group of physicists working on chain reactions in America. One possible way of achieving this might be for you to entrust with this task a person who has your confidence and who could perhaps serve in an inofficial capacity. His task might comprise the following:

a) to approach Government Departments, keep them informed of the further development, and put forward recommendations for Government action, giving particular attention to the problem of securing a supply of uranium ore for the United States;

b) to speed up the experimental work,which is at present being carried on within the limits of the budgets of University laboratories, by providing funds, if such funds be required, through his contacts with private persons who are willing to make contributions for this cause, and perhaps also by obtaining the co-operation of industrial laboratories which have the necessary equipment.

I understand that Germany has actually stopped the sale of uranium from the Czechoslovakian mines which she has taken over. That she should have taken such early action might perhaps be understood on the ground that the son of the German Under-Secretary of State, von Weizsäcker, is attached to the Kaiser-Wilhelm-Institut in Berlin where some of the American work on uranium is now being repeated.

Yours very truly,

A. Einstein

(Albert Einstein)

DOCUMENT 1.2 KENNETH BAINBRIDGE TO ALL CONCERNED WITH PROJECT TR SOURCE: DOE NNSA/NSO ALLA0000919

To: All Concerned with Project TR
From: K. T. Bainbridge

J. H. Williams has suggested that Project Y personnel having responsibilities with respect to the Trinity project should be circularized on all information which may affect the planning or performance of their work. This seems better than frequent meetings because of the large amount of travel ahead and the diverse duties of a considerable group of people. The individuals on the following list will be sent information which may affect their programs, and the attached sheets summarize the agreements and arrangements reached in the past three weeks since the formation of the project. The individuals on the list are responsible for the dissemination of information on travel and security regulations and other matters of interest to their men who will be going to Trinity. Some of you have already received memoranda relating to the subjects covered below, but to insure complete coverage to those omitted on earlier lists the information is included.

The Trinity project should be abbreviated "TR."

DISTRIBUTION LIST

H. L. Anderson
K. T. Bainbridge
Comdr. N. E. Bradbury
Dr. L. H. Hempelmann
S. Kershaw
G. B. Kistiakowsky
J. E. Mack
J. H. Manley
W. G. Marley
E. W. Marlowe
D. P. Mitchell
P. B. Moon
J. R. Oppenheimer
W. G. Penney
Ens. G. T. Reynolds
H. T. Richards
E. Segre
Lt. R. A. Taylor
R. J. Van Gemert
B. Waldman
V. Weisakopf
J. H. Williams
R. R. Wilson
Meteorologist

1. AIR SHOT DECISION—According to present plans the gadget test shot will be made with the gadget mounted on a 100 ft. steel tower.

The center of gravity of the gadget will be 103 ft. above the ground. The scheduled height for the 100 T shot is 28 ft. above the ground. Jumbo will be erected at a point bisecting the angle N 10,000 - 0 - W 10,000 at a point 800 yds. radially from 0. Dr. Oppenheimer's decision giving the air shot higher priority is given in enclosure No. 1 attached.

2. 100 FT. TOWER—The specifications of the 100 ft. tower are given in enclosure No. 2. The actual purchase of this tower is not firm until we hear from the New York office on or before March 30. Detailed drawings and stress analyses of the tower are given on a set of blueprints available in Room A-202 and may be inspected if desired.

3. 100 T SHOT—The 100 T shot is scheduled for May 5 with April 30 a desirable date for all installations to be completed so that rehearsal runs can be made on May 1, 2, 3 and 4. The actual date of firing is dependent upon satisfactory wind conditions, but from information available on the weather at the site it is not expected that one will have to wait for more than four days for a satisfactory wind direction and velocity during May. The 100 T pile will be an octagonal cylinder— i.e., octagonal sides and flat top and bottom surfaces. The 100 T pile will be detonated from six points. The shape of the pile and use of multiple detonation points should insure uniform blast conditions at quite small radii and this scheme is being carried out at the recommendation of Penney and Marley. Details of the 100 T set-up are given in enclosure No. 3. The tower will be located 800 yds. south from 0 on the line N 10,000 - 0 extended.

4. PROJECT TR RESPONSIBILITIES ON 100 T SHOT—The Project TR responsibilities on the 100 T shot are listed in enclosure No. 4.

5. ORGANIZATION CHART—The organization chart as of March 24 is given in enclosure No. 5.

6. ORGANIZATION AND SERVICES

    A. TRAVEL REGULATIONS—Regulations for civilian personnel are given in enclosure No. 6-A.
    S.E.D. personnel are allowed a per diem allowance ($5.00) while on route between A and Project 36. They do not receive any per diem allowance at Trinity. This has been checked with Army rules and regulations through the kindness of Capt. Smith.
    Officers on temporary assignment to Trinity from Project Y receive $7.00 per diem en route and $5.00 per diem in residence at Trinity.
    Usual transit time to Trinity, less than nine hours, equals 1/4 day.

    B. SECURITY REGULATIONS—The security regulations mutually agreed upon by Major de Silva, Lt. Bush, Lt. Taylor, K. T. Bainbridge and J. H. Williams are given in enclosure No. 6-B and should be read carefully by all of your men prior to going to Trinity.

C. PROCUREMENT OF EQUIPMENT—Information relative to procurement has been sent out by J. H. Williams March 20 to all but a few of the above list. It is included as enclosure No. 6-C to complete the distribution.

D. PHOTOGRAPHIC SERVICES AT TRINITY—J. E. Mack (G-11) has a photographic laboratory at the site under T/5 Ernest D. Wallis, and details of this arrangement are included in enclosure No. 6-D.

E. TIMING, FIRING, REMOTE CONTROL DEVICKS, PHONE COMMUNICATIONS—E. W. Marlowe of J. H. Williams' office is handling devices of this nature as indicated in enclosure No. 6-E. A detailed summary of the requirements of each group for the May 5 test should be ready for Mr. Marlowe not later than April 1. Mr. Marlowe or someone appointed by him and Mr. Williams will handle the telephone layout which, it is planned, will allow communication from preamp stations to the main shelters and from one main shelter to another or to the base camp.

F. TRANSPORTATION AND SHIPPING—Transportation to and from Trinity should be requested from J. H. Williams' office. Wherever possible groups should cooperate in their trips as the transportation is in a poor state because of the large number of vehicles in for repair. More vehicles will have to be obtained, but our request should be documented and any difficulties should be reported to J. H. Williams.

Shipping is handled through Harry Allen's office. No material may be taken in personnel vehicles without giving Allen and Williams a complete detailed list. Mr. Mitchell has asked that we avoid carrying anything to Trinity in group vehicles.

G. SPECIAL SHELTER BUILDINGS—R. W. Carlson (X-2), Room A-203, and Ens. G. T. Reynolds (X-5), Room B-102, will continue as consultants on the design of special shelter buildings for equipment or personnel. Their help should not be sought until after detailed plans of the interior arrangements of a shelter or instrument box are completed with a layout of the dimensions, access openings, etc. All requests for construction go to J. H. Williams.

H. LABORATORY BUILDINGS AT TRINITY—The west McDonald ranch house, No. 1, has been assigned to Group G-11 for print filing, print reading and laboratory work. The eastern ranch house, No. 2, will have one room for headquarters with detailed maps and air mosaics mounted for easy reference, and two steel files for safeguarding of classified reports. The southwestern base camp building is available for laboratory use for two-thirds of its length. The details of distribution of space for the latter two buildings can only be settled if group leaders will submit their estimated requirements for working space, if any, at the base camp. Requests should be submitted to J. H. Williams with a copy to Bainbridge not later than March 31. I hope that most of this can be taken care of at S 10,000, W 10,000, N 10,000 and the hutments which will be located near the main shelter buildings. These hutments should be in place not later than March 26.

i. RADIO COMMUNICATIONS—There are available a total of 20 25-watt FM Motorola transmitters and associated receivers and three 50-watt transmitting stations. One 50-watt and six 25-watt stations are used by the M.P. detachment. These are on frequency 38.860 megacycles with call letters WZZZ-1, 2. . . . . . .23 inclusive. All 23 of these radios are project property. Their major use will be to coordinate the work of Dr. Hempelmann's rough riders and M.P.'s after the gadget shot, and for communication outside the ABPO area on siting trips. Phone communication should be used for all testing work in setting up preamps, gauges, etc.
There are two SCR-299 450-watt transmitters in the band 4-8 megacycles. These are for ground-to-plane communication and for long distance ground-to-ground communication. No call letters or exact frequency band have yet been authorized on these. Major de Silva has been requested to get authorization for the use of these transmitters. Either or both 3,440 and 7.235 megacycles will allow ground-to-plane communication. The SCR-299 radios will only be used by B. Waldman, Lt. C. D. Curtis, J. H. Williams, K. Bainbridge or operators appointed and agreed to by them.
There are two S-29 Sky Travellar battery-operated receivers which cover the SCR-299 range and an additional six S-39 battery-operated receivers are on order. These are for receiving only at remote points to obtain advance warning of shot firing.
There are two SCR-511 Walkie-Talkie transeivers for use particularly in exploratory work, site hunting, etc. Their range is limited to 5 or 6 miles at best.
R. F. Bacher and W. Higinbotham have agreed to assign one man to take care of the radio communication equipment and the installation of the remaining FM radios.

J. ASSISTANCE IN TESTS REQUIRING H.E. SHOTS—Comdr. N. E. Bradbury (Group X-6) has very generously agreed to supply assistance on explosives for both the Trinity test and prior experimental work. All requests for such assistance should be addressed to Comdr. Bradbury with copies to Lt. W. F. Schaffer, J. H. Williams and K. Bainbridge. (See enclosure No. 6-J.)

K. COMBAT SUITS—We shall not be allowed to use combat suits for work at Trinity in spite of the primitive conditions there. Mr. Mitchell is trying to see if he can get ski pants and parkas as substitutes. All those who have not yet returned their combat suits should turn them in to S stock. I will keep you advised of future developments.

L. MAPS—Complete sets of maps, the best available of the Trinity region, have been requested through Capt. Davalos' office, and one set each will be issued to the meteorology group, R. R. Wilson, J. E. Mack, J. H. Williams, J. H. Manley, B. Waldman and two copies to Dr. Hempelmann. One set will be mounted in the headquarters office in ranch building No. 2. In addition there are good air mosaics of the region on hand which will be mounted in the headquarters office, and a special 6-inches-to-the-mile strip which includes N 10,000, S 10,000 and runs nearly as far west as W 10,000. The air navigation map for the region will be available too, which gives the position of radio beacons and restricted areas for the southern part of the state. At present detailed maps of the region are available in Lt. Bush's office. All the maps should be well taken care of and should be considered classified information. A detailed layout of all the roads and the survey of the main stations is available in Lt. Bush's office, Capt. Davalos' office or Room A-202.

M. WEATHER INFORMATION—General weather information for the region is given in Report No. 826, classified "SECRET" - "A Climatic Discussion of the Central Plateau Region of New Mexico." Mrs. Anderson will have this available in Room A-202 where it can be read. The more detailed information on wind directions at different levels, ceiling heights, distribution frequency of thunder storms, distribution frequency of clouds, etc., is given in copy No. 1147 of the Airway Meteorological Atlas for the U.S. However, this just summarizes weather data up to 1941 and does not include more recent and better information obtained from new stations set up at Army air fields during the past few years. The latter information will become available later when the meteorological group has started work. The atlas is available for reference in Room A-202.

N. MAIL—At present Lt. R. A. Taylor will take care of forwarding the mail between Y and Trinity. Letters for the personnel at Trinity should be brought to his office and will be sent to Trinity either by project personnel who are travelling there or with a member of Lt. Bush's detachment on the regular schedule of trips back and forth.

O. GENERAL SET-UP AT TRINITY—The basic general description of facilities and plans for Trinity vehicles and equipment is given in a memorandum classified "SECRET" which will be available from Mrs. Anderson in Room A-202.

P. SHOP WORK—E. Long has asked for a representative of project TR to whom he can go on questions of shop priority, design changes, etc. The representative will be K. Bainbridge and, in his absence, J. H. Williams.

Q. MATERIAL ORDERED FOR PROJECT TR—Harry Allen has circularized two lists of material ordered for TR. List A was reviewed by Manley, Wilson and Bainbridge and assignments made for equipment. The only correction is that the three mounted precision forks are for the SCR-584 equipment and do not represent open stock. List A covers material ordered and received; List B covers material ordered but not yet received. The Blaw-Knox tower due date should be 6–4–45 with the absolute latest date 6–15–45.

Attachments   K. T. BAINBRIDGE
    No.1 - 1 page - SECRET
    No.2 - 1 page - CONF.
    No.3 - 2 page - CONF.
    No.4 - 1 page - CONF.
    No.5 - 1 page - SECRET
    No.6-A - 1 page - CONF.
    No.6-B - 2 page - CONF.
    No.6-C - 1 page - CONF.
    No.6-D - 3 page - CONF.
    No.6-E - 1 page - not classified
    No.6-J - 1 page - CONF.

DOCUMENT 1.3 OPPENHEIMER AND KISTIAKOWSKY ACTIVITIES AT TRINITY SOURCE: DOE NNSA/NSO ALLA0004059

INTER-OFFICE MEMORANDUM
October 13, 1944

To: J. R. Oppenheimer
From: G. B. Kistiakowsky
Subject: Activities at Trinity

The following sets down the plan and scope of operations proposed for Trinity and will serve as a justification for the construction and equipment requirements for Trinity as submitted to you in a memorandum dated 10 October 1944 from K. T. Bainbridge.

1. The plans for Trinity have been drawn on the assumption that a field test of the gadget will prove a success, the nuclear explosion having occurred. In that case, we believe, it is most essential to obtain detailed and quantitative information on the various effects from the gadget, which will serve as the basic technical data for an intelligent development program on and tactical planning of the use of this weapon. The information will be useful in two ways. First, it will tell what is to be expected from a gadget of the same design as that to be tested, at Trinity. Second, as the design of the gadget is improved and greater TNT equivalent is hoped for from subsequent gadgets, it will be possible, on the basis of Trinity data, to predict with good accuracy the destructive effects from these improved models of the gadget.

2. We believe that this information will be very difficult to obtain from observations on the performance of the gadget over enemy territory, because observation of the actual phenomena taking place at the instant of the nuclear explosion will be scanty and incomplete at best, while a subsequent study of the damage inflicted upon the enemy installations will be complicated by the impossibility to correlate it with the precise position of the gadget at the instant of explosion, weather existing at the instant of explosion and, finally, incomplete knowledge of the blast, etc., that accompanied the explosion. Considering how difficult it is for the British and our Air Forces to evaluate accurately the performance of the bombs dropped over enemy territory, even though large numbers are dropped, and hence statistical averaging methods can be used, this statement is by no means too pessimistic. Hence, if we do not have accurate test data from Trinity, the planning of the use of the gadget over the enemy territory will have to be done substantially blindly, and only *gradually* enough information will be accumulated to make possible a more intelligent selection of targets, height of detonation, etc., etc.

3. It may be further noted that, if we have accurate information on the test gadget to be fired at Trinity and combine this information with the, by necessity, incomplete information on later gadgets dropped over enemy territory, we will be in a better position to judge whether the newly introduced changes in design are giving improved performance or not. This, quite obviously, is of prime importance for the success of the technical work at Y which is presumably to continue after the test at Trinity. Without this information it will be much more difficult to estimate whether the subsequent designs of the gadget do give improved performance or not.

4. In carrying out the test at Trinity, of course, one has to allow for the possibility that the gadget will fail to function. This very real

contingency is allowed for in the plans for the Trinity test by the proposal that the gadget be fired in the Jumbo if the design of the former, by the time the Trinity test gets under way, is such that Jumbo is likely to withstand the explosion of H. E., and the time is such that Jumbo is at Trinity. As you know, an alternate method has been proposed and is being actively worked on by Group X-2. This consists in mounting the gadget inside of a water tank with a weight of water being about fifty times the weight of the explosive. Present indications are that after an explosion under such conditions at least 50% of the material contained near the center of the tamper sphere can be recovered from the ground in the near vicinity of the explosion. The present bowl being constructed at the Two-Mile Mesa will be used for firing experimental gadgets on one-half linear scale. If these relatively large scale tests confirm the results obtained with small charges, we should seriously consider the recommendation to construct at Trinity a bowl of about 400 feet diameter with a tower in the center to support the water tank and the gadget. This construction has not been included in the proposals referred to above because the tests at Y have not as yet reached a stage where the method has been adequately proved. It may be pointed out that the construction of the bowl will not be a colossal task, and could be completed on relatively short notice—that is, eight to ten weeks. Its cost is difficult to estimate but perhaps the following considerations will be useful: The cost of the present bowl at Y is estimated at $10,000. The linear dimensions of the bowl at Trinity may be twice those of the bowl at Y. Hence one would suggest a figure of $80,000, calculating it on the cube of linear dimensions rule.

5. The phenomena accompanying nuclear explosion, which it is desired to measure at Trinity and which will be of interest in estimating the effects of the gadget over the enemy territory are the following:
   A. Air Blast
   B. Ground Shock
   C. Instantaneous neutron and gamma ray flux.
   D. Atmospheric phenomena, such as the rate of rise of the hot gases, the altitude they reach, their volume and their subsequent fate.
   E. The distribution of radioactive residue on the ground, both in the immediate vicinity of the explosion, and as a result of sedimentation from the "ball of fire" that is expected to rise to stratospheric heights.

6. In respect to practically all of these observations, one major fundamental difficulty faces the testing personnel, namely, the uncertainty as to the magnitude of nuclear explosion. If we knew, for instance, that the explosion would be equivalent to 1,000 tons of TNT, then the layout

of the test equipment could be roughly predicted by scaling up the data obtained from the study of small explosive charges elsewhere. Unfortunately even this scaling is so inaccurate and so little is known about the effects of large charges that it is almost indispensable to fire, sometime before the actual test, a rather large charge of H. E. (such as the proposed 100 tons), to be sure that the plans laid out are not completely erroneous and that the testing equipment will function satisfactorily in the actual test. But even after such a test, as stated above, the uncertainty will remain as to whether the nuclear explosion is of a magnitude comparable to 100 or 10,000 tons of TNT. Thus it is necessary to place gauges over quite a large range of distances from the gadget and to place recording equipment so far away that even the largest conceivable explosion will not damage it so that records are destroyed or that operating personnel is lost. It is this uncertainty which has led to a rather elaborate field layout, requiring much cable, roads, shelters, etc.

7. It is hardly necessary to discuss the reasons for measuring the air blast, since the present plans for the use of the gadget over enemy territory consider blast as the effective damaging agent. However, it may be noted that the problem of measuring blast of such long duration as that expected from the gadget has never been tackled before and therefore two types of gauges now contemplated are none too many, to insure useful records regardless of what happens.

8. In addition to the blast measurement on the ground, wanted to estimate the extent of damage, it is planned to measure blast high above the gadget by means of condenser gauges and informer circuits dropped from a plane flying at a safe distance from the explosion. This procedure is identical with that proposed for operation over the enemy territory and the data are essential to permit the correlation of the data to be obtained later over enemy territory with those expected from the Trinity test.

9. The operation of the gadget over enemy territory contemplates its detonation at such height above ground that damage from ground shock will be negligible compared with that from blast. This has been recommended on the basis of data obtained with small charges only. Consequently, the test at Trinity, in which the gadget would be detonated near the ground, would provide an excellent opportunity to determine once for all whether that decision is right or gadgets should be detonated next to the ground, major reliance being placed on the earthquake-like ground shock, aided by the somewhat reduced air blast. This is the reason why geophones are included in the test equipment and will be placed at varying distances from the gadget. Their

records will also be of great value in calculating the total energy release from the gadget.

10. The measurements of instantaneous neutron and gamma ray flux present great difficulties and, besides, the Jumbo or the water layer surrounding the test gadget will alter the flux in a manner not too easy to predict. In view of all this we consider such measurements of less importance than the others, but intend to carry them out if the difficulties prove to be not too great and if theoretical calculations going on meanwhile indicate that the data obtained will be of value. The method of carrying out these measurements is to expose gold foil, and possibly photographic films, to the action of the radiation. Unfortunately data thus obtained next to the ground will be difficult to interpret because of the uncertain nature of the scattering of neutrons by the ground. A relatively easy alternate method of getting data high above the ground is by means of shells shot from mortars and provided with parachutes in the manner of ordinary military flares. These would be shot upward an instant before the explosion and would contain the necessary gold foil, etc. Even though the final decision to use them has not been reached as yet, the nature of these observations is such that unless we procure the equipment in advance and develop the technique in good time, it will be impossible to use them on short notice.

11. The fate of the gases and active material rising into the atmosphere after the explosion is not only of academic interest because:

    A. It affects vitally the safety of aircraft flying near the site of the explosion, not only the one which is carrying the gadget but also all the accompanying planes which will undoubtedly be used to provide an armed escort, act as a blind, make observations, etc., etc.

    B. It is quite essential to follow the fate of these gases for a long time since they will contain, probably, the major portion of radioactive products, and it is of obvious military interest to determine where and how such products are precipitated, what intensity of radiation they create on the ground, etc.

12. In view of the uncertain nature of this "ball of fire", it is difficult to predict whether it will be observable by an ordinary photographic means over a sufficient length of time. Furthermore the weather conditions may be unfavorable for photographic observation but the urgency of the test at Trinity may be such that it will be impossible to wait for a completely clear day. Therefore it is intended to use duplicate type of equipment:

    A. Photographic and movie cameras of standard type, including spectroscopic equipment to determine the temperature of the gases.

B. Radar equipment (SCR-584). This equipment is particularly prom-
ising since it will register motions and the location of the "ball of
fire" even after it has been concealed by clouds, and even when the
temperature has dropped so low that the luminosity is too weak but
the refractive index of the gases is significantly different from that
of the surrounding atmosphere. Two radar sets are wanted for this
operation because with one set, even if it functions, the possibility
of losing the "ball of fire" is not negligible, and two sets operating
at the same time will increase the probability of successful observation very materially.

13. Accurate information on the weather expected during the test, as well
as that actually existing when the test has taken place is quite important to insure successful observation of the "ball of fire" and the pre-
diction of the behaviour of the "ball of fire" from gadgets dropped
over enemy territory. Unfortunately there exist no weather stations
near Trinity providing information on the condition of the upper air
layers and thus it has become necessary to obtain Radiosonde equipment, train our personnel in its use and then follow the weather in the
immediate vicinity of the test site.

14. It will be quite essential to approach the location of the explosion and
to study the terrain before the residual radioactivity has subsided.
Therefore it is planned to equip the M-4 tanks, now at Site Y, with
internal lead shields to protect the crew from the harmful effects of
radiation, and then to drive the machines to the site of explosion, collecting samples of the soil at various distances by means of automatic
sampling devices operating from the bottom of the tank. A determination of the ratio of the unchanged 25 to the fission products in these
samples will give the most accurate information on the efficiency of the
nuclear explosion.

15. In my opinion, these plans are not too elaborate, considering the importance of the test and the value of the technical information to be
obtained. However, if the present plans are carried through, the probability of obtaining adequate information is very high; in other words,
the plans are not inadequate.

16. As regards the construction of the various shelters, only brief remarks
should suffice in addition to plans submitted to you. It would be extremely difficult to place the gauges near the focus of the explosion
and then bring different electrical signals as far out as is necessary in
order to reach personnel shelters, if the latter are to be safe. Hence the
necessity for intermediate instrument shelters close enough to the explosion to make the electric signal transmission relatively simple and

far enough to insure that the equipment there located is not damaged.

17. It may be noted that the plans now submitted do not include any personnel shelters for visitors. If a larger number of visitors, not connected with technical work, come to observe the test, it will be necessary to design and build special shelters for them, since their presence in the now contemplated personnel shelters will interfere with technical work.

Distribution: Copies 1 & 2: J. R. Oppenheimer
Copy 3 W. S. Parsons
4 K. T. Bainbridge
5 N. E. Bradbury
Copies 6 & 8 File
Copy 7 Major W. A. Stevens

DOCUMENT 1.4 PHILIP MORRISON "IF THE BOMB GETS OUT OF HAND" SOURCE: EXCERPT FROM *ONE WORLD OR NONE,* NY, NEW PRESS, 2007

About a quarter-past seven on Monday morning, August 6, the Japanese early-warning radar net had detected the approach of some enemy aircraft headed for the southern part of Honshu, and doubtless for the ports of the Inland Sea. The alert was given, and radio broadcasting stopped in many cities, among them Hiroshima. The raiders approached the coast at very high altitude. At nearly eight o'clock the radar operators determined that the number of planes coming in was very small—probably not more than three—and the air-raid alert was lifted. The normal broadcast warning was given to the population that it might be advisable to go to shelter if B-29's were actually sighted, but that no raid was expected beyond some sort of reconnaissance. At 8:16 the Tokyo control operator of the Japan Broadcasting Corporation noticed that the Hiroshima station had gone off the air. He tried to use another telephone line to reestablish his program, but it too had failed. About twenty minutes later the Tokyo railroad telegraph center realized that the main line telegraph had stopped working just north of Hiroshima. And from some small railway stops within ten miles of that city there had come unofficial and rather confused reports of a terrible explosion in Hiroshima. All these events were then reported to the air-raid defense headquarters of the General Staff. The military called again and again the Army wireless station at the castle in Hiroshima. There was no answer. Something had happened in Hiroshima. The men at headquarters were puzzled. They knew that no large enemy raid could have occurred; they knew that no sizeable store of explosives was in Hiroshima at that time.

The young major of the General Staff was ordered in. He was instructed to fly immediately by army plane to Hiroshima, to land, to survey the damage, and to return to Tokyo with reliable information for the staff. It was generally felt in the air-raid defense headquarters that nothing serious had taken place, that the nervous days of August, 1945, in Japan had fanned up a terrible rumor from a few sparks of truth. The major went to the airport and took off for the southwest. After flying for about three hours, still nearly one hundred miles from Hiroshima, he and his pilot saw a great cloud of smoke from the south. In the bright afternoon Hiroshima was burning. The major's plane reached the city. They circled in disbelief. A great scar, still burning, was all that was left of the center of a busy city. They flew over the military landing strip to land, but the installations below them were smashed. The field was deserted.

About thirty miles south of the wrecked city is the large naval base of Kure, already battered by carrier strikes from the American fleet. The major landed at the Kure airfield. He was welcomed by the naval officers there as the first official representative of aid from Tokyo. They had seen the explosion at Hiroshima. Truckloads of sailors had been sent up to help the city in this strange disaster, but terrible fires had blocked the roads, and the men had turned back. A few refugees had straggled out of the northern part of the town, their clothes and skin burned, to tell near-hysterical stories of incredible violence. Great winds blew in the streets, they said. Debris and the dead were everywhere. The great explosion had been for each survivor a bomb hitting directly on his house. The staff major, thrown into the grimmest of responsibilities, organized some two thousand sailors into parties, which reached the city about dusk. They were the first group of rescue workers to enter Hiroshima.

The major took charge for several days. The rail line was repaired, and trainloads of survivors were shipped north. The trains came first from Onomichi, where, about forty miles north, there was a large naval hospital. Soon the hospital was filled, and its movable supplies exhausted. Then the trains bore the injured still farther north, until there too the medical facilities were completely used up. Some sufferers were shipped twenty-four hours by train before they came to a place where they might be treated. Hospital units were mobilized by Tokyo to come from hundreds of miles to set up dressing stations in Hiroshima. One bomb and one plane had reduced a city of four hundred thousand inhabitants to a singular position in the war economy of Japan: Hiroshima consumed bandages and doctors, while it produced only trainloads of the burned and the broken. Its story brought terror to all the cities of the islands.

The experts in the science of the killing of cities have developed a concept which well describes the disaster of Hiroshima, the disaster which will come to any city which feels the atomic bomb. That is the idea of saturation. Its meaning is simple: if you strike at a man or a city, your victim defends himself. He hits you, he throws up flak, he fights the fires, he cares for the wounded, he rebuilds the houses, he throws tarpaulins over the shelterless machinery. The harder you strike, the greater his efforts to defend himself. But if you strike all at once with overwhelming force, he cannot defend himself. He is stunned. The city's flak batteries are all shooting as fast as they can; the firemen are all at work on the flames of their homes. Then your strike may grow larger with impunity. He is doing his utmost, he can no longer respond to greater damage by greater effort in defense. The defenses are saturated.

The atomic bomb is preeminently the weapon of saturation.

PHOTO 1.5 MCDONALD RANCH CONTROL POINT *Source:* DOE NNSA/NSO 004039-30

DOCUMENT 2.1 DEAR DR. SHIELDS WARREN SOURCE: DOE NNSA/NSO
NV04087743

APPENDIX "A"
August 5, 1948

Dr. Shields Warren, Director
Division of Biology and Medicine
U.S. Atomic Energy Commission
Washington 25, D. C.

Dear Dr. Warren:

We have just returned from our resurvey of the Bikini and Eniwetok areas. The program as outlined for Bikini last spring (UWFL-10) was completed with all the stations occupied and sufficient data gathered that it will now be possible for us to evaluate the changes that have taken place.

We arrived at Bikini on July 3, 1948 and remained until July 20. The weather during our stay was uniformly fair so that we could work in the field each day. Collections were made in each collecting area with samples of the aquatic fauna and flora gathered for preservation by drying, ashing or chemical means. A total of 1878 ashed samples were prepared at Bikini. Material gathered for further study in our laboratories will greatly increase the number of samples.

The period from July 21 to July 30 was spent at Eniwetok where we collected extensively in six areas. Three of the collecting areas were in the relatively uncontaminated areas, with three stations near major sources of contaminating materials. Spot collections and plankton sampling helped to complete the sampling. We prepared 798 ashed samples while at Eniwetok and returned with frozen, dried, and chemically preserved samples for continuing the study at our laboratory.

The counting of the activity contained in the samples is getting underway. As fast as counts are made and the data analyzed we will prepare summary reports that will be sent to you.

It is entirely too early to predict with certainty the distribution of the fission products, it does seem however, that there has been a shift of active materials at Bikini up onto the land mass and into the vegetation. Some collections were made of land plants and animals to study the amounts contained in the various forms.

The organization of the data collected during this and previous years' expeditions into a complete study will be a very Herculean task. We hope that on your next trip to the west you can visit our laboratory so that we may review the problems and develop those that will contribute to an understanding of the most important phases of the work.

The Navy was very helpful in all phases of the program. They helped expedite the movement of personnel, equipment and materials. We are especially grateful for the assignment of Lt. J. J. Schmidt, U.S.N. as our liaison officer. Mr. Schmidt is a fine young naval officer with an understanding of the problems.

In all matters of administration, security, transference of reports and material we shall continue to work with the Atomic Energy Commission's representative at Richland as we have in the past.

Very sincerely yours,

Lauren R. Donaldson
Director
Applied Fisheries Laboratory

DOCUMENT 2.2 VICE ADMIRAL W. H. P. BLANDY FOREWORD TO BOMBS AT BIKINI SOURCE: *BOMBS AT BIKINI: THE OFFICIAL REPORT OF OPERATION CROSSROADS* (NEW YORK: WM. H. WISE & CO., 1947)

Operation Crossroads was directed by the United States for purposes of national defense; but its lesson has world-wide significance. The atomic bomb is definitely not "just another weapon"; its destructive power dwarfs all previous weapons. Observers at Bikini saw the bomb sink great steel warships and, with its penetrating nuclear radiations, reach into ships' interiors to kill test animals. The explosions in air and underwater were very different spectacles, but their end results mean the same: death and destruction on an enormous scale.

Only after the military implications of atomic energy have been grasped by the people of the world will the way be clear for working out effective international control. Throughout its ten-month tenure, Joint Task Force One attempted to give the world an intimate knowledge of the purposes, execution, and consequences of the Tests. The present volume not only summarizes much of the information already given out, but presents much material not previously disclosed. This volume, together with the recently published Pictorial Record, forms the final, and perhaps the most informative release on the Operation.

Vice Admiral W. H. P. Blandy, U.S.N.,

Commander, Joint Task Force One

DOCUMENT 2.3 DOSE SUMMARY FOR CROSSROADS SOURCE: *FOR THE RECORD—A HISTORY OF THE NUCLEAR TEST PERSONNEL REVIEW PROGRAM, 1978–1993, DEFENSE NUCLEAR AGENCY, DNA 001-91-C-0022, MARCH 1996.*

4.2.3 Dose Summary for CROSSROADS

CROSSROADS operations were undertaken under radiological supervision, intended to keep personnel doses below 0.1 rem of gamma radiation per day. About 15 percent of the participants were issued film badges. Personnel anticipated to have the most potential for exposure were badged, and a percentage of each group working in less radioactive areas were badged (3: 2, 3).

Because radiation dose data are not complete, reconstructions have been made of personnel doses for unbadged crewmembers of the ships involved. The calculations relied upon the radiation measurements recorded by radiation safety personnel in 1946 and used the types of methods discussed in chapter 7. The table below summarizes the available dosimetry information:

SUMMARY OF EXTERNAL DOSES FOR OPERATION CROSSROADS AS OF 1 MAY 1986

	GAMMA DOSE (REM)					
	0–0.5	0.5–1	1–3	3–5	5–10	10+
Army	3,250	25	15	10	0	0
Navy	28,436	4,883	2,939	4	0	0
Marine Corps	550	0	0	0	0	0

DOCUMENT 2.4 U.S. NATIONAL MUSEUM (SMITHSONIAN) CURATOR OF ICHTHYOLOGY, LEONARD P. SCHULTZ'S DIARY FROM ABLE DAY, JULY 1, 1946 SOURCE: SMITHSONIAN INSTITUTION ARCHIVES, HTTP://WWW.MNH.SI.EDU/ONEHUNDREDYEARS/PROFILES/LEONARD_SCHULTZ. HTML, LAST ACCESS 08/09/16

Since the air currents were greater velocity near the water and of different directions at various heights, the Bomb cloud did not drift as a vertical column. The lower part drifted westward leaving the cirrus cloud more or less suspended in the sky over the lagoon while the lower parts drifted from under it. The very lowest part hanging together as a unit down where the cumulus clouds go sailing by out here, perhaps ½ & a mile higher.

About an hour after the blast there was small rain squall that obscured the lower cloud and when it had passed we could no longer see the lower A-bomb cloud.

The cirrus or upper cloud finally spread out into a thin whish of a cloud and was blown to right.

Caption reads: "Carl Mydans was sent to the area to document the exodus of the people of Bikini. The story was published by *LIFE* (Mar 25 1946). The graveyard on Bikini Island, just outside a village on the southside of the island, held about thirty graves. Walking together between the tombstones, the children smile, probably not realizing that they would soon leave their island and its history behind."

PHOTO 2.5 CARL MYDANS'S GRAVEYARD ON BIKINI ISLAND, 1946 *Source:* Getty Images

DOCUMENT 3.1 PROJECT NUTMEG REPORT FAVORABLE WEATHER
(PAGES 39–40) SOURCE: DOE NNSA/NSO NV0411323

REPRODUCED AT THE NATIONAL ARCHIVES

CONTINENTAL WEATHER (UNITED STATES) FAVORABLE FOR ATOMIC TESTS

	FAVORABLE CONDITIONS ARID SOUTHWEST & OF TIME		FAVORABLE CONDITIONS HUMID SOUTHWEST & OF TIME	
	Aloft	Surface	Aloft	Surface
Midwinter (Nov., Dec., Jan)	99	75	100	41
Midsummer (July)	50	40	50	30

Because of the almost universal prevalence of favorable conditions aloft throughout the entire United States during winter, it can be assumed that tests in that period can be conducted 75% of the time in the arid Southwest and 40% of the time in the humid southeast. During summer favorable conditions aloft match pretty well the favorable conditions at the surface but the matching is not universal. It is estimated that favorable conditions at the surface and aloft for the arid southwest will prevail 30% of the summer, while in the humid southeast, favorable conditions will prevail 20% of the summer. For purposes of planning and logistics, these figures show that the arid southwest is more favorable as a location for atomic test sites than the humid southeast.

OTHER CONSIDERATIONS INFLUENCING CHOICE OF SITES

Wherever sites are chosen in the United States, it is estimated that qualified meteorological personnel will be capable of issuing forecasts three days in advance to alert the operating personnel of approaching favorable conditions for test. Other figures taken from the Air Force charts indicate favorable weather situations persist for eight days during winter in the arid southwest before interruption by unfavorable conditions while in the humid southeast, favorable periods persist from four to eight days before interruption.

Observations made in the tropics, transposed to the continent, with respect to the different meteorological regimes, indicate that a certain amount of radioactive waste will fall out of the atmosphere to the eastward of continental sites following atomic tests. This follows from consideration of the volumetric envelope of revolution containing fission products produced by the velocity vectors of the winds aloft and its vertical projection upon the earth's surface. The writer maintains, after study of the fall out figures for the tropics, that such fall out will not harm the population, the economy nor the industry of the nation. However, if this negligible possibility cannot be accepted for sites chosen in the arid southwest, the coastal region of the

United States, between Cape Hatteras and Cape Fear, is offered as a suitable area from which to choose sites. As has been shown, this area is favorable for tests 40% of the winter as well as 20% of the summer. During winter, the coastal islands and foreshore localities are relatively free of population. The complete substance of the waste products of nuclear explosions will move eastward out over the Atlantic Ocean. Trajectories of upper winds can be prognosticated to avoid the geographical coordinates of Bermuda as well as the shipping lanes. The Gulf Stream and the currents of the Gulf of Maine will be compared in succeeding paragraphs to show how the Gulf Stream can be depended upon to remove fission products eastward, thus obviating the accumulation of activity through biological processes in organisms inhabiting the coastal matters of the nation.

DOCUMENT 3.2 FREDERICK REINES, CONTINENTAL TEST SITE REPORT SOURCE: LOS ALAMOS NATIONAL LABORATORY RESEARCH LIBRARY, DOE NNSA/NSO, LAMS-1173

December 16, 1950
LAMS-1173

Washington Document Room
J. R. Oppenheimer
Los Alamos Document Room

1 thru 10
11
12 thru 40

DISCUSSION OF RADIOLOGICAL HAZARDS ASSOCIATED WITH A CONTINENTAL TEST SITE FOR ATOMIC BOMBS

Based on Notes of Meetings Held at Los Alamos
August 1, 1950
MORNING MEETING
Introduction: A. C. Graves

The purpose of the meeting is to consider, from the point of view of radiological hazard,[1] whether or not it is acceptable to conduct tests of atomic

---

[1] Other bomb effects, e.g., blast, thermal radiation, etc., have much smaller danger radii, and for these effects and a bomb yield of 250 kilotons, a distance of 20 miles is more than ample to guarantee safety.

weapons at the continental site which seems to best satisfy logistic and safety requirements: Tonapah Bombing Range in Nevada.[2] For the purpose of the present discussion, attention will be confined to this site only, with no consideration of other suggested possibilities (e.g., sites in Canada, Australia) which are ruled out for the immediate future by logistic and diplomatic reasons.

We will attempt to formulate a set of specifications for weather conditions, yield of the bombs, etc., which can be considered acceptable for this site, and then try to evaluate the possibility that such specifications can be met.

It is emphasized that these considerations are from a radiological point of view only, omitting insofar as possible the psychological and political implications.

The discussion is to be based on the assumption that, in the event of a shot in Nevada, meteorologists would pick the actual shot days. The term "acceptable" or "desirable" day as used herein thus means one in which the pre-set specifications as to wind direction and velocity, probability of precipitation, etc., are satisfied; moreover, such favorable conditions must prevail for the length of time specified. Thus, the approach would be not to set a shot date in advance as, for example, 1 April, but to be ready to shoot any time after a specified date when the meteorologists give the green light.

* * *

The following statement was made by Fermi: there is a probability of the order of a few percent (between 1 and 5%) with a 250-KT shot to irradiate a circle of 300 miles radius with 10 r total dose, and the total dose decreases roughly inversely proportionally to the distance squared.

Fermi then made the following argument: assume a certain density of population, excluding the cities and taking only the rural population. (Ogle supplied a number of one/mi^2 for the density of rural population in this area.) Let us consider that the zone of 100 miles about zero will be guarded, heavily monitored, evacuated, etc. The zone of interest, then, is

---

[2]   It might be added that Tonapah is much superior to Trinity as a continental site. A reasonable criterion for the hazard factor is given by the expression $H = \sum_i \dfrac{p(r_i)}{r_i^2}$

where $p(r_i)$ is the population at distance r_i from the detonation. A more complete "hazard factor" should take the wind direction into account. H. K. Stephenson computed H for both Tonapah and Trinity. Taking the least populated 90° sector out to 150 miles for these two sites, he found that Tonapah is favored over Trinity by a factor of 3. Tonapah is even more favored than this, however, because the 90° sector for Tonapah is in the direction of the prevailing winds, whereas, it is not so for Trinity.

the one between 100 and 300 miles in radius and enclosing an angle of one radian, an area roughly 4×10^4 mi^2. Now, 1% of this area will be exposed to doses ranging from ~ 10 to ~ 50 r, so that 400 mi^2 will actually be exposed to this dose. Associated with this area, then, are ~ 400 persons.

For a rural population, the mathematical expectancy will be some average number of people exposed to doses of this order of magnitude. In cities, of course, the mathematical expectancy will have less meaning since there are much wider fluctuations. The probability of 1% is assumed for both cases. This is the size of the risk. Any evaluation beyond this, Fermi felt, was up to the psychologists and physicians.

(There was some discussion of the 1% probability-of-rain figure, since most of the group felt it quite high. Suydam pointed out that even if it is 100% certain it will rain, it would probably be over only 1% of the area in question. As a result, the figure 400 might possibly be an order of magnitude high.)

CONCLUSIONS

The probability of risk as stated by Fermi for the rural population is based on somewhat pessimistic estimates. Kennedy thought that in addition to this statement, there should be included the much smaller probability of a hot spot occurring in a city, emphasizing the lesser probability but the much greater effects.

This risk, as stated above, is not a probability that anyone will be killed, or even hurt (if the yield is kept low enough to insure that the dosage is ≤6 r), but it does contain the probability that people will receive perhaps a little more radiation than medical authorities say is absolutely safe.

Fermi felt that our conclusions should stress the extreme uncertainty of the elements we had to go on, and that we did our best with these; that the group is attempting to agree on physical facts.

It is considered desirable that the meteorologists carry out further calculations and extensions of the studies they presented at the meeting in order to build up a body of statistics. Graves suggested that it might also be worthwhile to start making predictions. It is clear that if a continental site is to be used with a minimum of hazard there must eventually be worked out a set of rigid specifications for suitable weather conditions.

A large number of those present considered the assumptions as to expected doses to be unduly pessimistic.

Judging from the results stated in Table I and the conservative nature of the considerations which led to it, it is considered that a tower-burst bomb having a yield of 25 kilotons could be detonated without exceeding the allowed emergency tolerance dose of 6 - 12 r outside a 180° test area sector 100 miles in radius. The degree of conservation could be checked with such a small bomb and the hazard associated with larger weapons could then be more realistically assessed.

APPENDIX I: GAMMA AND BETA DOSE

Using the $t^{-1.2}$ decay law for fission product activity, the total gamma dose from a time, t (hours), to ∞ is related to the dose rate, R, in r/hr at the end of one hour by the formula

$$I(t) = \frac{5R}{t^{0.2}}$$

The weak 1/5 power dependence on time is notable. Table I lists I(t)/R versus time.

TABLE I

I(T)/R	T (HRA)
5	1
3.6	5
3.2	10
2.9	15
2.7	20
2.6	25
2.5	30

DOCUMENT 3.3 FREDERICK C. WORMAN, ANATOMY OF THE NEVADA TEST SITE SOURCE: LOS ALAMOS SCIENTIFIC LABORATORY, DOE NNSA/NSO, NV0016244, LAMS-1173

EARLY INHABITANTS OF NTS

There is every probability that man of a very respectable antiquity lived on and around the Nevada Test Site. Elements of early cultures have been found in surrounding areas. Confirmation has been found in radiocarbon dates from Gypsum Cave, near Las Vegas (10,450 years), Stewart Rock Shelter in Clark County (4,050 years) and Tule Springs, Nevada. Early excavations, at Tule Springs, by Fenley Hunter and M. R. Harrington of the Southwest Museum, uncovered an ash bed two feet below the present surface and about fourteen feet below the lake bed deposit that once covered it. The charcoal was thought to be of human origin and showed a radiocarbon date of over 23,800 years. (11). Work during the past year by Shutler and Rozaire may produce a conclusive man date for Tule Springs. While evidence of ancient man at NTS is still unproven, it may well be that future investigations may bring such evidence to light.

A knowledge of the later Paiute occupation is rather sketchy and must be based on information supplied by old informants among Southern Paiutes still living in nearby areas. These people occupied this area, in moderate numbers, until recent historic times. Their economy was probably little different than that of nearby bands who have been studied ethnologically.

Small bands or family groups of Paiutes wandered throughout the area sleeping where they happened to find themselves at dusk. They knew when and where to harvest certain plants and small camps were set up for the purpose. Campsites are abundant in watered areas. At Cane Springs (see page 9) the remains of two large campsites are very apparent. Sherds of Paiute brownware pottery lie intermingled with chips of obsidian, chalcedony and chert used for the making of projectile points and tools. Here the animals came to water and here the stalker lay in wait. Additional edible plants, such as the cattail (Tule) were available. Several rock-mounded graves (vandalized) give evidence that some Paiutes remained at Cane Springs.

That Cane Springs had visitors antedating the Paiutes is indicated by the finding of a sherd of North Creek black-on-gray ware which dates back to the Pueblo II period [(12), pp. 45–47]. Campsites and artifacts are found at Tippipah Springs and along the road extending from Shoshone Mountain north to the upper end of Forty-Mile Canyon. Cat Canyon, near its junction with Forty-Mile Canyon, has a number of sites and many petroglyphs. Occupation in Cat Canyon until recent times is confirmed by a cave shelter where a prospector read newspapers as late as August of 1928. Other campsite centers are found at Topopah Springs, White Rock Springs (see page 3) and in the piñon-gathering centers on the tops of Rainier Mesa and other higher elevations. The description of White Rock Spring, "Clear and cold, it rose in its rocky vase, and was found carefully covered by a great, flat rock," was written by a member of the Jayhawker party of Forty-niners after captured Indians had led some of the party, camped at Groom Lake in November, 1849, to the lifesaving water. Development of the spring by later settlers resulted in the gaping hole in the white-rock wall (13).

The name given to the historic group may be Paiute, Piute or Pahute. Suggested but uncertain interpretations are "true Ute" for the first two and "water Ute" for the last. The name "Paiute" has been applied to Shoshonean tribes in many parts of the West. In the Southwest the name is specifically applied to Shoshonean bands living in southern Utah and Nevada and northwestern Arizona. Exact population figures are uncertain but indications are that there are about 500 Paiutes living in this area (1940) (14).

Linguistically the Paiute is of Shoshonean stock of the large Uto-Aztecan family. Escalante, the first white explorer in the area (1776), observed that the Southern Paiute spoke a language similar to that of the Indians of the north "although with some differences" (15). Clothing was simple and scanty. Women wore short aprons of skin or fiber. Rabbit-skin blankets, caps and possibly foot covering were worn in the winter. I have found no evidence, or heard of any, that would indicate the Indians of this area wore foot-covering of any kind. Most Southern Paiutes, living in the desert, were habitually barefooted.

Basketry, the main craft, was of a twilled or diagonal weave and the few remnants found on the Test Site were of fine quality. That some of the bands carried on a trade with other Indians is shown by the presence of Paiute baskets, especially wedding baskets, among the Navajo and Apache to the south and east (16).

The Paiute home was a brush shelter or "wickiup" type dwelling. The simplest form was made by setting eight poles in shallow holes around a rough circle, bending over the tops and tying them together, and covering the framework with a rude thatch of grass or brush. In addition to the brush huts, caves or rock-shelters were occupied in this area. Two excavated rock-shelters and four observed ones were all occupied, at least sporadically by travelling bands, into fairly recent times.

Jewelry or ornamentation among the Paiutes was simple and either scarce or lacking entirely among some bands. Stewart's Southern Paiute informants denied the use of either stones or shells [(17), p. 235]. Two types of beads and several fragments of abalone pendants were found in one of the rock-shelters, excavated on Rainier Mesa, and definitely show trade relations with other areas. The artifacts will be discussed fully in the following section of this pamphlet. Hunt reports similar beads in some abundance from the Death Valley salt pan and considers them as rare in the Ash Meadows area south of the Test Site [(4), pp. 245–286].

Pottery at the Test Site is of a Southern Paiute variety of brownware and is found in abundance in widely scattered areas. Pueblo black-on-white sherds, found in several places, further emphasize trade relations with the outside. Pottery will be further discussed in the portion of the paper covering salvage archaeology.

The main food of the Paiute were plants, and animals were taken whenever possible. After a careful study of Paiute eating habits, one may maintain that they ate anything that did not eat them first. When Escalante discovered them he found them eating "grass seeds, hares, and dates (yucca fruit) in season". Both the fruits and the buds of the yucca were eaten. They planted no maize and, according to Bolton's observations, they acquired very little of it. [(15), p. 204]. Piñon nuts, acorns, and cactus fruits were also important. Of greatest value to the Indians of the area were piñon nuts which could be stored, either green or roasted, in caches, and used later pressed into balls or made into a mush. No seeds, roots or fruits of an edible nature were overlooked by these desert bands in their wandering economy.

Mammals, birds, reptiles and insects were eaten as a supplement to their plant diet. Under very fortunate conditions deer and antelope could be taken. The rabbit, used for both food and winter clothing was most important to the Paiute. It was probably taken with nets. The jack rabbit abounded in all parts of the area while the cottontail was more confined to higher areas and around springs. Kangaroo rats, mice, ground squirrels, wildcats, badgers, porcupines, prairie dogs and foxes found their way to the "table." Stewart's informants denied the eating of skunks [(17), p. 244], but Hunt reports that they were eaten in the Death Valley area [(4), p. 14]. The coyote was not eaten because of its place in Paiute beliefs. The coyote steals the souls of the ill [(17) p. 310] and recovery cannot be made unless the shaman can cause the coyote to return it to the owner. The stars are the "Coyote's children" [(17), p. 324]. Pictographs were made by the coyote when he was a man [(17), p. 321]. The Shivwits, in southern Utah, used coyote skins for winter capes and hats and were probably the only Paiute group to do so [(17), p. 279]. Young crows and ravens, owls, hawks, ducks, doves, mud hen, and quail were eaten. On the diet were snakes, lizards and the tortoise. Grasshoppers and crickets were collected in the early mornings while they were still cold and slow-moving. Caterpillars, ants and ant eggs were an easily collected food source.

The Paiute way of life may be summed up: "Living in the largely barren desert area in Utah and Nevada are many bands of Paiute and Shoshone speaking related dialects — the nickname "Digger" applied to them as well as to central California tribes—least developed of all Indians, perhaps of all people in the world — lived on a bare subsistence level on wild seeds, roots, insects and a little game, with no farming—the scantiest of clothing but makers of woven rabbit skin blankets—only brush windbreaks and huts—coarse, slightly decorated basketry the main craft, with some plain pottery and a little very fine basketry near the Nevada-California border— social and religious organizations at the most elementary level, just poor families or bands wandering on foot in search of food" (14).

Occupation for generations, and even hundreds of years, in such inhospitable places as the Nevada Test Site and even in Death Valley, is a tribute to man's ability to adapt to nearly any environment. The Paiute was a "Digger." He had to be—to live.

DOCUMENT 3.4 WHY NUCLEAR WEAPONS ARE TESTED, NEVADA TEST ORGANIZATION SOURCE: WILLIAM GEAGLEY COLLECTION ON NUCLEAR SAFETY, UNLV SPECIAL COLLECTIONS, MS-00792

In a world in which free people have no nuclear monopoly, the United States must keep its atomic strength at peak level. That is the primary reason why tests are held periodically in Nevada and in the Pacific.

Most of the tests are intended to advance weapons development. Four areas of work are involved in the laboratory and field test development of atomic weapons: primary experimental research, theoretical investigations and calculations, component development experimentation, and full-scale nuclear detonations. If anyone is neglected, the rate of weapons progress slows. The rate of testing required depends on the rapidity of generation of new ideas.

At least nine *developmental purposes* are served by full scale nuclear tests:

1. To proof test a weapon for desired military characteristics before it enters the national stockpile.
2. To provide a firm basis for undertaking extensive engineering and fabrication efforts which must be expanded to carry a "breadboard" model to a version satisfactory for stockpile purposes.
3. To demonstrate the adequacy, inadequacy or limitations of current theoretical approaches.
4. To explore phenomena which can vitally affect the efficiency and performance of weapons but which are not susceptible to prior theoretical analysis of sufficient certainty.
5. To provide a basis of choice among existing theoretical methods of weapon improvement so as to concentrate effort along lines of greatest practical significance.
6. To determine the validity of entirely new and untried principles proposed for applications to improve performance.
7. To provide entirely new information pertinent and valuable to weapon development and arising simply as a by-product of scientific observation of full-scale detonations.
8. To gain time in very urgent development programs by substituting tests for a portion of a possible but lengthy program of laboratory calculations and experiments.
9. To provide as a by-product basic scientific information to add to the stockpile of such knowledge.

Only for the first purpose, a proof test, would the detonation necessarily be of a weapon as such. In most circumstances, an experimental device is designed. The device tested is simplified as much as possible to answer the basic question. It minimizes the expenditure of active material. It has as low a yield as possible to minimize off-site fallout. It is seldom a useful weapon design. The information obtained from its testing will, however, immediately or eventually affect the design of stockpile weapons and improve the stockpile position.

The *Department of Defense* and *Armed Forces* have a deep interest in the conduct of full-scale tests. Full understanding of the output characteristics of nuclear weapons and their effects on various targets under varying conditions is essential to planning for the use of weapons, for planning military defenses against nuclear weapons, and for developing the desired characteristics of new weapons.

The *Federal agencies* charged with civil defense, biomedical studies, and with non-military applications of atomic energy have a continuing need for effects data paralleling the development of nuclear weapons. Essential civil effects information is generally in two categories, biomedical and structural, both distinct from the military effects data required by the Department of Defense. The Federal Civil Defense Administration has obtained such effects information, and additionally has trained its personnel in various test-conducted programs. In all of this broad field of study of the effects of atomic energy, it has been found that certain answers can only be obtained in the presence of a nuclear detonation. In this respect, the Nevada Test Site (and to some extent the Pacific site) is used as an outdoors laboratory for non-military applications.

While most field tests are therefore developmental in nature, the cost in material and effort is so great for any given test that every effort is made to answer with it as many other questions as possible.

DOCUMENT 3.5 U.S. ATOMIC ENERGY COMMISSION, "AN INTERIM REPORT OF BRITISH WORK ON JOE," SEPTEMBER 22, 1949

SOURCE: HARRY S. TRUMAN LIBRARY, PRESIDENT'S SECRETARY'S FILES, BOX 199, NSC-ATOMIC

(This document consists of 9 pages, Copy No. 2 of 6 Copies, Series C.)

AN INTERIM REPORT OF BRITISH WORK ON JOE

The British atomic energy authorities were alerted at 1130 AM (DST) on Saturday morning September 10, 1949. A conference was held by teletype in the American Embassy in London and the British were informed that a mass of air containing activity was about to pass north of Scotland. It was estimated that the activity would be approximately 1/4 of a disintegration per minute per cubic foot. The British were invited to attempt to collect activity and make independent assessments of its significance.

Two British meteorological flights, with the code names of NOCTURNAL and BISMUTH were in regular operation carrying filters of a type described at the American and British discussion held in September 1948 in Washington. The BISMUTH flights had shown no activity on the 9th of September and the NOCTURNAL flight had shown no activity on the 10th of September. The first flight to collect results from north of Scotland left at 2140 hours on the 10th of September and gave immediate results. Planes were deflected from the BISMUTH flights to north of Scotland, with the result that no BISMUTH flights took place between Saturday, the 10th of September and Wednesday, the 14th of September inclusively. The NOCTURNAL flights were not affected. A summary of all flights to date is given in Appendix I.

As a matter of interest, if the Americans had not alerted the British the first evidence of activity would have been obtained by the British on the NOCTURNAL flight from Gibraltar on Saturday the 10th of September, and results would not have been obtained before Wednesday the 14th of September, as there is a delay of approximately three to four days in getting the filters from Gibraltar into the laboratory at Harwell.

FILTER

The filter used for collecting the activity is one of the British standard gas mask filters. The material is made from esparto grass in the form of a cylindrical tube approximately 12 cm in diameter. The filter is mounted in a hollow steel tube, the leading edge of which is shaped to give good aerodynamic properties. This steel tube is bolted onto the wing of an aircraft and usually each aircraft carries a filter on each wing. A wire grid is usually mounted at the front end of the filter to protect it from hail.

The air flow characteristics and the flow efficiency of these filters were calibrated by appropriate tests. Details are given in Appendix II.

COUNTER

The counter consists of four Geiger counters, each approximately 14 cm long and 1.3 cm in diameter, made of glass 35 mgm/cm^2, and accepts Beta down to 0.3 mev. The four Geigers are used in parallel and are put inside of the filter on some guard rails so that the geometry is preserved from observation to observation. The counter efficiency is 7.65 and a count of 1 per minute is equivalent to 6.0×10^{-12} curies on the filter. (Area 358 cm^2.)

METHOD OF COUNTING AND ELIMINATION OF BACKGROUND

There are three counting units employed, and in one of them is placed the sample filter, in one of the others is placed an unflown filter taken from the same baton as the flown filter. The third counter records counts from an unflown filter which has been preserved and continuously used for counting since observations first began in 1948. The counting time is in every case taken to be sufficient to give a 1% standard error. When a set of readings has been obtained from the three counters, the filters are permuted among the counters and a new set of records taken. By taking averages and permuting again, it is possible to eliminate all statistical fluctuations and variations in counter performance. The results obtained are that the background is 90 counts per minute and the activity of flown filters is expressed in terms of this quantity. The symbol R^1 is used to denote the activity of a filter expressed as a multiple of the background. Thus for example: $R^1 = 1$ means no activity on the filter, but only background; while $R^1 = 2$ means as activity above background exactly equal to the background. The activity collected from the cloud is therefore R^1-1. Values of R^1-1 obtained from filters flown on the various flights are given in Appendix I.

RESULTS ON GROSS ACTIVITY

The activity of various filters was measured from day to day with the object of determining the time of origin. By assuming that the activity decreased with time according to an inverse 1.2 power law, it was estimated that the time of origin was between the 26th and 30th of August. There is a slight uncertainty in the exact time of origin and the dates given might need correction of the order of one day if the departures from Way and Wigner Law are taken into account. However, the spread in time of the original disturbance has been set widely enough to cover this uncertainty.

NOTE: It is perhaps worth noting that the maximum activity collected by the British filters, for flights of equal duration at similar altitudes, was roughly 20 times that obtained for any of the SANDSTONE tests. The maximum activity in the cloud was on September 14th, and was roughly 0.35 disintegrations per minute per cubic foot of air. This flight was at 20,000 ft. About two-thirds of this activity was found at 30,000 ft on September 11th.

RADIOCHEMISTRY

By applying standard radiochemical techniques, three fission elements have been isolated, namely Barium, Cerium and Iodine. Filter B3 on September the 20th was giving an iodine count of 0.8 ± 0.4 while barium is giving 7.8 ± 3. Further measurements are in progress but all radiochemical results so far obtained are consistent with the time of origin obtained from the gross activity.

AUTO-RADIOGRAPHS

The first auto-radiographs gave unsuccessful results, but, by increasing the time of exposure to 4 days, positive results have now been obtained. On filter B10, one fairly large particle and 34 extremely small ones have been located. The large particle is giving approximately 10 disintegrations per minute and is therefore about twice the radius of the largest particles collected by the American observers.

ACTIVITY VERSUS PARTICLE SIZE

The evidence so far obtained is that most of the activity collected by the filters is extremely fine and penetrates to some depth in the filter medium. In the case quoted in the last paragraph, only a small percent of-the total activity is due to the one large particle and the 34 small ones. Provided that the large particle proves to be authentic, special measurements will be made on it in the hope of measuring the efficiency.

PLUTONIUM AND URANIUM

Information sent by cable and therefore necessarily brief, showed that on September 19th it had been established that the amount of Plutonium on one of the most active filters was less than 3×10^{-12}. The results on Uranium were very unsatisfactory because of the relatively large Uranium concentration in the filter. All that can be said is that the amount of Uranium collected might have been approaching 10^{-7} gms.

It was planned to make two further measurements on alpha emitters. The first was to attempt to get alpha tracks in a photographic film and from standard methods to determine the energy of the alpha particle. A second method was to concentrate the Uranium from the filter and see if the isotopic ratio 235:238 departed from normal. In neither case has any result yet been reported.

This interim report has been written on the evidence existing at Harwell on Saturday, September 17th, supplemented by fragmentary information communicated by secret cable. A proper report of the British work will be written later when the experimental measurements have been more fully digested, and a copy of this report will be forwarded to AFOAT-1.

22 September 1949

APPENDIX II: PARTICULATE FILTERING AND FLOW EFFICIENCY OF FILTERS

Filters normally tested at 3 cu. ft. per minute air flow against a standard methylene blue cloud (90% of particles under 0.5 microns) giving efficiency averaging 99%. Efficiency falls off slightly with increased air flow, but is not expected to fall below 95% at 60. cu. ft. per minute – no measurements available at this speed.

Flow through the filter equals 1.764 v litres per second where v is the air speed in the filter entry. The air speed in the filter entry is given by the formula—(where V is the aircraft speed).

$$\frac{1}{2}\rho v^2 = \text{Pressure drop} = A\frac{\rho}{\rho_0}v^2 B\frac{uv}{\mu_0}$$

where P and P_0 and μu and μ_0 are the density and viscosity of air at the altitude concerned and at sea level. The values of A and B found by experiment are 0.349 and 1.826 respectively. The air flows deduced have been given you in a separate memorandum.

DOCUMENT 3.6 WARNING POSTER SOURCE: NATIONAL ATOMIC TESTING MUSEUM, EPHEMERA COLLECTIONS

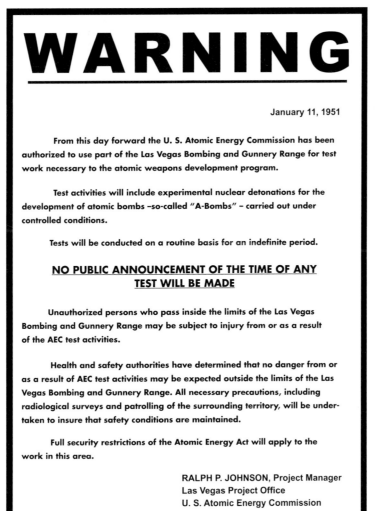

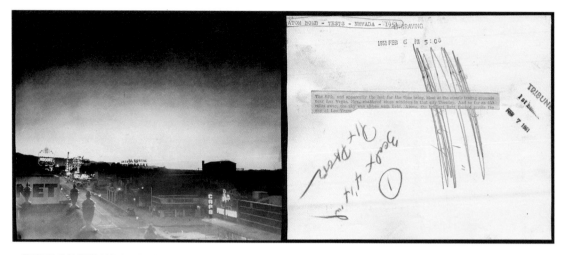

PHOTO 3.7 ATOM BOMB—TESTS—NEVADA—1951 (front and back) *Source:* National Atomic Testing Museum Photo Collections

DOCUMENT 4.1 GLADWIN HILL, "ATOMIC BOOM TOWN IN THE DESERT" SOURCE: *THE NEW YORK TIMES*, FEBRUARY 11, 1951, P. 158

Las Vegas, getting over its first shock, now takes near-by bomb tests with a poker face.
By GLADWIN HILL

GLADWIN HILL, head of The Times Los Angeles bureau, has been on, a "dawn patrol" vigil in Las Vegas since nuclear tests began.

LAS VEGAS, Nevada—A few short weeks ago betting men—of which this community has probably a record proportion—would have wagered large sums at long odds that Las Vegas would be one of the last places in the nation to experience the flash and roar of an atomic explosion. But Las Vegas has been through five of them, and while there has been a temporary halt in the tests the folks know that there are more to come in the future because Las Vegas is the site of a permanent atomic testing station.

A city of only 25,000, in the desert 250 miles from the Pacific Coast, it derives its livelihood primarily from two of the most peaceable pursuits imaginable—the sale of sunshine and the privilege of legal gambling. A third "industry" is short-order marriages and six-week divorces, of which there were last year, respectively, 18,060 and 2,805.

Altogether the city is one of the most amiably raffish communities in the nation—an assembly of glittering chrome and flaming colors by day, a flowering jungle of glowing neon and flashing lights by night. Las

Vegas pays little attention to calendar or clock. The sunshine seems to be permanent, regardless of season; breakfast is served twenty-four hours a day, because gambling goes on twenty-four hours a day. Not only does The Golden Nugget gambling hall and a dozen others like it offer the hazards of wheel and dice table; even the filling stations and grocery stores have their batteries of slot machines.

* * *

NOTHING in all this—or in the town's history—suggests that Las Vegas would be a likely spot for serious and critical scientific tests. The site nearly a century ago of a short-lived colonization effort by Mormon pioneers, the city came into modern being in 1905 as a division point on the newly constructed San Pedro, Los Angeles and Salt Lake Railroad, at present part of the Union Pacific. Now it has five modernly rustic luxury hotels, plus other flamboyant attractions, on the five-mile "Broadway-in-the-Sagebrush" strip of U. S. Highway 91 west of town.

Nevertheless, there were sound reasons for the A. E. C.'s choice of this region for its experiments. The commission had a protracted series of tests to perform, calling not only for privacy but for numerous other features such as specialized weather conditions and accessibility to urban communications and with a living center that provided separation from other communities. Las Vegas supplied these.

Furthermore, north of the city lies a 5,000-square-mile area of mountainous desert which is posted by the signs of the Air Force notifying the world to keep out. It is a bombing and gunnery range connected with the Nellis Air Force Base, located in Las Vegas. The land is dotted with sagebrush and here and there with the dirt piles of abandoned mine diggings. Surrounding the tract is a natural wall of mountains which, with the assistance of Air Force bomb craters on the plateau floor, has created a landscape with the lorn and dismal quality of one of those artist's impressions of the surface of the moon.

* * *

JUST what the nuclear scientists and the military men are up to is what every Las Vegan wonders. It is assumed that the experiments are concerned with such problems as the production of a lighter-weight bomb; with bombs in the form of guided missiles; with the most effective height of explosion and with size of "critical mass" of fissionable materials; with whether an atomic blast produces sufficient heat to "trigger" the infinitely more destructive hydrogen bomb.

The Las Vegans don't know the answers, of course. All they can do is "live with the bomb," tolerating it as they might any other perplexing visitor. As the light, noise and shock from each explosion are dispersed in different directions and intensities by the irregular array of mountains surrounding the proving ground, and by atmospheric conditions, the people of the city have widely varying stories to tell. Some see the light as a brief near-white flash, others as a long-flickering orange "ball." On a given day, people in one place will feel the shock as several times more powerful than the previous explosion, others as less. The number of "booms" in a single blast has been set at anything from one to ten.

Aside from the new topic of conversation, a visitor to Las Vegas will find little change from former times. Some 500 scientists, administrative personnel, technicians and construction workers connected with the project have settled down in the town's assorted hostelries.

* * *

ALL in all, Las Vegas can be described as pleased with its new acquisition. There has been an influx of visitors, rather than an exodus; the town's publicity man has had the local hairdresser create an "atomic" coiffure and has rushed out to the nation's press a collection of pictures of bathing beauties equipped with Geiger counters. And on a more solemn note, The Las Vegas Morning Sun has said: "We have glorified gambling, divorces and doubtful pleasures to get our name before the rest of the country. Now we have become part of the most important work carried on by our country today."

DOCUMENT 4.2 (A) CAMP DESERT ROCK I: A PSYCHOLOGICAL STUDY OF TROOP REACTIONS TO AN ATOMIC EXPLOSION AND (B) DESERT ROCK 1: SKETCH MAP DOE NNSA SOURCE: (A) DOE NNSA/NSO NV0006252; (B) NSO NV0767719

Reproduced by
Armed Services Technical Information
DOCUMENT SERVICE CENTER
KNOTT BUILDING, DAYTON, 2, OHIO
ACH1.950808.019
HumRRO-TR-I

DESERT ROCK I: A PSYCHOLOGICAL STUDY OF TROOP REACTIONS TO AN ATOMIC EXPLOSION

Peter A. Bordes
John L. Einan
Joseph R. Hochstim

Howard H. McFann
Shepard G. Schwartz
HumRRO
The George Washington University
HUMAN RESOURCES RESEARCH OFFICE
operating under contract with
THE DEPARTMENT OF THE ARMY

CALENDAR OF IMPORTANT EVENTS, DESERT ROCK I

D-day minus 45 (17 Sep 51)	Defense Department announces A-bomb maneuver
D-day minus 30 (2-3 Oct 51)	Questionnaire A (baseline test) administered, Fort Campbell
D-day minus 28 (4-5 Oct 51)	Phase 3 indoctrinations given at home-bases to participant troops
D-day minus 17 (15 Oct 51)	Troops arrive at Camp Desert Rock
D-day minus 9 (23 Oct 51)	Questionnaire B (post-indoctrination test) administered to non-participants, Fort Campbell
D-day minus 4 (28 Oct 51)	Special Camp Desert Rock indoctrination
D-day minus 3 (29 Oct 51)	Questionnaire B (post-indoctrination test) administered to participants, Camp Desert Rock
D-day minus 2 to 1 (30-31 Oct 51)	First polygraph test administered, Camp Desert Rock
D-day (1 Nov 51)	A-bomb explodes. Questionnaire C (post-bomb test) administered in the afternoon, immediately after return to Camp Desert Rock
D-day plus 13 to 36 (14 Nov-7 Dec 51)	Second polygraph tests administered to participants, Fort Campbell
D-day plus 14 to 33 (15 Nov-4 Dec 51)	Control polygraph tests administered to non-participants, Fort Campbell
D-day plus 18 (19 Nov 51)	Questionnaire D (delayed effects test) given to participants and non-participants, Fort Campbell
D-day plus 25 (26 Nov 51)	Questionnaire D (delayed effects test) given to participants and non-participants, Fort Lewis

DOCUMENT 4.3 BUSTER-JANGLE FALLOUT PLAN SOURCE: DOE NNSA/ NSO NV0404739

Office Memorandum • UNITED STATES GOVERNMENT

Date: August 23 1951
To: Dr. Walter D. Claus, Chief, Biophysics Branch, Division of Biology and Medicine, Washington
From: Merril Eisenbud, Director, Health and Safety Division, New York Operations Office
Subject: MOBILE FALLOUT STUDIES FOR "BUSTER" AND "JANGLE"
Symbol: HS:ME:srm

BEST COPY AVAILABLE

We are proceeding to develop plans for the mobile ground-air fallout studies for two clouds from Buster, and two from Jangle. This memorandum
will list certain questions which I would hope could be answered within
the next week or ten days in order to make it possible for us to develop the
final details of the operational plan.

1. Will AFOAT or some other branch of military provide air support?
   The operational success of this project may well depend on whether or
   not we are successful in obtaining planes and crews with the equipment and experience to facilitate cloud observation. In this connection
   I might recapitulate our concept of the kind of air reconnaissance that
   would be required:
   a. By 0200 of each day, we should have a report giving the dimensions
      of the cloud (or the principal cloud fragment in the event the origi-
      nal cloud becomes fractionated), the location of the cloud mass and
      its direction and speed of travel.
   b. Preferably no later than 0600, a member of the AEC monitoring
      group assigned to this project should be delivered at an airport lo-
      cated approximately two hours (cloud travel time) in front of the
      cloud nose. It is desirable that this location be as near as feasible to
      a point below the anticipated forward axis of the cloud.
   c. Observations aloft should begin immediately following delivery of
      the ground observer. This phase of the reconnaissance should be
      designed to obtain the best possible record of the cloud characteris-
      tics in passing above the observation station. We should record the
      time of arrival of the cloud mass and the total time of transit. During
      the period of transit, we should have a log of the cloud behavior as
      regards vertical and horizontal geometry and levels of radioactivity.
   d. The above operation should be repeated by a second observer be-
      ginning 1600. This would presumably involve a duplicate of equip-
      ment and personnel required for "c".
   e. To facilitate the above operation and in order to assure that its day
      to day planning is consistent with the ultimate objectives of the
      operation, it would be desirable for a member of my staff to be as-
      signed for liaison purposes to the AFOAT headquarters. This would
      be helpful regardless of which organization provides the actual per-
      sonnel and equipment for the above reconnaissance.
2. What is the anticipated ratio of beta-gamma activities within the clouds?[3]

---

[3] The answers to this and the following questions are necessary that we may plan for the
eventuality that we provide our own instrumentation for the aerial phase of
reconnaissance.

3. What is the range of beta and gamma activities that may be anticipated in a traverse through the center of the clouds at 1000, 2000 and 3000 miles?

4. What are the best available estimates of the anticipated specific activities of the dust from (a) Buster and (b) Jangle?

5. What beta and gamma spectrum may be anticipated at 1000, 2000 and 3000 miles?

US DOE ARCHIVES
326 U.S. ATOMIC ENERGY COMMISSION
RG DOE HISTORIAN (DBM)
Collection 1132
Box 3362
Folder #10

DOCUMENT 4.4 MIKE REPORT SOURCE: DOE NNSA/NSO NV0029277

UNITED STATES
ATOMIC ENERGY COMMISSION
WASHINGTON 25, D. C.

RG US DOE ARCHIVES 326 US ATOMIC ENERGY COMMISSION
Collection DMA
Box 3777
Folder MR+A7 Ivy (Downgraded TS papers)

November 3, 1952

Memorandum for Mr. Dean.
The President read the attached memorandum yesterday, about noon. He was very appreciative of our getting it to him. He did not want to retain it; nor did he wish a copy. I had the impression that he anticipates we will report at the end of the Operation in more detail.

I would suggest keeping only one copy of this memorandum, if any. Do you wish to keep it in your files, or should I keep it?

K. E. Fields
Brigadier General, USA
Director of Military Application

Attach:
Cy 1-A memo, 11-1-52
Dean to President

* * *

UNITED STATES
ATOMIC ENERGY COMMISSION
WASHINGTON 25, D. C.

November 1, 1952

Memorandum for the President.

The Atomic Energy Commission wishes to report that at 0715 November 1 (1415 October 31, Washington time), the first full scale thermonuclear experiment was conducted successfully at Eniwetok. You will recall that we discussed certain aspects of this operation with you on June 30, at which time Dr. Norris E. Bradbury, Director of the Los Alamos Scientific Laboratory, described this particular experiment in some detail for you.

From early and incomplete evaluation of results, the yield is estimated roughly to have been more than 6 megatons, possibly as high as 12 megatons; that is, 6 to 12 million tons of TNT equivalent. In comparison with atomic bombs of the Hiroshima type, this is equal to some 50 to 75 in terms of destructive effect.

If the more precise and lengthy methods of measuring yield, which are now in process, confirm the above yield, the detonation exceeds what we had anticipated. We are confident even now, however, that the principles of the recent discoveries that opened the way to accelerated thermonuclear effort, can be applied in full scale devices.

The shot island Eugelab is missing, and where it was there is now an underwater crater of some 1500 yards in diameter.

No significant fall-out of radioactive contamination occurred. As a precaution against fall-out, Joint Task Force 132 had evacuated Eniwetok Atoll for the shot. They expect to return to the atoll today.

Unfortunately, during the cloud sampling operation one aircraft, an F-84-G, and pilot, were lost in Eniwetok Lagoon. Otherwise the principal operational missions were conducted without incident and as planned.

Our present plan calls for the conduct of the second and final detonation of this operation not earlier than November 11, Eniwetok time. Actual conditions encountered on reentry to Eniwetok may, of course, cause delay beyond this date. This detonation will be a proof-test of a one-half megaton fission bomb dropped from a B-36 aircraft.

Gordon Dean
Chairman

PHOTO 4.5 DOROTHY GRIER (WHITCOMB), RANGER CERTIFICATE *Source*: NATM O 2004.126.008
BOX DA33

DOCUMENT 5.1 OPERATION DOORSTEP REPORT SOURCE: DOE NNSA/NSO
NV0014434

On March 17, 1953, more than 600 Civil Defense observers and representatives of the Nation's information media witnessed an atomic explosion at the Atomic Energy Commission's Nevada Proving Ground. Some news and radiomen called the event "Operation Doorstep." The name was appropriate, since the purpose of the program was to show the people of America what might be expected if an atomic burst took place over the doorsteps of our major cities.

"Operation Doorstep" was a combined Atomic Energy Commission, Department of Defense, and Federal Civil Defense Administration program, under the direction of a Joint Task Group made up of personnel of the three agencies.

The atomic explosion selected for the operation was one in which the Federal Civil Defense Administration had a limited test program. The program had three major projects: (1) Exposure of two typical American

X–19
This mannequin can only stay in the position in which he was placed, staring through the window at coming disaster. A real occupant of this house could prepare—and survive. (FCDA—Operation Doorstop—Yucca Flat, Nev., Mar. 17, 1953.)

homes to atomic blast in order to determine what would happen to the homes, to test the effectiveness of simple basement shelters; (2) exposure of eight outdoor home-type shelters, in a joint project with AEC, to test the structural strength of such shelters; and (3) exposure of a variety of typical passenger cars to determine the amount of protection afforded to passengers, and the effect on the mechanical operation of the cars.

Both the observer and technical programs were incidental to the main purpose of the atomic detonation, which was to test an experimental nuclear device. It is important to note that the explosion was part of the AEC developmental series. It would have taken place whether or not Civil Defense and the Department of Defense had participated.

"Operation Doorstep" marked the first time Civil Defense observers were allowed to witness a technical test program. The arrangement was made with the knowledge that it involved a certain amount of risk: that some observers might jump to conclusions, and that their conclusions might be wrong. However, the value to the Nation in demonstrating the effects of an atomic explosion on American homes and cars was so great it was believed the risk was warranted. Actually, very few persons reached wrong conclusions. These were mostly in regard to radiation hazard. The facts are contained in the preliminary report, starting on page 12.

An important angle of "Operation Doorstep" which has not received sufficient stress is the participation of industry. Without the cooperation of a number of business associations and concerns the program would have been far more limited in scope. For example, the test of passenger cars was made possible by the loan of vehicles by major manufacturers through the Automobile Manufacturers' Association and by public-spirited automobile dealers and dealers' associations. Technical evaluation of the program was provided by a special committee of the Society of Automotive Engineers. Gas and oil for the cars were donated by the Standard Oil Company of California.

Mannequins for the houses and shelters were loaned by the L. A. Darling Co. and transported to and from Las Vegas by North American Van Lines. The Atlas Trucking Co. of Las Vegas not only donated hauling service from Las Vegas to the Proving Ground but provided some items of furniture. Clothing for the mannequins was obtained from the J. C. Penney Co. through the National Retail Dry Goods Association.

Even with industry cooperation, however, the technical program was limited in the results which could be obtained. For example, there were no funds available for fully instrumenting the home shelters. Hence, conclusions reached were limited to the effect of blast on the shelters themselves with no evaluation of the effects of blast within the shelters.

Also we have been asked why we chose only a single type of dwelling for the test. Again, the reason was a financial one. No funds were available for additional houses of different types. FCDA has had for over a year a comprehensive program for testing a variety of typical American homes, including masonry dwellings of various kinds, other types of frame dwellings, and the "row house" type of structure. This test was designed by a leading firm of engineers under contract with FCDA, and was approved by the American Institute of Architects. In selecting the houses for "Operation Doorstep," FCDA chose a typical kind which could be built with the funds available. It was necessary to test at least two in order to determine the effect of the blast at different ranges, but since there were only two, we could not risk setting them on fire. Every possible precaution was taken to prevent this, and the houses did not burn. But because of this fact, we are not able to state how much fire hazard there would be in a house fully equipped with utilities.

FCDA expects to continue its test program in the future. Only by a continuing program of this kind can we provide information needed by the public and State and local Civil Defense organizations.

UNKNOWN FACTORS

In evaluating the results of any test, two important things must be kept in mind. We make tests with an atomic weapon of known size and power, and our test items are placed at known distances from ground zero. But in translating the test results into what would happen in case of atomic attack on our cities, we do not know the size and power of the enemy weapons which might be used against us. We do not know where those bombs would fall in our cities—i.e., what their ground zeros would be.

What Civil Defense and the public needs are general conclusions which will apply in the majority of cases under the principle of the "calculated risk" which is basic to all realistic Civil Defense planning.

Thus, when Civil Defense recommends a home shelter design, we are saying in effect: "Since no one knows where ground zero would be, the chances are that you would not be within the total destruction area of an atomic burst over your city. Therefore, this home shelter should give you good protection from blast, heat, and radiation. It probably would save the lives of yourself and your family in areas where persons with less protection might be badly hurt or killed."

With these things in mind, FCDA learned on March 17th that the shelters which were tested can withstand blast, heat, and radiation. We learned that with such shelters, the chances for survival under atomic attack are greatly increased. The reasons for this conclusion are given in detail in the report which follows.

FCDA owes a particular debt of gratitude to the Atomic Energy Commission and its Test Organization for the excellent cooperation and assistance which have made the Civil Defense test programs possible. The observer program of "Operation Doorstep" was made possible by the combined efforts of the Atomic Energy Commission, the AEC Test organization, the Department of Defense, the Las Vegas-Clark County Civil Defense organization, and the FCDA Atomic Test Operations Staff headed by Harold L. Goodwin.

It now remains for each of us to apply the lessons learned in "Operation Doorstep" toward greater family Civil Defense preparedness.

VAL PETERSON
Administrator
Federal Civil Defense Administration

DOCUMENT 5.2 OPERATION UPSHOT-KNOTHOLE, DIRECTIVE FOR EXERCISES, DESERT ROCK V SOURCE: DOE NNSA/NSO NV0767909

1. An indoctrination training exercise with the unclassified nickname DESERT ROCK V will be conducted in the vicinity of Las Vegas, Nevada, during the period 12 March to 22 May 1953, in conjunction with atomic tests UPSHOT and KNOTHOLE. DESERT ROCK V is a continuation of previous atomic tests of the DESERT ROCK series and will be conducted under supervision of Commanding General, Sixth Army, who has appointed Colonel William C. Bullock Exercise Director, Exercise DESERT ROCK V, with the concurrence of this Office.
2. Mission.
    a. Provide indoctrination training in tactical operations featuring tactical employment of atomic weapons.
    b. Provide training in essential physical protective measures.
    c. Provide indoctrination training for participating troops and troop observers on the effects of an atomic explosion on animals and equipment.
    d. Within limits or restrictions established by AEC and AFSWP, demonstrate influence or modifying effects of atomic weapons on field fortifications and defensive structures.
    e. Measure ability of trained staff officers to estimate target damage.
    f. Observe psychological effects on individuals resulting from atomic explosion.

DOCUMENT 5.3 USEFULNESS OF DESERT ROCK EXERCISES
SOURCE: DOE NNSA/NSO NV0751015

CLASSIFICATION: SECRET OPERATIONAL PRIORITY

From: CO Cp Desert Rock Nev
To: CO Sixth Army
Info: OCAFF G3 DEPTAR Wash DC
Nr AMCDR-CO 04237
Signed Bullock. This mag in 2 parts.

1. In occupying a trench at 2000 yards from ground zero the volunteers have approached ground zero as closely as my criteria for nuclear radiation will permit. I recommend one of the following courses of action be taken.
   a. Increase tolerances for nuclear radiation to permit moving volunteers closer to ground zero or
   b. Termination of the volunteer program.
2. I believe there is little to be gained in repeatedly placing volunteers in trenches at 2000 yards from ground zero on successive shots, as any additional information to be derived there from will be insignificant.

MEMO BY SDO: Red by SDO 1725 22 Apr 53. No immediate action required.
PARAPHRASE NOT REQUIRED. CONSULT CRYPTOCENTER BEFORE DECLASSIFYING
NO UNCLASSIFIED REPLY OR REFERENCE IF THE DATE TIME GROUP IS QUOTED

ACTION, 03
INFORMATION: Secy, AG Control
T-254723 Apr 53

DOCUMENT 5.4 NORRIS BRADBURY MEMO TO C. L. TYLER ON HOW TO EXPLAIN ATOMIC TESTING, 1953 SOURCE: DOE NNSA/NSO NV0124371

To: C. L. TYLER
From: N. E. Bradbury
Subject: Nevada Briefings
Symbol: DIR
RG326 US ATOMIC ENERGY COMMISSION
Location ALOO

Collection _____
Folder PLSYL (NTS, Eniwetok, BIKINI - FY-53)

1. There follow some suggestions for your use in your talk at the Nevada
   briefings relative to the relationship of the Nevada test programs to the
   weapon development program of the Atomic Energy Commission.
   The primary responsibility for the development of new atomic weapons as well as the improvement of existing devices is carried out for the
   Atomic Energy Commission by the Los Alamos Scientific Laboratory.
   Supplementary work in this field is also being carried out by the Radiation Laboratory of the University of California at Livermore.
   Research in the field of atomic weapons is always directed at getting
   the most for one's money (i.e. fissionable material) under the particular
   conditions required by the use or delivery system of the weapon. Accordingly, the LASL directs its efforts both towards increasing the efficiency of use of active material in a given weapon system, and to
   increasing the scope and flexibility of atomic weapons so that they be
   available for the maximum number of applications to problems of
   warfare.
   Research on atomic weapons means, of course, not only research on
   the best ways under various circumstances to use fissionable material
   but research on the use of cheaper materials for atomic weapons. Thermonuclear reactions, sometimes publicly described as the H-Bomb,
   fall in this field.
   Laboratory research and study can investigate nuclear phenomena or
   the other phenomena of potential nuclear weapons only up to the point
   before a nuclear chain reaction starts. There are two reasons for this:
   one, a chain reaction requires the use of expensive fissionable material;
   and two, after the chain reaction starts, one has an atomic bomb and
   it would be impractical to build and staff a new Los Alamos after
   every experiment!
   With stand-in materials the LASL can investigate in considerable detail
   most of the behavior of an atomic bomb up to the time when, with real
   materials, it would actually start to explode. However, the explosive
   phase of the reaction is not only the most interesting and the most
   important phase, but it is the phase which is least susceptible to calculation. It involves temperatures as hot as the interior of stars and the
   properties of materials at temperatures, pressures, and densities obtained nowhere else on earth. Temperatures of ten million degrees,
   densities that would make a cubic foot of water weigh a ton, pressures
   of millions of atmospheres, and times of a hundred millionths of a
   second (the "shake") are commonplace in these circumstances.

As an example of how difficult the exploding phase of an atomic bomb is to calculate, one may go back to the Trinity bomb of 1945. After all the theorists had made their best calculations (really, their best guesses), they nodded wisely and said it will probably be about 5 to 10 kilotons. But it came out nearer 20. A few years ago the LASL made the most extensive calculation that could be devised using the most modern electronic computers of this same system. This time, however, the answer came out nearly twice as *big* as the bomb actually went. Clearly, only experiment can really say exactly what is going to happen and can point the way to real improvements in atomic weapons. This our empirical formulae cannot do.

The details of the Los Alamos and Livermore experiments are technically so complicated that little use would be served by describing their intimate details. None of these particular experiments are models of actual weapons although this is, of course, not necessarily true of the shots being conducted for other agencies. Moreover, all of the LASL experiments have as primary objects additional information (generally of many sorts) related to the process which go on when an atomic bomb explodes under one or another type of nuclear system. Thus, an extremely detailed and complicated program of experimental observations is both fundamental and essential and the actual "bang" or yield of the explosion is, in many cases, of secondary interest or of diagnostic interest in furnishing information as to what went on, and how, inside the chain reacting system.

The accompanying slide shows the list of bombs and the rather affectionate names assigned to them, the agency responsible for the particular test, and the probable yield. This latter figure, as indicated above, is not of significance in itself in experiments of this sort, but is mentioned here only to give some relative idea of how the size explosion which will be seen compares in appearance with the explosions from conventional weapons in the stockpile.

To give some idea of what sorts of fields are being explored by the LASL, the first and eighth shots, Annie and Harry, are primarily explorations of the hydrodynamics of the assembly of fissionable material and what goes on in the very late stages of this assembly, particularly if the initiation of the chain reaction is delayed. Annie is actually the third one of a series, two of which have been conducted in earlier test operations. The result of the series will give us much information which can be applied to increasing the efficiency of use of fissionable materials in new weapons.

The second and seventh shots, Nancy and Simon, are explorations of scientific phenomena urgently needed by the LASL in connection with the research program on thermonuclear and related systems. These are *not* thermonuclear weapons; indeed, they have little relationship to any actual weapons, real or imaginary. They are actually pure nuclear experiments in the realm of temperatures and pressures which can only be obtained by setting off an atomic bomb.

The fourth shot, Dixie, is an experimental observation of a new and cheap method for initiating a nuclear chain reaction as well as furnishing more light on the question of when and how such reactions start.

The fifth shot, Badger, is an experiment to explore a potential new technique of not only increasing the efficiency of burn-up of fissionable materials in atomic bombs, but an exploratory experiment in the further use of cheap materials in nuclear explosions. Again, the device is not a weapon, but, if it works, the ideas found effective therein will speedily find their way into weapon application.

The two Radiation Laboratory experiments (Ruth and Ray) are explorations of the nuclear properties of certain systems, a knowledge of which may prove useful for both conventional and thermonuclear research programs.

It will be noted that most of the LASL shots are on towers rather than dropped as air burst bombs. This is primarily because of the detailed instrumentation which requires that not only the precise time of detonation be known, but that the device be exactly placed and that complicated instruments with electronic recording be in its immediate vicinity. With yields of the order of magnitude indicated, such tower shots can be conducted with complete safety. Only when the necessary information can equally well be obtained from a free air experiment are these employed.

It should be apparent that these tests cover a wide spectrum of atomic weapon research and development. They supplement in an absolutely essential way the laboratory investigations at Los Alamos. In reality the Nevada Test Site is only an extension of the physics, explosives, chemical, and metallurgical laboratories at Los Alamos to cover the temperatures, pressures, and other phenomena which can only be obtained by an actual atomic bomb explosion. To the LASL, Nevada is a fundamental and imperative part of the laboratory just as are cyclotrons and test tubes. One part supplements and complements the other in the continual race to make sure that the United States is always ahead in the rapidly expanding field of atomic warfare.

2. I have clearly only indicated ideas and possibly phrases which you may want to use. No attempt has been made to put this in any form which you could quote since I presume you will be speaking informally. Nor have I included any quantitative remarks on the stockpile gains which have

arisen out of LASL work including these field experiments. This latter gets pretty classified but could be included in general terms if you wish.

NEB/hrg
N. E. Bradbury
Director
Orig. and 1 cc - C. L Tyler
cc - J. C Clark
D. M. Stearns
File

DOCUMENT 5.5 DONALD ENGLISH INTERVIEW EXCERPT

SOURCE: NEVADA TEST SITE ORAL HISTORY PROJECT, UNLV SPECIAL COLLECTIONS, HTTP://DIGITAL.LIBRARY.UNLV.EDU/U?/NTS,1178

When some of the first blasts happened, you see stories in the newspaper of windows being knocked out of shops and that sort of thing.
Oh absolutely. In fact I understand later that they tried to fashion the shots so that they had enough explosive power or whatever it was to skip over Las Vegas, to kind of jump over it, but we would wake up in the mornings sometimes and the water would be sloshing out of the pool, just exactly the same thing as an earthquake. Chandeliers would swing, water would slosh out of swimming pools, the elevators inside the elevator transoms would swing back and forth.

Was there a sound along with it or—?
Maybe kind of a rumble a little bit, but mostly the motion more than sound. One time we did a stint in the Mint Hotel. Silver dollars were big in those days and we took silver dollars and lined them up just as high as we could, piled one on top of the other. We had this huge column of silver dollars, and we photographed the silver dollars with the background of the main street, Fremont Street, and started the camera before we thought the blast was going to occur, and you could see the flash in the sky. Then, oh maybe five or six minutes after, the shock wave would hit and you could see the chandeliers swinging. We shot pictures of that, and of course the silver dollars all tumbling down. Anything to give a graphic illustration of what was happening.

So what other shots or photographs did you do with your job at this time? Beyond what some of these other guys were doing, what were you doing for photography?

Well, assorted things. Sometimes we would cover it from Angel's Peak, take pictures of the mushroom cloud. Sometimes we'd take dancers up to the top of the peak. I'd have one girl, Sally McCloskey, we did a little series that was called Angel's Dance. And she was a ballet dancer, not a showgirl, and she did an interpretive dance to the mushroom cloud as it came up and we shot a series of pictures and sent it out on the wire and they called it Angel's Dance. We just did anything we could to make the picture a little bit different because the newspapers would run the mushroom cloud pictures, but they were always hungry for anything that had any kind of a different approach. I always thought if I didn't get up to go to Mount Charleston or missed the boat, I would try to go downtown, Fremont Street, and see if there's any possibility from the top of one of the buildings to see the mushroom cloud over the city. So sure enough I didn't wake up or I didn't get up in time to get to Mount Charleston so I rushed downtown and I climbed up I think it was a drugstore and it was overlooking Vegas Vic and some of the neon signs that were on Fremont Street. And I saw the flash in the sky and waited around for a little while and by gosh all of a sudden there was the mushroom cloud right between Vegas Vic and the Pioneer Club, absolute perfectly in the center. I started shooting like crazy, and you were talking about the shock wave, and there were some fellows on a building right below me and they were working [00:20:00] on a glass transom and they said, what are you doing over there? I said, Listen, I'm taking pictures of the atomic cloud. If you go out to the end of the building you can see it. From their point it was hidden by other buildings. And so they walked out to the end of the building to take a look at it and right about that time the shock wave hit and it shattered that transom. That glass just went all over the place. Then after I took the pictures of the cloud over the city, I got done, I thought well, I'll see what kind of damage—it was a pretty good shock wave, and Sears and Roebuck used to be on Fremont Street so I went down there and by gosh the window was all blown out. And the manager was picking up some of the glass in the display window and picking up the mannequin that had fallen, so I took a picture of that and it ran in all the papers, the manager of Sears lifting up a mannequin that had fallen after the shock wave had reached the city.

That shot you did from the top is the one that's used in a lot of postcards, the one that you see these days yes?
Yes, the picture of the cloud over the city ran in papers all over the country and *Life* magazine ran it as picture of the week, so that was nice. They said, There's danger everywhere you look in Las Vegas. That's the way they captioned it [laughing].

Did people start showing up to see the bomb like tourism or was it working as a promotional thing as years went on to get Las Vegas on the map or was it a measurable thing?

You know, I'm sure some statistician could give you some—however, it had to have had an effect on tourism because Las Vegas was in the headlines almost every day. Another thing that happened with that, we had as I said press from all over the United States, all over the world out here and they were on pretty big expense accounts. And day after day they would cancel the shots; they still had to be here to cover it. And if for any reason the wind was wrong or something happened in their calculations or whatever, they would cancel a shot. They'd postpone it until future notice or until tomorrow or for next week. And there were all these writers, reporters, and photographers on assignment out here, eating up these expense accounts, so they started dreaming up stories about Las Vegas to kind of justify their keep. So we got a real, real bonus of publicity. Everybody was looking for any kind of a sidebar, any kind of a story on Las Vegas. So it was just a bonanza for us.

You talked about News Nob earlier. When was the first time that you visited that area to see a shot?

I'm lousy on dates. I think it was 1951 or 1950.

Could you describe what News Nob is what it looks like?

OK, News Nob actually is just a spot in the desert on the atomic proving flats, seven miles from the blast. And they had bleachers out there. By the way, afterwards I'll show you a picture taken recently from those bleachers. And of course most of the tests were done at predawn, so just right after the test the light would start coming. So people were there, the press, hundreds of writers and photographers, everybody lined up, checking their equipment. And there was a little red light, like if it was a tower shot there'd be a little red light—this was seven miles away—and you'd kind of train your lens on that, trying to find it anyways if you had good eyes, so you'd be aimed in the proper direction. Also we had explicit instructions—we were given heavy dark glasses for eye protection but even with that you couldn't look at the bomb. You had to turn around a hundred and eighty degrees of the area where the bomb was going to be detonated [00:25:00] because the intensity was still so great. Nobody would look at the test while it really went—

The light or the heat?

As soon as it went off, then you could turn around. That didn't mean the cameras weren't going. And you know you think—it was ethereal. I remember one time the bomb went off and the yucca plants, all the desert plants, caught on fire for miles around, and it was ghostlike because it looked like a city that had been incinerated. You could see these little flames of fire. But other than that, another interesting thing, you'd think, what would there be? Would there be a hush? Would there be absolute silence? Maybe people shouting? I'll tell you what happened. Everybody out there was responsible for—getting stories was the one thing but for photographers they better have the picture. There's no way they could go out there—and so the first thing that happened after the flash went off, *Life* magazine and AP and a lot of these people that had very expensive equipment, they had light sensoring devices so that as soon as the light went off from the bomb it would trigger the camera, and they had what they called Hulcher cameras. They were high speed cameras that took I don't know how many frames a second, and you'd hear them *chug-chug-chug-chug-chug-chug-chug-chug-chug-chug*. You'd see the flash, you'd hear the *chug* of the Hulcher cameras, and then you'd hear oaths from one end to the other, everybody fighting their equipment. OK, first of all, the blast kind of—you couldn't see too well and everybody was fighting their—they were taking—in those days a lot of people had four-by-five cameras with film packs in them and film holders and they had to take them out and change them and change their f-stops. And anyway everybody was fighting their equipment and somebody would—their leg would kick a tripod leg and they'd be upset. But anyway that was the impression—that was the first thing that happened. Of course then a few seconds later, *bam!* the shock wave hit, so you got that. It wasn't damaging, didn't set you on your fanny or anything like that that, but it was a pretty good jolt. Then another few seconds or half-a-minute, something like that—first of all the shock wave goes out and then it comes in, so then you got it again from the opposite direction. So it was exciting.

Being that close, I mean, how large are these explosions? Seven miles doesn't seem like it's too terribly far.
They were huge.

And then also you mentioned you have these goggles and you can't see through them, they're so dark. The lenses of the camera, did you have to do anything special with the cameras because of that or no?
Yes. Well, we put all kinds of filters on the camera for the initial blasts, and close the aperture down to the smallest opening, then just by guess or by golly, kind of open up the aperture and continue shooting. Then as soon as you could, you'd take off the goggles and start shooting the mushroom cloud.

What were the restrictions on what you could shoot and could not shoot?
There were no restrictions. There was nothing to—seven miles away, you know, what. . .? One time we went out and they said, OK, we're going to allow one photographer to go in the trenches one mile from the blast and shoot and media, you can make up your mind who goes. So I was with the Las Vegas News Bureau and I shot sixteen millimeter. I did a lot of newsreel photography, and stills. So everybody said, well, English, you're neutral. We know that if you [00:30:00] go out there you're not going to shoot a special camera for yourself and have some film that's exclusive, and you'll be fair, won't you, and distribute the film to everybody? So you're elected. So I was elected to go into the trench one mile from the—

And this is with the Army troops?
With the Army troops. Said, oh gosh, I got my equipment together and went out there and we had a general that gave us a briefing before we went. He said, Men, he said, when they start counting down for that bomb, ten, nine, eight, seven, when he gets to that last second, that's going to be the longest second in your life. You better believe that you won't realize how long that second is going to take, and I thought, Well, this guy. . . That's what we do is we have to time for time exposures and in the darkroom printing, you time one-thousand-one, one-thousand-two. I said, this guy's full of baloney. Anyway, we were in the trenches and had the camera on a tripod and I had to keep the camera just below the surface of the trench because I didn't want any part of me or any equipment exposed. And there came the countdown, five, four, three, two, one, and I thought, By God, that guy's right. This is the longest second. Well, as it turned out it was a misfire [laughing]. So anyway, that was the longest second. I was very disappointed, of course.

He climbed a hundred foot up to the tower and the door was locked. He said whoever armed the bomb and came down, nobody was going to go up there, but it was procedure, you had to lock the door. And they never thought about it, so he had to go all the way down the tower again, get the key, and then climb back up and disarm the bomb.

They gave us badges that were supposed to detect [00:35:00] any radiation and we would wear them and then turn them in at the end of the time. I never heard of anyone being called, saying, Gee, you were radiated. But we just—kind of the age of innocence and everybody believed what was going on. Well, I mean we didn't know about the things that were happening with the downwind in Utah and all that until later.

It was a lot of pride.

PHOTO 5.6 MANNEQUIN FAMILY IN A DOOM HOUSE *Source:* National Archives, Records of the Office of Civil and Defense Mobilization, 1947–1962, Record Group 304, Civil Defense Photographs, 1951–1961 series

DOCUMENT 6.1 LOS ALAMOS CONFERENCE ON LIVESTOCK LOSSES
SOURCE: DOE NNSA/NSO NV0404967

October 27, 1953

Damage to the skin of animals from radioactive fall-out has been recognized in horses during the last series of tests at the Nevada Proving Grounds and in cattle during the Spring of 1952 tests. In both cases the animals were located within a few miles from the site of detonation and in areas of relatively heavy fall-out. About the first of June, there were reported incidents of sheep, originally grazing in Nevada, showing lesions and also about 1400 owes and 2900 lambs had died within the preceding few months. The question was raised as to the possibility of radiation damage causing or contributing to the lesions or deaths.

The same lesions were noted on sheep in areas of little or no fall-out with approximately the same incidence as in areas of relatively heavy fall-out. The general amounts of fall-out in the areas under question have been determined. These quantities of radiation dosage are not known to be sufficient to produce the lesions noted.

Evidence has been gleaned from microscopic examinations and comparisons of tissues both from the sheep in fall-out areas and some sheep on which skin beta burns were produced experimentally.

All of these data present a preponderance of evidence to support the conclusion that the lesions were not produced by radioactive fall-out. However, due to some anomalies in the evidence, it is recommended that studies be continued in order to determine the causative agent and to explain its isolated occurrence.

In considering radiation damage to the internal organs, the most critical is the thyroid, due to the uptake of radioactive iodine from the fall-out material. The amount of highest radiation dosage to the thyroid has been calculated to be far below the quantity necessary to produce detectable injury.

Bernard F. Trum
Joe B. Sanders
M. A. Holmes
Arthur H. Wolff
F. F. Lushbaugh
R. E. Thompaett
F. H. Melvin

DOCUMENT 6.2 ESTIMATED THYROID DOSES AND PREDICTED THYROID CANCERS IN UTAH INFANTS EXPOSED TO FALLOUT I^{131}

SOURCE: DOE NNSA/NSO NV0403156

Charles W. Mays
Physics Group Leader, Radiobiology Div.,
Anatomy Dept., U. of Utah

ABSTRACT: The inadvertent exposure of about 250,000 Utah infants to average thyroid doses estimated at 1.3–10 rads may provide a unique opportunity to establish the effects of low doses of I^{131} irradiation in children.

INTRODUCTION

Iodine-131 is produced in nuclear explosions. If cows eat forage which is contaminated with fresh fallout, I^{131} appears in their milk. If a child drinks this radioactive milk, I^{131} concentrates in his thyroid gland and irradiates it. Infants are considered to be the critical members of the population.

Dr. Robert C. Pendleton[4] was the first to discover that fallout from the Nevada nuclear tests of 1962 would cause significant contamination from radioactive I[131] in Utah. Following his vigorous urging that steps be taken to reduce the exposure, the Utah State Department of Health recommended: (1) transfer of cows from highly contaminated pasture to stored feed, and (2) diversion of highly contaminated milk from the fresh market. This protective action set a precedent: it marked the first official attempt in this country to prevent the intake of fallout-contaminated food.

In analyzing the 1962 incident I became fascinated with the implications of exposures from the previous years of testing. Unknown to me at the time, this problem was also being investigated through different approaches by Dr. Harold A. Knapp then with the AEC, and by members of the St. Louis Committee on Nuclear Information. Working independently, we all came to the same conclusion: significant exposures were indicated.

The problem was complicated enormously by the fact that I[131] was not properly recognized as a fallout hazard during the early years of testing (1951, 1952, 1953 & 1955), and, unfortunately, I[131] was not measured in milk during that time. Therefore, attempts to reconstruct the probable exposures during this period must be indirect. Knapp used the gamma-ray intensity above a contaminated field as an index of its I[131] content, while the St. Louis Group used this and the beta-particle disintegration rate from fallout collection trays. I used the observed beta activity in the air and the fission yield. Knapp and the St. Louis Group were concerned chiefly with exposures in Southern Utah near the Nevada Test Site, because that was where the highest individual doses were indicated. My major concern was the North-Central portion of Utah, because it contained so many more people.

During the 1963 Congressional Fallout Hearings, Dr. Eric Riess of the St. Louis Group and I both urged that a study be made of the irradiated Utah children. This study, supported by the U. S. Public Health Service, is now in progress.

Originally, the study had 2 objectives: (1) search for medical effects, and (2) estimation of radiation dosage. The medical phase is progressing well, but the dose program has lagged. An unfortunate decision was made to neglect dosimetry unless significant medical effects could definitely be established. In my opinion, this is the most serious defect in an otherwise excellent study. Waiting for possible medical effects may forfeit forever the opportunity to make the best estimates of dose. Memories fade, records are destroyed, and these children will soon reach adulthood and scatter

---

[4]   Associate Professor of Genetic and Molecular Biology and Head, Department of Radiological Health, University of Utah.

across the nation. Even if no effects appear, the exposures should be evaluated as accurately as possible. If a safe dose exists for I^{131} in children, proper study of the 250,000 irradiated Utah infants may provide the unique chance to establish it.

In this paper I present lower and higher limits for the average doses received by Utah infants. I do this for 2 reasons. First, I hope that the uncertainty in these limits will stimulate interest in improving the dosimetry. Secondly, despite dose uncertainties, the indicated exposures are sufficient to justify continued study of the Utah children.

DOSIMETRY

Prior to the 1963 Fallout Hearings, I calculated the number of radiation-induced cancers predicted for the total population of 250,000 Utah children exposed to fallout I^{131} as infants. I have never before published these predictions nor discussed them in public, primarily because I felt that most of my estimates of dose might be somewhat unreliable. Working in isolation at the time, I was aware of I^{131} milk measurements for only 1 of the 7 years of Nevada testing: doses for the other 6 years I estimated from measurements of beta-activity in the air or from fission yield during the growing season. New information now permits improved estimates for 5 of the 7 test years, and for the remaining 2 I have set lower and higher limits.

For 1962, our analysis of milk from Pendleton's 39 stations scattered throughout Utah indicated that for the daily consumption of 1 liter (1.06 quarts) of milk, the average I^{131} intake for the year was 45,000 picocuries[5] assuming a 3 day delay from milking to consumption. This agreed closely with the 37,000 pCi intake reported by the U. S. Public Health Service for the Salt Lake milk pool. The corresponding infant thyroid doses[6] were 0.77 or 0.63 rads[7] respectively.

For 1958 and 1957, USPHS analysis of the Salt Lake milk pool indicated average yearly intakes of 11,242 and 73,840 pCi I^{131} with associated infant thyroid doses of 0.2 and 1.3 rads, respectively.

For 1953 and 1952, the beta activity in fallout-collection trays at Salt Lake City was 15,000,000 disintegrations per minute/ft^2 at 12 hours after the detonation of shot "Nancy" on 24 March, 1953, and 23,000,000 dpm/ft^2

---

[5]   A picocurie is 2.22 disintegrations per minute.

[6]   Assuming 30% uptake in a 2 gram thyroid with a subsequent effective retention half-time of 7.6 days.

[7]   A rad is the absorption of 100 ergs of energy per gram of tissue.

at 12 hours after the detonation of shot "Easy" on 7 May, 1952. Infant thyroid doses have been calculated by the St. Louis Group as 2–12 rads for this 1953 shot and 3–13 rads for this 1952 shot (see pp. 529–530, ref. 3). A number of limitations exist in using these values. First, they are for only one shot during each year: additional shots may have caused additional contamination. Second, the measurements were made in Salt Lake City, not in the pasture lands: pasture contamination could have been higher or lower. I have used these values for yearly exposures only because I am unaware of better data (although it may exist and could be uncovered). My presumably less reliable estimates (see pg. 561, ref. 3) for these average yearly exposures were 6.3 rads for 1953 (from the fission yield) and 1.6 & 5.9 rads for 1952 (from the fission-yield and air beta activity, respectively).

For 1955 and 1951, I only have my estimates of 2.0 and 0.4 rads from the fission yields of 84 and 18 kilotons during the growing season (see pg. 561, ref. 3). Comparing my approximate fission yield estimates of dose with more reliable methods suggests that the fission-estimates averaged over a year of testing might be accurate within a factor of 10. Therefore, I have assigned dose ranges of 0.2-20 rads for 1955 and 0.04-4 rads for 1951. It is not my intent to deceive the reader into believing that the true doses are well established for the years 1955, 1953, 1952 and 1951. More work is needed.

My best estimates of the average thyroid doses for all Utah infants is summarized in Table 1 for each year of Nevada testing. Individual doses were much higher: Knapp estimated doses of 120–440 rads for infants in St. George, Utah, following the "Harry" shot of 19 May, 1953. The dose for our highest station in 1962 was 9–26 times greater than our average.

TABLE 1: ESTIMATED AVERAGE THYROID DOSES TO ALL UTAH INFANTS

YEAR OF TESTING	LOWER LIMIT	RADS	HIGHER LIMIT	METHOD OF DOSE ESTIMATION
1962	0.63	–	0.77	S.L. MILK POOL & PENDLETON'S MILK STA.
1958		0.2		USPHS SALT LAKE MILK POOL
1957		1.3		USPHS SALT LAKE MILK POOL
1955	0.2	–	20	FISSION YIELD
1953	2	–	12	FIELD BETA ACTIVITY AFTER SHOT "NANCY"
1952	3	–	18	FIELD BETA ACTIVITY AFTER SHOT "EASY"
1951	0.04	–	4	FISSION YIELD

DOCUMENT 6.3 OPERATION CUE TEST PROJECT 36.1

SOURCE: OPERATION CUE: THE ATOMIC TEST PROGRAM, FEDERAL CIVIL DEFENSE
ADMINISTRATION NEVADA TEST SITE, SPRING 1955, DOE NNSA/NSO, NV0324290

Supreme Victor mobile home.

CIVIL EFFECTS TEST PROJECT 36.1: UTILIZATION OF TRAILER COACH MOBILE HOMES FOLLOWING EXPOSURE TO NUCLEAR EFFECTS

PROJECT SPONSORS

Mobile Homes Manufacturers Association
Mobilehome Dealers National Association
Trailer Coach Association (California)
with Federal Civil Defense Administration

PROJECT OFFICER

Ebe R. Shaw, Trailer Coach Association

Any nuclear attack on our cities would leave large numbers of people homeless and in need of aid. A thermonuclear attack would not only result in greater numbers of people in need, it would also destroy many of the facilities on outskirts of target areas that normally would be available to care for the homeless. Trailer coach mobile homes would be an important resource under these conditions.

Trailer parks and dealer facilities are generally located on the outskirts of cities. Hence, for this project, distances from ground zero were selected that would simulate damage that might be expected from low blast pressures reaching out to the suburbs, as would be the case if a thermonuclear weapon were exploded over the center of the target area.

Two clusters of nine trailers each will be exposed. After the blast they will be examined to determine the general pattern of damage, ease with which damaged trailers might be restored for emergency use, and possible design changes that might make such mobile homes more resistant to blast.

The trailers will be typical of those in common use throughout the country.

Additional trailers will be placed in the zone of expected fallout for use in comparison radiation intensity studies described under project 38.4.

DOCUMENT 6.4 PROJECT GABRIEL REPORT SOURCE: DOE NNSA/NSO
NV0404830

US DOE ARCHIVES
326 U.S. ATOMIC ENERGY COMMISSION
RG DOE HISTORIAN (DBM)
Collection 1132
Box 3363
Folder #24

November 12, 1953

Report: Status of Project Gabriel
Prepared by: Division of Biology and Medicine
Reference: Request dated October 22, 1953 from Honorable W. Sterling Cole, Chairman, Joint Committee on Atomic Energy, to Mr. Strauss, Chairman, U. S. Atomic Energy Commission.

OBJECTIVE OF PROJECT GABRIEL

1. The objective of Project GABRIEL is the study of the probable effects, with particular reference to the inhabitants of affected regions, of the fall-out of radioactive materials from the use of nuclear weapons in warfare. Depending upon the conditions under which such weapons are used, the major interest may lie in the short range contamination from the use of a single weapon or in the number of weapons required to produce levels of contamination hazardous to the population of a major area.

2. The terms "short range" and "long range" as used in this discussion refer to time, although in general short range hazards will occur at relatively small distances from points of detonation. A large fraction of the dust (or water) swept up by the detonation of a nuclear weapon characteristically falls out in a limited area at some distance downwind from the point of detonation. The distance, size, and average level of radioactivity of this area will depend upon the altitude of

detonation, characteristics of the weapon, and meteorological conditions. The short range hazard from a single event of this nature is due to the high levels of radiation from the fall-out during the first several hours or days after deposition, and may occur at distances of several scores of miles from the point of detonation. Long range problems are associated with the possibility of occurrence, over periods of months or years, of hazardous quantities of long-lived radioactive materials in the general food supply. Such a problem might result, on a local scale, from the intensive use of surface weapons over a few thousand square miles of area. However, the long range problem which has received the most consideration is that of evaluating the hazard from the use of large numbers of weapons under conditions such that the radioactive debris would be spread generally over a large fraction of a continent or, perhaps, over a large fraction of the earth's surface.

STATUS OF THE PROJECT

3. The program involves the following phases:
   a. Probable distributions of fall-out from a single event or from a small number of closely related events under various conditions;
   b. Long range behavior of fall-out from multiple events; and
   c. Evaluation of health hazards resulting from radioactive fall-out under the range of conditions which may be anticipated from actual warfare.
4. Several programs currently supported by the Division of Biology and Medicine were initiated specifically to supply information on the distribution and probable effects of radioactive fall-out from nuclear detonations. These include:
   a. Studies of environmental effects of continental tests by the Atomic Energy Project at the University of California at Los Angeles, started at the Trinity test site in 1947 and extended to include the Nevada Proving Grounds;
   b. Monitoring of the radioactivity of fall-out from weapons tests at approximately 100 stations in the United States and 70 stations outside the United States;
   c. A theoretical study by Rand Corporation of the probable physical behavior of fall-out under conditions of interest; and
   d. Studies of the occurrence in soils, vegetation, dairy products, animals and humans of strontium 90 and other fission products from nuclear weapons tests. Principal participants are identified in Paragraph 9.

5. The Atomic Energy Project of the University of California at Los Angeles has, in connection with the several series of tests at the Nevada Proving Grounds, studied the occurrence of radioactive materials in soils, plants and small animals taken within a radius of one or two hundred miles of the test site. These studies are supplemented by laboratory investigations of the uptake by plants of radioactive materials from soils containing fall-out from the test site, of the inhalation by small animals of radioactive dusts from the test site, and of related subjects.

6. Rand Corporation was given a contract in 1952 to make a theoretical study of those aspects of GABRIEL which, on the basis of available information, are amenable to such study. Their principal effort has been aimed at predicting probable fall-out from a single detonation under various conditions of use. A complete report on this phase of their studies is expected about January 1954.

7. Rand's primary contribution to the long range aspects of GABRIEL has been related to the organization of a conference in July 1953 to provide a critical review of the entire project by qualified personnel in related fields, and to the writing of a report on the conference. The final version of this report is complete.

8. At the 1953 Rand Conference, the code name SUNSHINE was adopted to identify that portion of Project GABRIEL dealing with direct sampling of the occurrence of strontium 90 as the result of weapons tests.

9. Of the radioisotopes resulting from the detonation of nuclear weapons, strontium 90 appears to be critical in the determination of hazardous long range effects. An exploratory sampling of the occurrence of strontium 90 in humans, animals, milk, vegetation and soils is in progress. Through the cooperation of the Bureau of Plant Industry, U.S. Department of Agriculture, samples of soil, vegetation, milk and animals from selected areas of the United States and samples of soil and vegetation from several foreign countries are being obtained. Human samples are being obtained through individual arrangements with hospitals and practicing physicians.

10. Assays of the materials sampled for strontium 90 are being made by W. F. Libby of the University of Chicago, by J. L. Kulp of Columbia University, and by the New York Operations Office of the U. S. Atomic Energy Commission. Studies of other characteristics of the samples bearing on the soil-plant-animal relationships involved are being made by the New York Operations Office, the Department of Agriculture, and others. It is expected that these studies will contribute to GABRIEL in the following ways:

   a. Actual samples of the present human content of strontium 90 from some 40 detonations of nuclear devices under partially known conditions will add to the confidence with which one can estimate orders of magnitude of human uptake from other devices detonated under similar conditions. In general it will be difficult or impossible to evaluate the relative contributions of individual detonations.

b. Correlation with fall-out data and with the results of controlled experimental studies will permit better estimates of quantities of material which may be hazardous under the various conditions which may be anticipated in nuclear warfare.

c. The extent to which actual sampling of strontium 90 is desirable can be determined only on the basis of results from the exploratory program now in progress.

11. Although a reliable estimate of the present distribution of strontium 90 will represent a substantial contribution to GABRIEL, additional information is needed to permit reliable estimates of changes in availability for human uptake as a function of time and of biological effects as a function of dose and of dose rate. Studies of radiotoxicity have continually constituted an important phase of the research program of the Division of Biology and Medicine, but at present, aspects of particular interest to GABRIEL are being augmented and emphasized.

12. The first studies of the long range aspects of Project Gabriel were undertaken in 1949 for the Atomic Energy Commission by Dr. Nicholas Smith, a theoretical physicist then at the Oak Ridge National Laboratory. His revised estimate (November, 1951) stated that the number of nominal atomic bombs required to reach lethal levels of residual radioactivity on 10% of the earth's surface "is in the order of 10^5 under expected circumstances. This estimate may be 100 times too low or 10 times too high." Limitations in our knowledge of the physical and biological properties of the radioactive products of a nuclear weapon, together with inherent uncertainties as to the conditions which might be involved in the use of such a weapon, impose a high degree of uncertainty on estimates of this nature. While continuing studies are increasing our knowledge of the behavior and effects of the radioactive materials involved, the range of known possibilities of design and use of nuclear weapons is continuing to broaden, adding to the unavoidable uncertainties inherent in predicting the results of their extensive use. The present stage of studies does not justify new numerical estimates of the possible long range effects of the use of large numbers of weapons. However, the trend of results indicates that to produce serious hazards over a large fraction of the earth's surface, a number larger than that estimated by Dr. Smith would be required.

13. In the event that GABRIEL develops a substantial basis for apprehension concerning the long range effects of strontium 90 in the

environment as a result of nuclear warfare, it may become desirable to initiate further projects to study means of minimizing the hazards from such occurrence—as for example, reallocating affected areas to the production of foodstuffs less inclined to utilize strontium (e.g., seed crops rather than dairy products), or development of methods to minimize uptake of strontium by plants as by liming.

DOCUMENT 6.5 CHECKLIST OF ACTIONS TO REDUCE WORLD ANTAGONISMS TO U.S. NUCLEAR WEAPONS TESTS. SOURCE: DOE NNSA/NSO NV0304906

OPERATIONS COORDINATING BOARD
Washington 25, D. C.
August 12, 1954

1. Associate friendly foreign governments in the conduct of the tests, either as observers or participants, with weapons or test problems of their own initiation, including civil defense problems.
2. Publicize and stress specific applications of scientific data achieved by such tests in the past to the peaceful application of problems of nuclear engineering.
3. Release data on global effects of Soviet weapon tests.
4. Stimulate speeches, articles, and commentary emanating from other than U.S. sources which stress the protective role of U.S. weapons superiority against Soviet aggression.

DOCUMENT 6.6 ATOMS FOR PEACE ADDRESS DRAFT SOURCE: DWIGHT D. EISENHOWER PRESIDENTIAL LIBRARY C.D. JACKSON PAPERS, BOX 30

Draft #5*
November 28, 1953

DRAFT OF PRESIDENTIAL SPEECH BEFORE
THE GENERAL ASSEMBLY OF THE UNITED NATIONS

When Secretary Hammarskjold's invitation to address this General Assembly on its closing day reached me in Bermuda, I was just beginning my conferences with the Prime Ministers and Foreign Ministers of Great Britain and France on some of the problems that beset our world.

During the remainder of the Bermuda conferences, I had constantly in mind that ahead of me lay a great honor. That honor is mine tonight as I stand here, privileged to address the General Assembly of the United Nations.

At the same time that I appreciate the honor and privilege of addressing you, I also have a sense of excitement as I look upon this assembly.

Never before in history has so much hope for so many people been gathered together in a single organization. Your deliberations and decisions during these somber years have already realized some of this hope.

But the great tests and the great accomplishments still lie ahead. And in the confident expectation of these accomplishments, I would use the position which, for the time being, I hold, to assure you that the Government of the United States will remain steadfast in its faith that from this body will flow a great share of the wisdom, the courage, and the decision which will bring to this world lasting peace for all nations, and happiness and well-being for all men.

* * *

As the brief Bermuda hours ticked away, I considered what would be an appropriate message for me to give you today.

Clearly it would not be fitting for me to take this occasion to present to you a unilateral American report on Bermuda. Nevertheless, I can assure you that our deliberations projected the detailed problems at hand against those same great vistas of universal peace and human dignity so cleanly etched in your Charter.

I also knew that it would not be a measure of this great opportunity merely to recite, however hopefully, pious platitudes.

I therefore decided that this occasion warranted my saying to you some of the things that have been on the minds and hearts of myself and my

---

* Ellipses in this document indicate where material is illegible in the original draft.

closest associates for a great many months—thoughts I had originally planned to say primarily to the American people.

I know that the American people share my deep belief that if a danger exists in the world, it is a danger shared by all—and equally, that if a *hope* exists in the mind of one nation, that hope should be shared by all.

Finally, if any proposal designed to ease world tensions, is to be advanced by the United States, what more appropriate audience could there be than the members of the General Assembly of the United Nations.

* * *

In a sense, I am speaking today in a language that is new—a language which I who have spent so much of my life in the military profession would have preferred never to use.

That new language is the language of atomic warfare.

* * *

On _____, the United States set off the world's first atomic test explosion at Alamagordo in New Mexico. Since that fateful day, the atomic age has moved forward at such a pace that today I consider that certain facts should be taken out of the realm of conjecture and stated officially.

I beg you to believe that the facts I shall reveal concerning the atomic power of the United States are not presented boastfully, or truculently, or threateningly. *On the contrary*, I, who know better than most the language of destruction, utter them with sober sadness.

This recital of atomic danger and power is necessarily stated in United States terms, for these are the incontrovertible facts which I know. You must, however, bear in mind that no area of the world, no matter how remote, could consider itself completely immune to some of the results were atomic warfare to occur on our planet.

Since that day in _____ we have conducted 42 atomic test explosions.

Bombs in today's . . . are more than 30 times as destructive as were those of 1945.

In these eight years, our mass of atomic weapons, with its ever-increasing annual growth, exceeds by *many times* the explosive equivalent of the *total* of *all* bombs and *all* shells that came from *every* American plane and *every* American gun in *every* theatre of war through all the *years* of World War II.

Any single *one* of the air wings of our Strategic Air Command could deliver in *one* operation atomic bombs with an explosive equivalent greater than *all* the bombs that fell on Germany through all the *years* of World War II.

One aircraft carrier of our Navy could deliver in *one sortie* atomic bombs exceeding the explosive equivalent of *all* the bombs and rockets dropped by Germany on the United Kingdom through all the *years* of World War II.

* * *

But the dread secret and the fearful engines of atomic might are not ours alone.

In the first place, the dread secret is shared by our friends and allies, Great Britain and Canada, whose scientific genius made a tremendous contribution to our original development and perfection of the atomic bomb.

The secret is also shared by the Soviet Union.

I am sure that it will be no surprise for you to hear that we possess very considerable evidence of the progress over the past four years of the Soviet Union's development of atomic and thermo-nuclear weapons. In this period, the Soviet Union has exploded a series of atomic devices, including one involving thermo-nuclear reaction.

If at one time the United States possessed what might have been called a monopoly of atomic power, that monopoly no longer exists. Therefore, although our earlier start has permitted us to accumulate what is today a quantitative advantage, the awful arithmetic of today's atomic realities is such that two facts emerge.

First . . . already two nations possess sufficient atomic resources so that either could inflict terrible damage upon any nation it might choose to attack.

Second, a vast superiority in numbers of weapons and a consequent capability of devastating retaliation, comprise no preventative . . . against the terrible material and human damage that could be inflicted in surprise aggression,

The United States is already embarked on a large and . . . program of warning and defense systems. That program will be increased and accelerated. I shall have more to say to the people of my own country on this subject at an early date.

The massive defense of the United States is forced upon us by more than reasons of selfish national protection. Within the Continental United States lies the vast arsenal of production which, since 1947, has been at the service not just of the United States, but of the free world. If that arsenal were to be gravely damaged, the whole free world would lie at the mercy of any powerful aggressor.

But let no one think that the expenditure of vast sums for defense of an industrial system can guarantee one hundred percent safety for the cities and people of the nation. Even with the most powerful defense, an aggressor in possession of the effective minimum number of atomic bombs for a surprise attack could place a sufficient number of his bombs on the chosen targets to cause grave damage.

* * *

Should this happen to the US, the nation could be violent. But for me to say that the defense capabilities of the United States are such that they could inflict terrible losses upon an aggressor—for me to say that the retaliation capabilities of the United States are so great that such an aggressor's land would be instantly laid waste—for me to say that if and wherever United States forces are involved in repelling *aggression*, these forces will feel free to use atomic weapons as military advantage dictates—all this, while fact, is not the true expression of the purpose and the hope of the USA. To pause there would be to confirm the hopeless finality of a belief that two atomic colossi are doomed malevolently to eye each other indefinitely across a trembling world. To land only on this . . . would be to accept, helplessly . . . and the beginning again, by men of the age old struggle toward decency, justice, and right.

Surely no sane member of the human race could discover victory in such disorder— if indeed military victory could be achieved by anyone.

Occasional pages of history do record the faces of the "Great Destroyers", but the whole *book* of history reveals mankind's never-ending quest for peace and mankind's God-given capacity to build.

It is with the *book* of history, and not with isolated pages, that the United States will ever wish to be identified. My country wants to be constructive, not destructive . . . it wants agreements, not wars, among nations. It wants to live in freedom itself, and confident that every other nation enjoys, equally, its right of choosing its own way of life.

* * *

So my country's purpose is to help us move out of this dark chamber of horrors into the light, to find a way by which the minds of men, the hopes of men, the souls of men everywhere, can move forward toward peace and happiness and well being.

In this quest, I know that we must *not* be impatient.

I know that in a world divided, such as ours today, salvation cannot be attained in one dramatic . . .

I know that many small steps will have to be taken over many months before the world can look at itself one day and truly realize that a new climate of mutually peaceful confidence is abroad in the world.

But I know, above all else, that we must start to take these steps, be they ever so small—*NOW*.

* * *

The United States and its allies, Great Britain and France, have over the past months tried to take some of these steps. Let no one say that it is we who shun the conference table.

On the record still stands the request of the United States, Great Britain and France, to negotiate the problems of a divided Germany.

On that record still stands the request of the same three nations to ne-gotiate an Austrian State Treaty.

On the same record still stands the request of the United States, Great Britain and France to negotiate with the Soviet Union the problems of Asia.

Most recently, we have received from the Soviet Union what is in effect an acceptance of our proposal of _____ for a Four Power meet-ing. Along with our allies, Great Britain and France, we were pleased to see that this note did not contain the unacceptable conditions previously put forward by the Soviets. Therefore, our final Bermuda communique, issued today, conveyed our agreement to meet with the Soviets at the earliest date to discuss the urgent problems at hand.

The Government of the United States approaches this conference with hopeful sincerity. And we will bend every effort of our minds to the single purpose of emerging from that conference with tangible results toward peace, which is the only true way of lessening international tension.

We have never, and never will, propose or suggest that the Soviet Union surrender what is rightfully hers.

We will never say that the peoples of Russia are an enemy with whom we have no desire ever to deal or mingle in friendly and fruitful relationship.

And beyond the hopeful prospect of this conference, our peaceful vision sees further opportunities for building the miraculous edifice of a world truly at peace.

We see, instead of the winter of discontent which is now settling upon Eastern Germany, occupied Austria, and the seething countries of Eastern Europe from the Baltic to the Black Sea, a family of free European nations, with none a threat to the other, and least of all a threat to the peoples of Russia.

We see beyond the turmoil and strife and misery of Asia and Southeast Asia a time when these nations . . . sprung after years of preparation for statehood, from the obsolete colonial mold, shall have the peaceful time to practice the techniques and responsibilities of independence, to develop their priceless natural resources, and to elevate the lot of their people.

These are not idle words or shallow visions. Behind them lies an ex-traordinary record of peaceful accomplishment.

Since 1918, out of the overseas possessions of the United States, Great Britain, and France, has come freedom and independence for _____ millions of people and _____ nations. For no instance has inde-pendence come about a result of war; all have been . . . through negotiation.

These are deeds of peace.

But I do not wish to rest our case either upon the reiteration of past proposals or the restatement of past deeds. The gravity of the time is such that every new avenue of peace, no matter how dimly discernible, should be explored.

In its resolution of November 18, 1953, this General Assembly suggested—and I quote—"that the Disarmament Commission study the desirability of establishing a sub-committee consisting of representatives of the powers principally involved, which should seek in private an acceptable solution and report to the Disarmament Commission as soon as possible in order that the Commission may study and report on such a solution to the General Assembly and to the Security Council not later than 1 September 1954."

The United States heeding the suggestion of the General Assembly of the United Nations, is instantly prepared to meet privately with such other countries as may be "principally involved" to seek "an acceptable solution" to the atomic armaments race which overshadows not only the peace, but the very life, of the world.

In this great peaceful endeavor, the United States looks beyond the mere reduction or elimination of atomic materials available for military purposes.

The United States knows that if the fearful trend of atomic military buildup can be reversed, this greatest of *destructive* forces can be developed into a great *constructive* force for the benefit of all mankind.

The United States knows that peaceful power from atomic energy is no dream of the future. It is *here—now—today.*

Pending the day when atomic fear will begin to disappear from the minds of the peoples and the Governments of the East and the West it should be possible for the Governments of the Soviet Union, Great Britain, and the United States jointly to take a . . . step in this direction for the benefit of mankind.

The three Governments could begin to make joint contributions of fissionable material to an Atomic Power Authority of the United Nations, which would be responsible for its impounding, storage, and protection. Our scientists already know of special safe conditions under which this fissionable material would be physically immune to seizure by surprise attack.

The Atomic Power Authority would have the responsibility of exploring the power-starved areas of the world in order to devise the methods to make this fissionable material available to provide electrical energy in those areas.

Thus, the United States, Great Britain, and the Soviet Union jointly would be dedicating some of their strength to serve the *needs* rather than the *fears* of the world—to make the deserts flourish, to warm the cold, to feed the hungry, to alleviate the misery of the world.

* * *

The United states would be . . . even proud, to take up with others principally involved . . . the development of plans . . . and powerful uses of atomic energy . . . Against the dark background of atomic bombing, the United States does not wish merely to present strength, but also the desire and hope for peace.

The coming months will be fraught with fateful decisions. In the Chanceries and military headquarters of the world; in this Assembly; in the hearts of men everywhere, be they governors or governed, may they be the decisions which will lead this world out of fear and into peace.

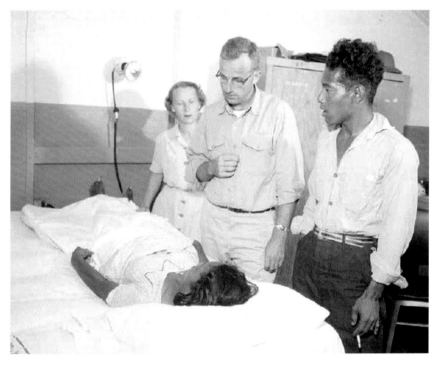

PHOTO 6.7 TREATMENT OF RADIATION VICTIMS AFTER BRAVO *Source:* National Atomic Testing Museum Photo Collections.

DOCUMENT 7.1 DEAR MR. GEAGLEY SOURCE: WILLIAM GEAGLEY
COLLECTION ON NUCLEAR SAFETY, UNLV SPECIAL COLLECTIONS, MS-00792

FEDERAL CIVIL DEFENSE ADMINISTRATION
NATIONAL HEADQUARTERS
BATTLE CREEK, MICHIGAN

April 25, 1957

Mr. William C. Geagley
526 West Ottawa St.
Lansing, Michigan

Dear Mr. Geagley:

This is to inform you that you have been tentatively selected to participate in the FCDA sponsored Radiological Defense Operations Program which is one of the phases of Operation PLUMBBOB which will be conducted at the Nevada Test Site during the summer of 1957. You have been tentatively assigned to Project 36.1 and it is estimated that your arrival time at the Test Site will be June 8th and that you depart on June 30, 1957.

The following enclosed items should be filled out and returned as quickly as possible.

1. Personnel Data card
2. Badge Request card (fill in only two first lines)
3. AEC waiver
4. Medical statement

Should the response to the program exceed the maximum possible enrollment, an adjustment may be necessary to insure that we have as representative a distribution of the various geographical locations as possible. Confirmation of your participation in this program will be forwarded at the earliest possible date after receipt of the information requested.

Sincerely,

Hugh D. Ivey
Director
Program 36, CETG

Enclosures

DOCUMENT 7.2 GLADWIN HILL SPEECH ON ATOMIC TEST COVERAGE SOURCE: UCLA CHARLES E. YOUNG RESEARCH LIBRARY, GLADWIN HILL PAPERS (1706), BOX 50

April 5, 1953
Las Vegas, Nevada

Suspicions have been murmured from time to time that covering the Nevada atomic tests consisted of sliding chips onto numbered squares with one hand, while manning a ten-ounce glass with the other, while glancing over one's shoulder past a nearby palm tree to corroborate the latest nuclear cataclysm.

Tragic to report, this idyllic conception is at least 75 miles from the truth geographically, and considerably farther in principle. The rigors of atom-bomb watching are such as to have given rise to two main schools of thought. One, espoused by Hanson Baldwin, is that the resultant exhaustion calls for sleeping before getting anything to eat. The other, espoused by this correspondent, is to eat first. What system is followed by Bill Laurence, the third side of the Times' answer to atomic bombs, remains a mystery. After each test, he disappears into the neon-lighted fastnesses of Las Vegas' casino strip, whence come vague but intriguing reports of crap-table coups, trills of feminine laughter, and general/high life as limned by E. Phillips Oppenheim.

There are two kinds of atomic tests. On one, the Atomic Energy Commission not only lets observers on its desert reservation for a close-range look, but runs virtual Cook's tours, hauling newsmen from all over the country in buses by the hundreds from downtown Las Vegas to "News Nob," the hummock nine miles from the detonation area.

On the other occasions, the A.E.C., with its curious policy schizophrenia, suddenly decides that newsmen are to be treated as potential spies, and bars the gates. Then it's a matter of trekking up some 8,000 feet to the top of Mount Charleston, 50 miles away, and peering over intervening hills at the blasts.

In either case, it's a matter of staggering out of the sack at ungodly hours like 1 A.M., freezing through the pre-dawn hours, later baking in the sun, and seldom getting the last query from the National Desk—asking plaintively yet once again whether it's "Yucca Flat" or "Yucca Flats"—disposed of until well-nigh sundown. It makes for a long day.

The atmosphere at each test is supercharged with the knowledge that something new is being tried, and the suspicion that *this* time they may have put in too much vermouth and will touch off the end of the world.

Amid the be-goggled sandwich-munching and coffee-gulping throngs at News Nob, Atomic Laurence is the Dean of Nucleonics, ever surrounded by a covey of brain-pickers to whom he patiently explains how they did it at Alamogordo and Hiroshima. Admiral Baldwin is Dean of Military Significance, surrounded by similar coveys of inquirers on whether this is good or bad for the Pentagon and the Kremlin, and how it felt in that forward foxhole. (Hanson's response recalled Stuart Little, the mouse who went down the bathtub drain and reported: "It was all right.") The undersigned, having seen a dozen or so blasts, is Dean of Comparative Phenomena, queried as to how the fireball this time stacked up against the fireball on Number 4, which he can never remember.

At News Nob the initial flash, which can be looked at only through dense dark glasses, is an overwhelming sheet of light. Then you count three and yank off the glasses, and it looks like somebody out on the desert had over-fuelled his Zippo but good. From Mount Charleston, the explosions, which can be watched entirely without glasses, are less overwhelming but quite distinguishable in their details. The location doesn't seem remote at all on such occasions as the morning a 100-mile-an-hour wind whisked the atomic cloud right onto the mountain and all but enveloped several observers.

An un-omittable figure in the Times' atomic coverage is its between-tests ear-to-the-ground man, Donley Lukens, Las Vegas correspondent for the Times and a bewildering array of other periodicals. Asked by an A.E.C. official as he scrutinized the recent bomb-shelter dummies if he was gleaning more news fit to print, Lukens replied: "Hell, no. I'm checking their clothes—for Women's Wear."

Each explosion is followed by a reportorial hassle for communications. The Signal Corps runs a wireless teletype system from News Nob to Las Vegas. On the St. Patrick's Day test it managed to transmit three or four hours of the A.P.'s copy into sheer oblivion, but the A.E.C. has been considerate enough to schedule the tests at hours permitting the NYTimesters to get into Las Vegas to file.

DOCUMENT 7.3 GLADWIN HILL FIELD NOTEBOOK, MAY 1957. TEXT OF FOUR-PAGE SERIES READS IN PART, "WAITRESS, THEY'RE GOING TO KILL US OFF. ROBERT MURRAY AGED 9: THE RAYS— HOW LONG THEY GOING TO BE HERE? BROWN: OH, THEY ARE OUT IN 3–4 HOURS." SOURCE: UCLA CHARLES E. YOUNG RESEARCH LIBRARY, GLADWIN HILL PAPERS (1706), BOX 50

DOCUMENT 7.4 PLUMBBOB PRE-SERIES BRIEFING, NEVADA TEST ORGANIZATION OFFICE OF TEST INFORMATION, LAS VEGAS, NV (MAY 1957) SOURCE: WILLIAM GEAGLEY COLLECTION ON NUCLEAR SAFETY, UNLV SPECIAL COLLECTIONS, MS-00792

OTI-57-NN

NEVADA TEST ORGANIZATION
OFFICE OF TEST INFORMATION
1235 South Main Street
Las Vegas, Nevada

Pre-Series Briefing
May 1957

Telephone: Dudley 2-6350
Remarks by: James E. Reeves
Director Test Division AEC Albuquerque Operations Office Test Manager, Operation Plumbbob

If all continues to go well, we will get the full scale testing portion of this Summer 1957 series under way Thursday morning. As Mr. Elliott has mentioned, the total series actually began with the detonation of a safety experiment on April 24.

As you know, the first scheduled shot had to be postponed from May 15 for 24 hours to give more time for installation of technical equipment. I am advised by my construction and technical people that everything is now moving on schedule. So, if no troubles develop and if we have reasonably good weather, we should get under way Thursday morning.

This new series is again designed to attain new knowledge important to the defense of the Free World. The development of weapons for defense against attack is a major objective. Studies of weapons effects will be continued in order to improve military and civil defense against nuclear attack. Many of the shots will, as usual, be used additionally as the occasion for civil defense and military training programs.

As some of you have already speculated, this will be the most extensive series held in Nevada, both in length of time and in number of shots. We have already had one safety experiment and three to six more will be fired in-between our full scale shots. As usual, we can't give you at this time a firm number for total nuclear detonations. We don't know what the total will be, as some shots may be cancelled, and others may be added. We can add up those which are certain, and of which you have already been told in one way or another.

First, there are nine shots to which news media will be admitted, scheduled between mid-May and September 1. Of these, seven are tower shots and two are from balloon suspensions. There will be at least two additional tower shots, an air burst rocket test, one detonation in a deep underground tunnel, and other balloon tests. These total more than the 14 shots fired in the Spring 1955 series, in addition to four or more safety experiments.

Additionally, our schedule of ready dates is somewhat more relaxed than in the past to provide more time for construction and greater intervals between scheduled shots for our scientists and technicians to get their experiments ready.

These various factors mean that we will use the Test Site for testing throughout the summer. If all goes well, we expect to conclude the series while there is still a day or two of summer left.

This adds up to a very demanding test operation. It will include many technical and training programs, of which later briefers will speak. As always, public safety has remained uppermost in our minds as we planned the operation. As we advised you Monday in a statement on radiological safety procedures:

None of the shots in the Plumbbob series is expected to produce as much fallout on the nearby region as did some of the shots in the 1955 Teapot series; and

The total fallout on the region around the Test Site from all shots in the new series is expected to be less than that for any Nevada test series since 1952.

Dr. Graves will report to you tomorrow morning on how we were able to manage this.

I want to add one thing here because it has definite public safety implications. Those of you who were with us during Teapot may be wondering about the shot which you are scheduled to see, and which will be fired from a 500-foot tower. Please do not be misled by the height of the tower into thinking this will be a difficult shot, in the sense of potential fallout created. The explosive yield of Thursday morning's device will be in the range of about one-half nominal. It will be the lowest yield detonation which will have been witnessed by newspapermen from on-site, although of course not as low in yield as others we will test in this series or others which you have viewed during the past series from Angel's Peak. The fireball from Thursday's detonation will not reach the earth's surface, and heavy fallout will not be created.

The tests are as usual being conducted by a joint organization of AEC, Department of Defense, contractor, and other Agency people. As the AEC's Test Manager, I am in effect the field agent for all participating organizations.

We are now at a peak strength here in Mercury, with large numbers of construction people still at work and with the influx of operating people.

Our peak for Spring 1955 was about 2700, and our present Test Site population is about 3500.

With us here this morning are two of my assistants who direct the many operations involved in construction, in general site and camp housekeeping, and operating jobs such as off-site radiological safety. I want you to meet them. Bill Allaire is my Deputy Test Manager and Director of Support Services. Max Smith is Manager of the AEC's Las Vegas office and directs the organization providing site construction, services, and general housekeeping.

It is nice having you with us, and be assured that we will do everything we can to make your visit instructive and rewarding.

DOCUMENT 7.5 AEC 141/33—RADIOLOGICAL CRITERIA FOR THE NEVADA TEST SITE SOURCE: DOE NNSA/NSO NV0408756

REPOSITORY NARA—College Park
COLLECTION RG326 office of Secretary 1951-58 Correspondence
BOX No. 186
FOLDER MR & A 7-1, Vol. III
1246th AEC Meeting 11-14-56 c

AEC 141/33 - RADIOLOGICAL CRITERIA FOR THE NEVADA TEST SITE (PP. 23–52)

Dr. Dunning discussed with the Commissioners the establishment of radiological safety criteria for exposures to gamma radiation from fallout to populations around the Nevada Test Site.

Mr. Murray referred to the statement in the staff paper that the operational guide be arbitrarily established at 10 roentgens in a period of 10 years and said this matter raised the question of the extent of the exposure to the people living in the neighborhood of NTS. Mr. Murray added that he believed this matter also raised the question of the desirability of establishing a second or third test organization in order that tests could be conducted in the Pacific without raising such questions as arbitrary determinations on the extent of exposures to gamma radiation from fallout. He suggested that consideration should be given to establishing a second test organization so that tests could be conducted in the Pacific more frequently. Mr. Strauss referred to his previous suggestion that all tests be moved to the Pacific and said that he believed if this were done, the Commission would not be faced with many problems such as a determination of radiological safety criteria. He expressed particular concern over the proposed underground shots.

Dr. Dunning then referred to Mr. Murray's comment on the establishment of 10 roentgens and said that during discussion of this matter by the Advisory Committee on Biology and Medicine, the ACBM had indicated that the National Academy of Science had also arrived at its figures of 10 roentgens in a 30-year period in an arbitrary manner. Dr. Dunning observed that there was no precise method of measurement in establishing these criteria. In response to a question by Mr. Murray, Dr. Dunning said that the ACBM had discussed this subject and that there was general agreement among its members that the recommended numbers were reasonable.

Mr. Strauss asked about the possibilities of conducting all tests in the Pacific and avoiding the extensive facilities and instrumentation connected with tests. Mr. Fields said that increased costs and time would be involved in conducting all tests in the Pacific. He then commented on the time required for constructing additional facilities, organizing the operational supporting groups, and transporting the necessary technical personnel from the various laboratories to conduct their own tests.

Mr. Libby commented on the possibility of establishing the 10-year limit at 5 roentgens and transferring additional but not all shots to the Pacific. He then discussed with Dr. Dunning ways of revising firing conditions of continental shots in order to remain within a 5 roentgen level. Mr. Libby then said he believed the recommendations of AEC 141/33 should be approved and that the record of the discussion at the meeting should be a guide to the test organization in further study of operational means of limiting fallout. He also suggested that there should be further study of the practicality of establishing a 5 roentgen level for a 10-year period and the effect on the test program of such a limit.

Dr. Dunning said that he believed it was much easier to announce a 10 roentgen level and to point out later that this level had not been exceeded rather than to explain why a more stringent 5 roentgen level, if adopted, had been exceeded.

Mr. Murray proposed that the 10-year level be established at 5 roentgens and that a study be made of the delay in the small weapons program as a result of the consequent need to transfer any shots to the Pacific. He said that he did not believe the matter of cost was so important to this question as the delay in the weapons program. He added that it would be a very serious matter if the study showed that going to the Pacific would delay the small weapons program.

The Commissioners discussed at length with Dr. Dunning the problems involved in establishing a 5 roentgen level. Dr. Dunning said that the 10 roentgen level would permit more flexibility and suggested that this level be accepted with the understanding that the test organization would be encouraged to review operational factors of the proposed test in order to reduce fallout and to remain well below the 10 roentgen level.

Mr. Libby inquired about reports on fallout patterns from earlier tests in Nevada and suggested that he review these reports to determine to what extent this information has affected planning for Operation PILGRIM. Dr. Dunning said that studies were being made of fallout data from previous tests and that he would obtain the latest reports.

Mr. Strauss suggested, in view of the uncertainty regarding the 10-year figure to be established and in view of the Commission's approval of AEC 944 which recommended approval in principle only, of the test program, that the recommendations of AEC 141/33 be approved, subject to final Commission consideration of this matter after review by Mr. Libby of the reports on fallout patterns of previous tests. Mr. Strauss also indicated that the staff should study the various factors involved in the transfer of all tests to the Pacific. Mr. Libby requested that the staff paper on the specific shot program contain figures on the estimated roentgens dosage from offsite fallout for the shots conducted at NTS.

The Commissioners then discussed at length with the staff the advisability of requesting Presidential approval of the test activities for CY 1957 and issuing a press release in view of the uncertainty regarding the Commission's final decision on radiological criteria and the possible transfer of tests to the Pacific.

Mr. Libby said he agreed with Mr. Strauss' proposal that the Commission approve the recommendation of the paper under discussion, subject to review of reports on fallout data. Mr. Strauss said that with respect to the letter to the President (AEC 944), he could delay this letter in order to permit Mr. Libby to review the reports.

Mr. Salisbury then commented on the desirability of including a statement on the radiological criteria in the public announcement on the test series. In response to a question by Mr. Strauss, Dr. Dunning said there was nothing in the recommendations of AEC 141/33 which would prevent the Commission from referring to the NAS report as an authority on the matter of radiological criteria.

Mr. Murray referred to Mr. Salisbury's comments on the need to include the established radiological criteria in the public announcement and suggested that the press release be delayed until Mr. Libby reviewed the reports on fallout data. Mr. Murray said that he did not wish to approve the paper with the ten roentgen figure in it until this had been done. The Commissioners then discussed the problem involved in delaying the public announcement in AEC 944.

General Starbird commented on the time involved in obtaining DOD approval of the test activities outlined in AEC 944. Mr. Salisbury observed that the announcement would be reviewed by the OCB after Presidential approval of the test activities, and Mr. Libby observed that there appeared to be ample time to review the fallout data reports prior to a public announcement.

Mr. Libby then requested that it be determined whether the ACBM has changed its position on the 10-year limit at 10 roentgens, Mr. Strauss requested that the ACBM position be confirmed in writing.

After further discussion, the Commissioners indicated that they favored adoption of AEC 141/33 with the understanding that Mr. Libby would establish the 10-year limit on exposure at a figure not exceeding 10 roentgens.

The Commission:

1. Approved the radiological safety criteria for gamma radiation set forth in paragraph 3 of AEC 141/33, with the understanding that after review of radiation effects data, Commissioner Libby may establish the 10-year limit at a lower level than that referred to in subparagraph 3b of AEC 141/33;
2. Noted that the criteria finally established in accordance with a above will be made public in the NTS test series announcement similar to that in Appendix "H" to AEC 944;
3. Noted that operational means for giving effect to the criteria finally established in accordance with a above will be developed by the Test Manager and the Division of Military Application with the technical guidance of the Division of Biology and Medicine; and
4. Noted that when the criteria are finally established, the Joint Committee on Atomic Energy, the GAC, and the MLC will be advised of this action by letter similar to that in Appendix "B" to AEC 141/33.

DOCUMENT 7.6 GLADWIN HILL, "AEC MEN DEFEND TESTS IN NEVADA" SOURCE: *THE NEW YORK TIMES*, MAY 26, 1957, P. 24

Discount Fears of Radiation Dangers—Note Virtually Perfect Safety Record
By Gladwin Hill

LAS VEGAS, Nevada, May 25—In addition to the ordinary vagaries of weather, atomic scientists this year must cope with an invisible cloud hanging over the Nevada nuclear tests.

It is a cloud of doubt generated by the international controversy over radiation dangers.

The scientists are confronted with the paradox that, despite a virtually perfect safety record through forty-five Atomic Energy Commission nuclear detonations here, more apprehension is being expressed than when the tests started in 1951.

The first of the current test explosions was rescheduled again today. The blast is now scheduled for Monday. It has been postponed eleven times.

Just as the new test work was getting under way a fortnight ago, Japan formally urged that the series be stopped in the name of public safety. Recently published articles have implied that the Nevada tests involved considerable hazards for people in the vicinity if not the nation at large. While most Nevadans seem unconcerned about the tests, at least one community civic organization, heretofore unheard from, recently expressed alarm about continuance of the program.

The scientists regard this apprehension generally as fallacious and far more of a threat to national security than the radiation itself. Several of them are scheduled to testify next week before the Joint Congressional Committee on Atomic Energy.

The test personnel—from the Atomic Energy Commission's laboratories in New Mexico and California, and its Civil Effects Division in Washington—have generally avoided involvement in the international debate.

Their assignment is to help maintain national superiority in nuclear weapons. Their basic contention in that the Nevada tests are essential to nuclear developmental work and that they are conducted well within long-established safety limits set by independent agencies for radiation work in industry, medicine and science.

The Nevada tests involve nuclear detonations of considerably less than 100-kiloton explosive force, meaning the equivalent of 100,000 tons of TNT, whereas the Pacific tests involve blast forces in the millions of tons, the scientists say.

Moreover, a test in Nevada costs only about one-third as much as it would if conducted in the Pacific. The difference is significant to the scientists mainly as an index of reduced complexity and time saved.

YARDSTICK SET

The National Academy of Sciences asserted last year that it was safe for an individual to receive, cumulatively, up to fifty roentgens during the first thirty years of his life, and up to another fifty during the following ten years.

The Nevada tests use a yardstick based on safety limits enunciated by the National Committee on Radiation Protection, an arm of the United States Bureau of Standards. This sets a maximum cumulative exposure total of 3.9 roentgens a year for people outside the test site.

The highest cumulative total for individuals generally in any community in the test region for the entire six-year period of atomic testing is said to be 4.3 roentgens at Bunkerville, Utah a town 100 miles southeast of the test area. This, the scientists contend, is infinitesimal, over a six-year period, compared to standard medical X-ray radiation doses, which may run fifteen roentgens or higher. It takes from twenty-five to fifty roentgens, received at one time to cause perceptible physical effects.

A few individuals within a 200-mile radius of the test site have received higher doses than the community levels, but none, so far as is known, has been exposed to more than seven or eight roentgens.

For the United States as a whole, the tests are calculated by scientists to have exposed people to considerably less than one roentgen.

In the six years of testing here there has not been a single court-established case of radiation injury to anyone outside the 640-square-mile test site— and only a half dozen cases of injury to people immediately involved in the test work.

In the only cases in which test damage has been established, the A.E.C. paid, without court action, $44,000 for shock damage to distant buildings, and $6,000 for sheep and horses that received secondary injuries on rangelands within twenty miles of the explosions.

What the scientists would like to see, in the public appraisal of nuclear testing, particularly in Nevada, is fuller appreciation of the balance of "calculated risk" that they maintain enters into any sensible consideration involving unknowns.

"Radiation can cause leukemia," on scientist explained this week. "But a person's chances of getting leukemia are something like 1 to 100,000. But the chances of a middle-aged person having something wrong with his heart are around 1 in 6. If he refuses to have a heart X-ray because of the possibility of getting leukemia, he's just plain silly."

"There's another risk to be calculated in connection with nuclear testing. That is long-range hazards, which are largely a matter of theory, against unpreparedness in the field of nuclear weapons. The casualties that could result from this aren't a matter of theory at all."

DOCUMENT 7.7 LINUS PAULING TO BARRY COMMONER, JUNE 11, 1957 SOURCE: AVA HELEN AND LINUS PAULING PAPERS, 1873–2013, OREGON STATE UNIVERSITY SPECIAL COLLECTIONS, BOX #5.002, FOLDER 2.1

June 11, 1957

Dear Barry:

I may try to get foreign scientists to sign the Appeal too.

Do you not think that it would be good to get more American scientists to sign? If you and other Washington University professions do, won't you go about sending out new copies for signatures? I suggest 10 October 1957 as deadline, to give some time during the Fall term.

Also, I suggest adding the material written below. I feel well pleased with the success of the Appeal.

Sincerely,
Linus Pauling

In a few days before, 1 June 1957, 2000 signatures were obtained, including the following:

(Here I copied the names at the bottom of p. 5 + on p. 6 of statement 7 June 1957 to Holifield, omitting those on printed form.)—sent by Mrs. Welf

[Barry—omit any of these that you want—add others from mimeographed list if you want.]

PHOTO 7.8 WILLIAM C. GEAGLEY I.D. PHOTO FROM MERCURY SECURITY ENTRY POINT, 1957

Source: William Geagley Collection on Nuclear Safety, UNLV Special Collections, MS-00792.

DOCUMENT 8.1 THE LITTLE GREEN BOOK, ATOMIC TESTS IN NEVADA, UNITED STATES ATOMIC ENERGY COMMISSION, MARCH 1957 SOURCE: WILLIAM GEAGLEY COLLECTION ON NUCLEAR SAFETY, UNLV SPECIAL COLLECTIONS, MS-00792

ATOMIC TESTING IN NEVADA

The Nevada Test Site of the U.S. Atomic Energy Commission is used periodically for experiments or tests involving nuclear detonations of relatively low yield (explosive energy).

Forty-five nuclear fission weapons, weapon prototypes, and experimental devices were fired at the Nevada Test Site from January 1951 to June 1955. They ranged in yield from less than 1 kiloton up to considerably less than 100 kilotons. (A kiloton is equivalent to 1,000 tons of TNT.)

Despite their relatively low yield, Nevada tests have clearly demonstrated their value to all national atomic weapons programs. They have made important contributions to the development of a whole family of weapons, including ones for defense against attack. Because of them our Armed Forces are stronger and our Civil Defense better prepared.

Each test fired in Nevada is justified, before it is scheduled, as to national need for the data sought. Each Nevada test has successfully added to scientific knowledge needed for development and use of atomic weapons, and needed to strengthen our defense against enemy weapons. Most tests have been used additionally for basic research, such as biological studies, which could be conducted only in the presence of a full scale nuclear detonation.

Conducting low-yield tests in Nevada, instead of in the distant Pacific, also has resulted in major savings in time, manpower, and money. The saving of time is particularly important because of its contribution to the Nation's defense capability.

PROTECTION OF THE PUBLIC

You people who live near Nevada Test Site are in a very real sense active participants in the Nation's atomic test program. You have been close observers of tests which have contributed greatly to building the defenses of our country and of the free world. Nevada tests have helped us make great progress in a few years, and have been a vital factor in maintaining the peace of the world.

Some of you have been inconvenienced by our test operations. Nevertheless, you have accepted them without fuss and without alarm. Your cooperation has helped achieve an unusual record of safety.

To our knowledge no one outside the test site has been hurt in six years of testing. Only one person, a test participant, has been injured seriously as a result of the 45 detonations. His was an eye injury from the flash of light received at a point relatively near ground zero inside the test site. Experience has proved the adequacy of the safeguards which govern Nevada test operations.

POTENTIAL EXPOSURE IS LOW

Any atomic detonation, even though small enough to be fired in Nevada, involves powerful forces. The effects of a detonation include flash, blast, and radioactive fallout. Your potential exposure to those effects will be low, and it can be reduced still further by your continued cooperation.

The low level of public exposure has been made possible by very close attention to a variety of on-site and off-site procedures.

Public protection began with selection of the site. Nevada Test Site was selected only after extensive studies of other possible locations. The testing site covers an area of more than 600 square miles, with an adjoining U.S. Air Force gunnery range of 4,000 square miles. The controlled areas are surrounded by wide expanses of sparsely populated land, providing optimum conditions for maintenance of safety.

EVERY TEST IS EVALUATED

Every test detonation in Nevada is carefully evaluated as to your safety before it is included in a schedule. Every phase of the operation is likewise studied from the safety viewpoint.

An advisory panel of experts in biology and medicine, blast, fallout, and meteorology is an integral part of the Nevada Test Organization. Before each nuclear detonation, a series of meetings is held at which this panel carefully weighs the question of firing with respect to assurance of your safety under the conditions then existing.

A complete weather unit is operated at the test site, drawing upon the extensive data available from the U.S. Weather Bureau and the U.S.A.F. Air Weather Service, plus additional weather stations ringing the test site. The data are evaluated up to one hour before shot time. A shot can be canceled at any time up to a few minutes before the scheduled detonation. In past Nevada test series, there have been more than 80 postponements due to forecasts of unfavorable weather at shot time or for the hours immediately thereafter.

Off-site radioactive fallout is the most critical test effect with regard to public health. You who live near the test site know that experience in each series and technical developments have brought improved controls and procedures for each series.

MINIMUM EXPOSURE IS GOAL

Past improvements include: Improved forecasting of wind speed and directions; improved methods of predicting fallout and blast intensity and location, including use of high-speed "electric brain" analog computers; reducing fallout by means such as yield limitations and increasing the height above ground of detonations; and intensified off-site radiological monitoring operations.

DOCUMENT 8.2 Q CLEARANCE FORM WITH EXECUTIVE ORDER NO. 10450 RESTRICTIONS SOURCE: WILLIAM GEAGLEY COLLECTION ON NUCLEAR SAFETY, UNLV SPECIAL COLLECTIONS, MS-00792

FEDERAL CIVIL DEFENSE ADMINISTRATION
NATIONAL HEADQUARTERS
BATTLE CREEK, MICHIGAN

April 25, 1957

Mr. William C. Geagley
Lansing, Michigan

Dear Mr. Geagley:

This is to inform you that you have been tentatively selected to participate in the FCDA sponsored Radiological Defense Operations Program which is one of the phases of Operation PLUMBBOB which will be conducted at the Nevada Test Site during the summer of 1957. You have been tentatively assigned to Project 36.1 and it is estimated that your arrival time at the Test Site will be June 8th and that you depart on June 30, 1957.

The following enclosed items should be filled out and returned as quickly as possible.

1. Personnel Data card
2. Badge Request card (fill in only two first lines)
3. AEC waiver
4. Medical statement

Should the response to the program exceed the maximum possible enrollment, an adjustment may be necessary to insure that we have as representative a distribution of the various geographical locations as possible. Confirmation of your participation in this program will be forwarded at the earliest possible date after receipt of the information requested.

Sincerely,

Hugh D. Ivey
Director
Program 36, CETG
Enclosures

***

FEDERAL CIVIL DEFENSE ADMINISTRATION
NATIONAL HEADQUARTERS
BATTLE CREEK, MICHIGAN

April 4, 1957

Dr. W. C. Geagley
Chief, Clinical Laboratory Division
Michigan Department of Agriculture
DeWitt Road
Lansing, Michigan

Dear Dr. Geagley:

Attached are the forms required in order that you may be granted a Class "Q" clearance from the Atomic Energy Commission. This clearance is necessary in order that you may have access to Restricted Data in connection with your activities for the Federal Civil Defense Administration in the forthcoming Tests in Nevada. The enclosed instruction sheet provides all information needed in completion of each form. Extra copies provided are for your personal files.

A self-addressed envelope, which requires no postage, is enclosed for your convenience.

Your cooperation in this matter will be appreciated.

Sincerely,

T. J. Harte
Director, Security Office

Attachments

PERSONNEL SECURITY QUESTIONNAIRE

INSTRUCTIONS: All sections must be completed. Write "None" when applicable. Type or print all answers. If space not adequate for complete answers, attach a supplemental sheet to this form. All addresses must show street number, street, city, and State.

1. NAME (Last, first, middle) _____

2. OTHER NAMES (Include maiden name, if married woman) _____

3. PRESENT   ADDRESS _____
   DATE _____

4. ALL OTHER ADDRESSES FOR PAST 15 YEARS _____
   DATE _____

5. DESCRIPTION: (Check which)   ☐ MALE   ☐ FEMALE
   RACE _____ HEIGHT _____ WEIGHT _____ COLOR
   EYES _____
   COLOR HAIR _____

6. (Check which)
   ☐ SINGLE   ☐ DIVORCED
   ☐ MARRIED   ☐ WIDOW(ER)

7. BIRTH DATE
   MONTH _____ DAY _____ YEAR _____
8. BIRTHPLACE (City, county, State, and country)
9. CITIZENSHIP: U. S. ☐ ALIEN ☐
   IF U. S. CITIZEN, INDICATE WHETHER:
   A. BY BIRTH ☐
   B. DERIVATIVE ☐
   DATE _____
   CERTIFICATE NO. _____
   PLACE _____
   (C) BY NATURALIZATION ☐
   PETITION NO. _____
   DATE _____
   CERTIFICATE NO. _____
   PLACE _____
   IF ALIEN, INDICATE ALIEN REGISTRATION NO. _____
   DATE OF ENTRY _____
   PORT OF ENTRY _____
10. DRAFT BOARD NUMBER AND ADDRESS WITH WHICH REG-
    ISTERED _____
11. SOCIAL SECURITY NO. _____
12. PERMANENT STATION, RANK, AND ADDRESS IF NOW IN
    MILITARY SERVICE _____
    _____

12A. MILITARY SERVICE (Past or present)
    SERIAL NOS. _____ BRANCH _____
    FROM (Yr.) _____ TO (Yr.) _____
    None _____ National _____
13. EDUCATION (All schools above elementary)
    NAME OF SCHOOL _____ ADDRESS _____ FROM (Yr.)
    _____ To (Yr.) _____ DEGREES _____
14. EMPLOYMENT (List ALL employment dates including present em-
    ployment and ALL dates and addresses when unemployed. If any of
    employments required AEC security clearance ("Q"), indicate the
    company or organization which requested the clearance. Give name
    or names under which employed if different from name now used.)
    DATE FROM _____ TO _____
    NAME OF EMPLOYER (COMPANY OR ORGANIZATION)
    _____
    TYPE OF WORK _____ ADDRESS (Where employed)
    _____
    REASON FOR LEAVING _____

15. FOREIGN COUNTRIES VISITED (Since 1930) (Exclusive of military service)
COUNTRY _____ DATE LEFT U.S.A. _____ DATE RETURNEDU.S.A._____PURPOSE_____

APPENDIX

Set forth below is a list of the organizations designated by the Attorney General pursuant to Executive Order No. 10450, as Totalitarian, Fascist, Communist, or Subversive, or as having adopted a policy of advocating or approving the commission of acts of force and violence to deny others their rights under the Constitution of the United States, or which seek to alter the form of Government of the United States by unconstitutional means.

Abraham Lincoln Brigade
Abraham Lincoln School, Chicago, Ill.
Action Committee to Free Spain Now
Alabama People's Educational Association (See Communist Political Association)
American Association for Reconstruction in Yugoslavia, Inc.
American Branch of the Federation of Greek Maritime Unions
American Christian Nationalist Party
American Committee for European Workers' Relief (See Socialist Workers Party)
American Committee for Protection of Foreign Born
American Committee for the Settlement of Jews in Birobidjan, Inc.
American Committee for Spanish Freedom
American Committee to Survey Labor Conditions in Europe
American Committee for Yugoslav Relief, Inc.
American Council for a Democratic Greece, formerly known as the Greek American Council; Greek American Committee for National Unity
American Council on Soviet Relations
American Croatian Congress
American Jewish Labor Council
American League against War and Fascism
American League for Peace and Democracy
American Lithuanian Workers Literary Association (Also known as Amerikos Lietuviu Darbininku Literaturos Draugija)
American National Labor Party
American National Socialist League
American National Socialist Party
American Nationalist Party

American Patriots, Inc.

American Peace Crusade

American Peace Mobilization

American Poles for Peace

American Polish Labor Council

American Polish League

American Rescue Ship Mission (A project of the United American Spanish Aid Committee)

American-Russian Fraternal Society

American Russian Institute, New York, also known as the American Russian Institute for Cultural Relations with the Soviet Union

American Russian Institute, Philadelphia

American Russian Institute of San Francisco

American Russian Institute of Southern California, Los Angeles

American Slav Congress

American Women for Peace

American Youth Congress

American Youth for Democracy

Armenian Progressive League of America

Associated Klans of America

Association of Georgia Klans

Association of German Nationals (Reichsdeutsche Vereinigung)

Association of Lithuanian Workers (Also known as Lietuviu Darbininku Susivienijimas)

Ausland-Organization der NSDAP, Overseas Branch of Nazi Party

Baltimore Forum

Black Dragon Society

Boston School for Marxist Studies, Boston, Mass.

Bridges-Robertson-Schmidt Defense Committee

Bulgarian American People's League of the United States of America

California Emergency Defense Committee

California Labor School, Inc., 321 Divisadero Street, San Francisco, Calif.

Carpatho-Russian People's Society

Central Council of American Women of Croatian Descent, also known as Central Council of American Croatian Women, National Council of Croatian Women

Central Japanese Association (Beikoku Chuo Nipponjin Kai)

Central Japanese Association of Southern California

Central Organization of the German-American National Alliance (Deutsche-Amerikanische Einheitsfront)

Cervantes Fraternal Society

China Welfare Appeal, Inc.

Chopin Cultural Center

Citizens Committee To Free Earl Browder

Citizens Committee for Harry Bridges

Citizens Committee of the Upper West Side (New York City)

Citizens Emergency Defense Conference

Citizens Protective League

Civil Rights Congress and its affiliated organizations, including:

    Civil Rights Congress for Texas

    Veterans against Discrimination of Civil Rights Congress of New York

    Civil Rights Congress of Texas (See Civil Rights Congress)

Columbians

Comite Coordinador Pro Republica Espanola

Committee to Aid the Fighting South

Committee for Constitutional and Political Freedom

Committee to Defend Marie Richardson

Committee for the Defense of the Pittsburgh Six

Committee for a Democratic Far Eastern Policy

Committee for Nationalist Action

Committee for the Negro in the Arts

Committee for Peace and Brotherhood Festival in Philadelphia

Committee for the Protection of the Bill of Rights

Committee to Uphold the Bill of Rights

Committee for World Youth Friendship and Cultural Exchange

Commonwealth College, Mena, Ark.

Communist Party, U.S.A., its subdivisions, subsidiaries, and affiliates

Communist Political Association, its subdivisions, subsidiaries, and affiliates, including:

    Alabama People's Educational Association

    Florida Press and Educational League

    Oklahoma League for Political Education

    People's Educational and Press Association of Texas

    Virginia League for People's Education

Congress of American Revolutionary Writers

Congress of American Women

Connecticut Committee to Aid Victims of the Smith Act

Connecticut State Youth Conference

Council on African Affairs

Council of Greek Americans

Council for Jobs, Relief, and Housing

Council for Pan-American Democracy

Croatian Benevolent Fraternity

Dai Nippon Butoku Kai (Military Virtue Society of Japan or Military Art Society of Japan)

Daily Worker Press Club

Daniels Defense Committee

Dante Alighieri Society (Between 1935 and 1940)

Dennis Defense Committee

Detroit Youth Assembly

Emergency Conference to Save Spanish Refugees (Founding Body of the North American Spanish Aid Committee)

Families of the Baltimore Smith Act Victims

Families of the Smith Act Victims

Federation of Italian War Veterans in the U.S.A., Inc. (Associazione Nazionale Combattenti Italiani, Federazione degli Stati Uniti d'America)

Finnish-American Mutual Aid Society

Florida Press and Educational League (See Communist Political Association)

Frederick Douglass Educational Center

Freedom Stage, Inc.

Friends of the New Germany (Freunde des Neuen Deutschlands)

Friends of the Soviet Union

Garibaldi American Fraternal Society

George Washington Carver School, New York City

German-American Bund (Amerikadeutscher Volksbund)

German-American Republican League

German-American Vocational League (Deutsche-Amerikanische Berufsgemeinschaft)

Harlem Trade Union Council

Hawaii Civil Liberties Committee

Heimuska Kai, also known as Nokubei Heieki Gimusha Kai, Zaibel Nihonjin, Heiyaku Gimusha Kai, and Zaibei Heimusha Kai (Japanese Residing in America Military Conscripts Association)

Hellenic-American Brotherhood

APPENDIX

This Appendix is an integral part of the Personnel Security Questionnaire of the U.S. Atomic Energy Commission

Executive Order 10450—Security requirements for Government employment The provisions of Executive Order 10450 of Apr. 27, 1953, appear at 18 FR 2489, 3 CFR, 1949-1953 Comp., p. 936, unless otherwise noted.

WHEREAS the interests of the national security require that all persons privileged to be employed in the departments and agencies of the Government, shall be reliable, trustworthy, of good conduct and character, and of complete and unswerving loyalty to the United States; and

WHEREAS the American tradition that all persons should receive fair, impartial, and equitable treatment at the hands of the Government requires that all persons seeking the privilege of employment or privileged to be employed in the departments and agencies of the Government be adjudged by mutually consistent and no less than minimum standards and procedures among the departments and agencies governing the employment and retention in employment of persons in the Federal service:

* * *

FEDERAL CIVIL DEFENSE ADMINISTRATION
NATIONAL HEADQUARTERS
BATTLE CREEK, MICHIGAN

May 6, 1958

Mr. William Carl Geagley
Lansing, Michigan

Dear Sir:

Attached herewith are three copies of an Atomic Energy Commission Security Termination Statement which it is requested that you sign in duplicate and return. The other copy is for your personal files.

This will cancel the "Q" clearance which you have held through FCDA for purposes of the 1957 Atomic Test Series. This cancellation is in accordance with AEC regulations since you will no longer require access to Restricted Data for this facility.

As you may know, the AEC grants "Q" clearance to each facility with which an individual is associated where his work will require access to Restricted Data. It is therefore possible that you have clearance with several facilities simultaneously. This cancellation through FCDA will not affect any "Q" clearance you may have with other facilities.

Enclosed for your convenience is a self-addressed envelope which requires no postage. Thank you for your cooperation in this matter.

Sincerely yours,

T. J. Harte
Director, Security Office

Enclosures

DOCUMENT 8.3 NTS BULLETIN PLUMBBOB, VOL. 1:23, FRIDAY, JUNE 21, 1957 SOURCE: WILLIAM GEAGLEY COLLECTION ON NUCLEAR SAFETY, UNLV SPECIAL COLLECTIONS, MS-00792

VOL. I, NO. 23
MERCURY, NEVADA
FRIDAY, JUNE 21, 1957

HOTTEST SPOT IN NTS

Did you know that ground zero in Test Area 9 is now the "hottest" spot at NTS? Sun suits and shorts are taboo in that location however, because it is not the heat that makes the area "Hot". The area is "radiologically hot". Protective clothing and Rad-Safe clearance is required for entry into that area. For latest information about Area 9, and all of the other "hot" spots at NTS, please consult the REECO Rad-Safe Division, Phone 8273.

PICNIC AREA NOW COMPLETE

Last Monday evening, June 17th, a dedicated group of men completed an excellent picnic area for all Mercury residents, located just 200 yards east of our city. This group of fourteen men, under the direction of their popular leader Bill Benner, call themselves the "Blue Hill Cork Club", and feel that they and others will occasionally enjoy barbecued meals under the stars. Without any fanfare or noise, this group obtained permission and scraped together lumber, shovels, charcoal, etc., and calmly built, in one evening, a lovely picnic spot. Their only request is that the area be used and left clean for the next users to enjoy. They have water, soap for dishes, tables, chairs, and have even erected a shelter from the sun. They have advised that barbecue materials and food can be obtained at the PX. Charter members of this group are - Bill Benner, Buck Buckman, Chuck Jordan, J. Pulse, Dave Cummings, Homer White, Gilson Reed, Jim Bittle, Bill Evans, Jack Cavanaugh, Hal Aronson, George Back, Bob Gangwer and Ed Shoemaker. Our thanks and appreciation to a swell bunch of guys. . . . .

WEARING APPAREL

Informal dress is quite acceptable and expected at Mercury. Shorts are permissible casual wearing apparel for both ladies and gents, provided they are worn with blouses or shirts. Ladies wearing brief sun top apparel and gentlemen without shirts should restrict this type clothing to their places of residence. It should not be worn, for example, to the cafeterias for meals.

POLKA & SQUARE DANCING

Recently, there has been a lot of interest in, and numerous requests for, polka and square dancing. We would like to hear from you folks who would like to take part in initiating a polka and square dancing program on Monday evenings. We have, here at Mercury, a professional square dance caller who has all the records, etc. If you don't know how to polka and square dance, there are a number of people here who can teach you. Learning is a lot of fun too. Let's hear from you. Call the Recreation Office, 9331.

GOLF DRIVING RANGE

An official opening of the Golf Driving range will be held at 5:30 PM, Monday, June 24. Everyone is cordially invited to attend this opening. THINK: Safety is no accident and has no quitting time.

DOCUMENT 8.4 GEAGLEY'S NOTES FROM RADIATION TRAINING AT NTS SOURCE: WILLIAM GEAGLEY COLLECTION ON NUCLEAR SAFETY, UNLV SPECIAL COLLECTIONS, DOE NNSA/NSO, NV0519243, MS-00792

Sky - Schenck - Training Branch KEEO-RADS

Natural Rad. Background.

Cosmic Rays   50 mR/yrs (males etc)

earth sources   70 mR/yr

own Bodies   20 mR/yr

=   140 mR/yr

Atom Tests etc.   1 mR/yr
                    141

Luminous Watch   40

X Ray teeth   500

Chests   1500

Shoes - Operation etc.   20000 mR/yr

N.T.S. - Tests year around problem

must know at all times Radiation intensity.

Rad. Safe.
   Supt

   SOS   Hanzel

m - PLB   Decon   T.R.   Log
                              Spassig.

DOCUMENT 8.5 DNA 6004F, SHOT SMOKY: A TEST OF THE PLUMBBOB SERIES, AUGUST 31, 1957 SOURCE: U.S. ATMOSPHERIC NUCLEAR WEAPONS TESTS NUCLEAR TEST PERSONNEL REVIEW

Force Special Weapons Center (AFSWC) and Exercise Desert Rock (EDR). AFSWC personnel flew the radioactive cloud sampling and tracking missions and were responsible for controlling air operations; EDR conducted troop tests to develop tactics for the nuclear battlefield.

1.1 THE SETTING FOR SMOKY[8]

In the early Saturday hours of 31 August 1957, several thousand men gathered at various observation and control points in the Nevada Test Site.[9] At 0445 the decision was made to detonate shot SMOKY at 0530 hours. The shot had been delayed three days by weather unfavorable to fallout. The latest meteorological data had been evaluated, advice from participating agencies had been considered, and all factors were deemed favorable. The Nevada Test Site had been secured and cleared of all unauthorized personnel. The nearest personnel were eight miles from the SMOKY test location and security guards manned stations and barricades on access roads to prevent unauthorized entry. Military and civilian observers, who had received training on procedures for observing the detonation, were ready at their respective observation posts. Survey teams were standing by to determine the extent of radioactive contamination as soon after the detonation as possible. Scientific project personnel were prepared to enter test areas and recover experiments. Military troops were ready to embark upon a tactical maneuver subsequent to the shot. The center of interest was the tower at the northern edge of the Nevada Test Site where the SMOKY nuclear device would be detonated.

The weeks preceding SMOKY had seen both preparation and delay. Originally planned for 19 August, SMOKY was not ready for firing until August 28, and then had been postponed twice due to weather conditions and the environmental effects of preceding nuclear tests. Even as late as 0445 on 31 August, the shot was postponed from 0500 to 0530 to provide

---

[8] The University of California Radiation Laboratory, which provided the nuclear device, chose to name its tests after mountains and mountain ranges.

[9] General description of the test site is drawn from reference 2. (All sources cited in the text are listed alphabetically by author and numbered in the Reference List, appended to this volume. The number given in the citation in the text is the number of the source document in the Reference List.)

time for collecting the weather data essential to predict fallout and to conduct supporting aircraft operations.

At the time of the test, approximately 5,800 men occupied two settlements at the Nevada Test Site (Camp Mercury and Camp Desert Rock). An estimated 2,800 men were present at Camp Mercury, a permanent installation located at the southern boundary of the NTS (Area 23), set up by the AEC in 1951 to provide office and living quarters for its temporary and permanent personnel participating in test activities. Personnel at Camp Mercury were responsible for performing the AEC and DOD's Armed Forces Special Weapons Project activities at the Nevada Test Site.

Another 3,000 military men occupied Camp Desert Rock, a temporary encampment which was maintained by a small garrison (9). Sixth Army troops from Camp Irwin, California, reopened and resupplied Camp Desert Rock to accommodate exercise troops during the various weapons tests. Personnel at Camp Desert Rock were responsible for conducting military maneuvers, training, and a few technical projects in an area set aside for them by the AEC Test Manager so as not to interfere with other test activities. In the weeks and hours preceding the detonation, certain of these troops prepared for the maneuvers they would conduct immediately after the shot.

At the shot tower, pre-shot preparations were completed well in advance of the firing. In order to record the effects within the fireball, AFSWP personnel had extended cables from the top of the tower to distant points on the ground; they had also installed ground cables running from the base of the tower like the spokes of a wheel. These cables were instrumented to measure such phenomena as blast effects over uneven terrain and neutron flux during initial radiation. Military equipment and field emplacements were located at varying distances around the tower so that nuclear effects on these items could be studied. In the hours after the detonation, when the levels of radiation permitted, scientific project teams re-entered these areas to retrieve and read the instruments. At test time, however, all areas out to a radius of about eight miles were cleared of personnel.

The shot was to be fired from the control center (CP-1) in Area 6, about 15 miles from the SMOKY tower. The control board in this center could avert the firing of the device up to the last moment. Even after a weapon was armed and readied for firing, and the automatic sequence for the firing was in progress, the instrumentation at the control board could stop the shot. The control center building had a strategic location, on a rise with a view of Yucca Lake to the north and Frenchman Lake to the south. A landing strip on the dry bed of Yucca Lake made the control center readily accessible by air, and the nearby Mercury highway made it accessible by ground vehicle. In addition, CP-1 provided storage maintenance and supply facilities and was a safe area for operations.

SMOKY was fired at 0530 hours. While the predicted yield for shot SMOKY was 45 kilotons, the output as actually measured was 43.8 kilotons. After the firing, the first step was the radiological safety survey to map contaminated areas around ground zero. Then the scientific and military teams could begin their planned activities. The succeeding portions of this report will specify those agencies present, their goals and responsibilities, and will describe the post-shot activities.

1.2 OVERVIEW OF DEPARTMENT OF DEFENSE PARTICIPATION

DOD was actively involved in two organizations — the Nevada Test Organization (NTO) and Exercise Desert Rock (EDR) — which had been set up at the Nevada Test Site to execute the plans for Operation PLUMBBOB.

The Nevada Test Organization was a joint AEC/DOD organization headed by an AEC Test Manager and containing elements of the AEC, DOD/AFSWP, and the FCDA. Functions of the NTO were to fire the planned shots and to perform the scientific weapons-development tests, military effects tests, and civilian tests. DOD personnel were involved at almost every level in the NTO. Military and scientific personnel were assigned to staff activities essential to testing the nuclear device itself and were included in NTO staff offices which coordinated various DOD operations. The AEC, FCDA, and AFSWP technical projects were accomplished by technical groups from various laboratories or organizations, both civilian and military. These technical group activities were coordinated by the Test Director, who was a member of the Test Manager's NTO staff. . . . Each state was requested to nominate two representatives and two alternates. Proper scheduling of applicants was difficult owing to shot-schedule changes, security clearances, and late receipt of nominees' names. Many were asked to attend a course at a time that was not convenient to them. These and other difficulties resulted in combining the May and June classes of Project 36.2 and the June class of Project 36.1 into one class. This class met from June 17 through 28.

The date for conducting the combined projects was determined primarily by the status of security clearances for participants and by funds for fiscal year 1957. The Restricted-Data security-clearance requirement for Project 36.1 was based on joint participation with projects of Program 35. Program 35 withdrew from June participation, allowing Project 36.1 to reduce clearance requirements to Limited Restricted Data. There were 35 participants of the combined project waiting for clearances the first week in June.

On June 7, all participants were mailed Government Transportation Requests and were advised that those not having security clearances could expect notification of clearance momentarily. Secret clearance for all nominees had been completed by June 12, and on June 10, 11, and 12, the 35 nominees were advised that security clearances had been completed.

Twenty-one participants, cleared for access to Restricted Data, were invited to attend the August–September session of Project 36.1. Sixteen participants accepted the invitations and arrived at the NTS on August 7.

DOCUMENT 8.6 CIVIL EFFECTS TEST GROUP, PROJECTS 36.1 AND 36.2, OPERATIONAL PLAN, MONDAY, JUNE, 17, 1957

SOURCE: WILLIAM GEAGLEY COLLECTION ON NUCLEAR SAFETY, UNLV SPECIAL COLLECTIONS, MS-00792

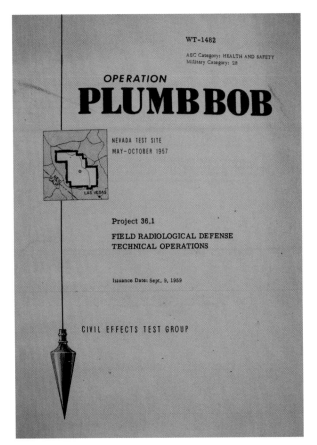

INTRODUCTION

1.1 OBJECTIVES

Project 36.1 was conducted to give practical training and to provide field experience in radiological defense to federal, state, and local civil defense officials. Project activities included monitoring techniques for performing radiation surveys on foot, in vehicles, and in aerial flights. The participants assisted in evaluating standard Federal Civil Defense Administration

(FCDA) instruments and in conducting beta-gamma absorption studies by using instrumentation designed for Project 35.4.

1.2 BACKGROUND

The first FCDA participation in nuclear test operations was in the fall of 1951; it was limited to a brief course in radiological monitoring for FCDA staff members. During the spring of 1952 the FCDA participated in Operation Tumbler-Snapper by conducting a study of radiological defense. The purpose was to familiarize FCDA personnel with radiological safety operations and problems of radiological contamination resulting from atomic detonations.

After these tests plans were made for a training program for state and local radiological defense personnel at the Nevada Test Site (NTS) during the 1953 series. The FCDA submitted a proposal for participation in a training project to the Atomic Energy Commission for these tests.

The first training project was conducted for three weeks during the 1953 series. Fourteen persons attended; each person was recruited by the FCDA from state and local civil defense organizations. The project was successful, and the FCDA decided to continue this type of field training in future test series.

During Operation Teapot (1955) at the NTS, the FCDA sponsored its second training project. The 24 participants were required to have radiological defense responsibilities and to have a background of knowledge and training in radiological health, safety, or defense. This project, which lasted about three and one-half weeks, was successful. However, the recommendations were that in the next series of continental tests consideration be given to conducting two separate courses for participants with varying backgrounds, and a proposal was submitted to the Civil Effects Test Group (CETG) for the inclusion of such a program in the next continental tests in which the FCDA would participate.

In addition to Project 36.1, there were two other training projects, Projects 36.2 and 36.5. They were designed to give more-advanced field training in radiological defense operations and technical experiments. Project 36.2 was titled Radiological Defense Monitoring and Data Evaluation, and Project 36.5 was titled Radiological Defense Training Operations.

The program for recruiting state and local radiological defense personnel for the training projects began Feb. 27, 1957, and was conducted through the FCDA regional offices.

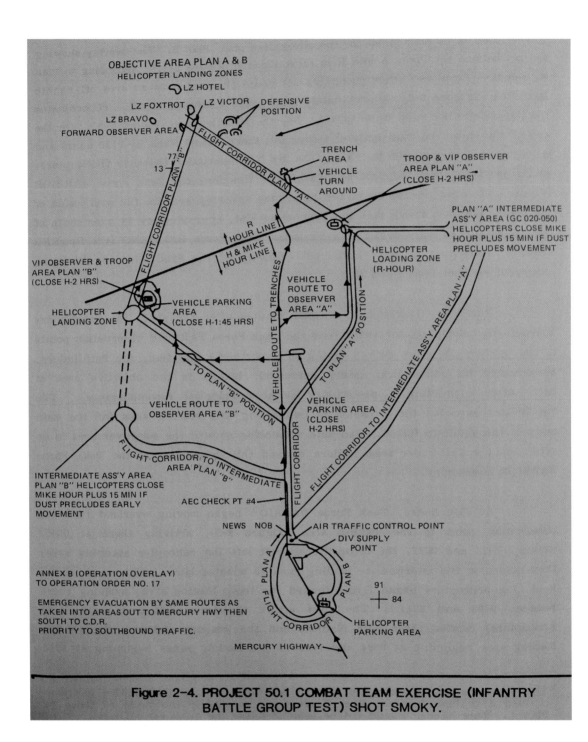

Figure 2-4. PROJECT 50.1 COMBAT TEAM EXERCISE (INFANTRY BATTLE GROUP TEST) SHOT SMOKY.

DOCUMENT 8.7 GEAGLEY FOLLOW-UP RADIATION DOCUMENTS,
DEAR MRS. GEAGLEY SOURCE: WILLIAM GEAGLEY COLLECTION ON NUCLEAR
SAFETY, UNLV SPECIAL COLLECTIONS, MS-00792

DEPARTMENT OF HEALTH, EDUCATION, AND WELFARE
PUBLIC HEALTH SERVICE
CENTER FOR DISEASE CONTROL
ATLANTA, GEORGIA 30333
TELEPHONE: (404) 633-3311

July 19, 1977

Mrs. William C. Geagley
3621 Cambrey Drive
Lansing, Michigan 48906

Dear Mrs. Geagley:

Thank you for contacting us regarding personnel involved in nuclear testing in Nevada. The Cancer Branch, Chronic Diseases Division, Bureau of
Epidemiology, Center for Disease Control, is primarily interested in developing a cohort of men exposed to a particular atomic device detonated on
August 31, 1957 (Smoky). If the data show these men were at increased risk
for development of malignancies, we may study other groups of men exposed in some of the other tests for confirmation. However, until the
Smoky study is completed, we will hold all material related to other tests
for future study.

Thank you for your interest.

Sincerely yours,

Glyn G. Caldwell, M.D.
Deputy Chief, Cancer Branch
Chronic Diseases Division
Bureau of Epidemiology

***

May 19, 1959

To: Participants in Program 36, CETG, Operation Plumbbob
From: Director, Program 36, CETG, Operation Plumbbob
Subject: Total Dose Recorded for Operation Plumbbob

Below is the reported total dose resulting from your participation in Program 36, Operation Plumbbob.

Name: William C. Geagley
Total Dose: 0 mr

Since, in many cases, partial doses resulting from film badge measurements were punched into cards and machine tabulated to obtain the total dose, there may be an occasional error.

If you have reason to believe that an error has been made in your reported dose, please inform me, together with the reasons, so that the information can be furnished to the AEC people for inclusion in their study of this approach to dosimetry records.

Hugh D. Ivey
OCDM BC 32480

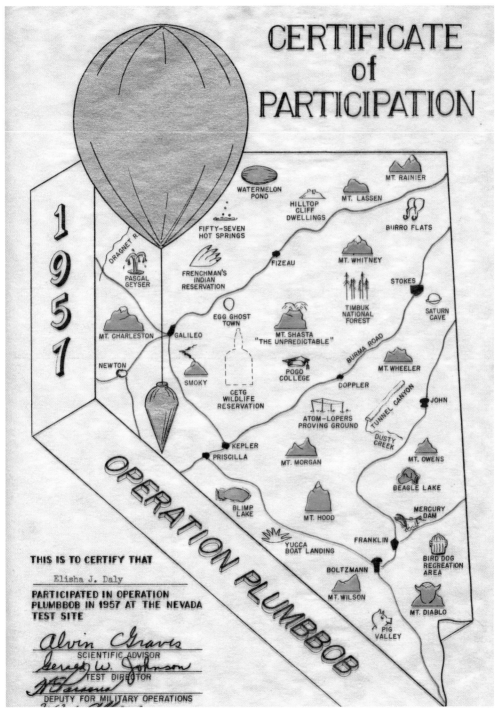

PHOTO 8.8 PLUMBBOB CERTIFICATE *Source:* Marie McMillian Collection, UNLV Special Collections.

DOCUMENT 9.1 RADIATION EXPOSURE COMPENSATION ACT
(RECA), 1990 SOURCE: U.S. DEPARTMENT OF JUSTICE HTTP://WWW.JUSTICE.GOV/
CIVIL/COMMON/RECA.HTML, LAST ACCESSED 08/09/16

RADIATION EXPOSURE COMPENSATION ACT (RECA)

NOTICE: Clarification of Definition after the Supreme Court's Decision in
United States v. Windsor. The Radiation Exposure Compensation Act uses
the following definition: "the spouse of an individual is a wife or husband
of that individual who was married to that individual for at least one year
immediately before the death of that individual." 42 U.S.C. § 2210 note,
Sec. 6(c)(4)(C) (2011); 28 C.F.R. § 79.2(0). Consistent with the Supreme
Court's decision in United States v. Windsor, the Department of Justice
clarifies that this definition, as well as any reference to "marriage" or "married" in the Department's implementing regulations, 28 C.F.R. Part 79,
will be interpreted to include same-sex spouses. All spouses, regardless of
gender, must establish their eligibility to file a claim as set forth in 28 C.F.R.
§ 79.71(e), which lists documents that may be used to establish a marriage
and includes documents issued by the jurisdiction in which the marriage
was celebrated, such as a public record or certificate of marriage.

PROGRAM SUMMARY

The United States conducted nearly 200 atmospheric nuclear weapons development tests from 1945 to 1962. Essential to the nation's nuclear weapons development was uranium mining and processing, which was carried
out by tens of thousands of workers. Following the tests' cessation in 1962
many of these workers filed class action lawsuits alleging exposure to
known radiation hazards. These suits were dismissed by the appellate
courts. Congress responded by devising a program allowing partial restitu-
tion to individuals who developed serious illnesses after exposure to radiation released during the atmospheric nuclear tests or after employment in
the uranium industry: the Radiation Exposure Compensation Act (the Act,
or RECA), 42 U.S.C. § 2210 note (2006), was passed on October 5, 1990.
The Act's scope of coverage was broadened in 2000.

The Act presents an apology and monetary compensation to individuals who contracted certain cancers and other serious diseases:

- following their exposure to radiation released during the atmospheric
  nuclear weapons tests, or
- following their occupational exposure to radiation while employed in
  the uranium industry during the Cold War arsenal buildup.

This unique statute was designed to serve as an expeditious, low-cost alternative to litigation. Significantly, RECA does not require claimants to establish causation. Rather, claimants qualify for compensation by establishing the diagnosis of a listed compensable disease after working or residing in a designated location for a specific period of time. The Act provides compensation to individuals who contracted one of 27 medical conditions. It covers all states where uranium was mined and processed, as well as specified counties in Nevada, Utah, and Arizona, where significant fallout from the atmospheric nuclear testing was measured.

The U.S. Attorney General established the Radiation Exposure Compensation Program within the Constitutional and Specialized Tort Litigation Section in April 1992. The DOJ promulgated regulations for carrying out the program that permit use of existing records so claims could be resolved reliably, objectively, and non-adversarially, with little administrative cost to either the individual filing the RECA claim or the United States government. The initial 1992 regulations were updated in 1997 and revised on March 23, 2004.

RECA establishes lump sum compensation awards for individuals who contracted specified diseases in three defined populations:

Uranium miners, millers, and ore transporters – $100,000; "Onsite participants" at atmospheric nuclear weapons tests – $75,000; and individuals who lived downwind of the Nevada Test Site ("downwinders") – $50,000.

Although the Four Corners Region (Utah, Colorado, New Mexico, and Arizona) residents have filed the majority of RECA claims, the program has awarded compensation to individuals residing in each state, as well as several foreign countries.

Indian Country. The claimant population includes many Native American tribes. The Program regularly cooperates with members of the Navajo, Hopi, Yavapai Apache, and Spokane nations. The Program has also visited more than a dozen reservations to meet with tribal leaders and assist members filing RECA claims. The map below illustrates the areas covered by the Act.

RECA COVERED AREAS

The Act describes three broad areas of application, and within each, specific geographic limits are defined.

Uranium Worker States: Arizona, Colorado, Idaho, New Mexico, North Dakota, Oregon, South Dakota, Texas, Utah, Washington, and Wyoming. The dates of coverage are from January 1, 1942, and ending on December 31, 1971.

Onsite Participants: Pacific Test Sites, Nevada Test Site, South Atlantic Test Site, Trinity Test Site, any designated location within a naval shipyard, air force base, or other official government installation where ships, aircraft or other equipment used in an atmospheric nuclear detonation were decontaminated; or any designated location used for the purpose of monitoring fallout from an atmospheric nuclear test conducted at the Nevada Test Site. "Atmospheric detonations of nuclear devices" means only those tests conducted by the United States prior to January 1, 1963.

Downwinder Areas: in the State of Utah, the counties of Beaver, Garfield, Iron, Kane, Millard, Piute, San Juan, Sevier, Washington, and Wayne; in the State of Nevada, the counties of Eureka, Lander, Lincoln, Nye, White Pine, and that portion of Clark County that consists of townships 13 through 16 at ranges 63 through 71; and in the State of Arizona, the counties of Apache, Coconino, Gila, Navajo, Yavapai, and that part of Arizona that is north of the Grand Canyon. The dates of coverage are from January 21, 1951, and ending on October 31, 1958; and from June 30, 1962, and ending on July 31, 1962.

INTER-AGENCY RADIATION NETWORK

Today, the RECA Program is at the center of a broad inter-agency network that comprises the comprehensive federal radiation compensation system. The Department of Labor processes claims filed under a compensation program created by the Energy Employees Occupational Illness Compensation Program Act (EEOICPA), 42 U.S.C. §§ 7384 et seq. (2006). This program pays uranium workers (or their eligible survivors) who were approved for compensation under Section 5 of RECA an additional $50,000 and future medical benefits related to the condition for which they were approved for compensation under RECA. In addition to the $50,000 compensation noted above, RECA Section 5 claimants may be entitled to compensation and benefits pursuant to Part E of EEOICPA. For more information, please review the Department of Labor's Office of Workers' Compensation Programs website at www.dol.gov/owcp/. The RECA Program works closely with DOL to coordinate this additional compensation.

The RECA Program also relies on cooperation from the Departments of Veterans Affairs, Energy, and Defense to determine the eligibility and compensation available to onsite participant claimants under RECA. Finally, the Radiation Exposure Screening and Education Program (RESEP), administered by the Department of Health and Human Services' Health Resources Services Administration, provides grants for education, prevention, and early detection of radiogenic cancers and diseases. RESEP has awarded grants to seven clinics in Nevada, Colorado, Utah, Arizona, Washington, and New Mexico. In addition to its outreach and educational programs, the RESEP clinics provide medical screening for specified compensable diseases under RECA, conduct follow-up services, make referrals to medical specialists, and assist with RECA and EEOICPA claims processing by providing necessary medical documentation.

RECA UPDATES

ONSITE PARTICIPANT INQUIRIES

Since 2012, the Radiation Exposure Compensation Program has processed an increased number of claims from individuals filing under the Onsite Participant provisions of the Radiation Exposure Compensation Act. Many of those claims were filed by individuals serving in Japan after the atomic bombing of Hiroshima and Nagasaki; other claims were filed by World War II veterans stationed in the Pacific Theater. Notably, the Act's coverage is limited to the atmospheric nuclear testing program conducted by the United States that followed the war. Also, the Act only provides compensation for an individual who has contracted a "covered" cancer following their exposure to radiation.

The U.S. Department of Veterans Affairs offers a benefits program for service members who participated in the Hiroshima and Nagasaki operations or who were part of the Japanese occupation forces following World War II. More information about that program can be found at: http://www.benefits.va.gov/compensation/claims-postservice-exposure sionizing_radiation.asp

For a full description of the claim categories and requirements for compensation under the Act, please see the RECA Claimant Categories Summary. Claim forms are also available at the link provided.

It is helpful if specific information can be provided regarding the test site location, assignment of duties, and a description of duties for the service member. This would include a DD-214 or other relevant service report.

Because of the significant number of calls to our toll free line, you may have to leave a message. We will return every call we receive and the Program appreciates your interest in this unique statute. Please feel free to call this line at 1-800-729-7327. If a RECA staff member is not immediately available, you will be directed to a voice mailbox. Your telephone call will be returned as soon as possible.

You may also leave an e-mail message at the following email address: civil.reca@usdoj.gov

EXPENSES AND COSTS UNDER THE RADIATION EXPOSURE COMPENSATION ACT

In light of the Federal Circuit Court decision in Hackwell v. United States, 491 F.3d 1229 (10th Cir. 2007), the Justice Department no longer enforces the regulation concerning attorney fees whereby attorneys are prohibited from receiving reimbursement for expenses and costs in addition to the statutory fee limits, pursuant to 28 C.F.R. § 79.74(b). Accordingly, attorneys who represent clients under the Radiation Exposure Compensation Act may receive reimbursement for expenses and costs related to the claim, in addition to the statutory attorney fee. On October 23, 2008, the Department published a Notice in the Federal Register (73 F.R. 63196) regarding its regulation concerning attorney's fees and costs.

POLICY GUIDANCE REGARDING THE COMBINATION OF PERIODS OF EMPLOYMENT FOR MINERS, MILLERS, AND ORE TRANSPORTERS

It has been the Department's practice to permit claimants to combine periods of employment as miners, millers, and ore transporters to meet the statutory one-year duration of employment requirement. For all three categories of uranium workers (mining, milling, and ore transporting), the Act specifies six common diseases: primary cancer of the lung, fibrosis of the lung, pulmonary fibrosis, cor pulmonale related to fibrosis of the lung, silicosis, and pneumoconiosis. Therefore, in cases involving these six illnesses, the Act's exposure criteria can be satisfied by combining periods of employment that include mining, milling, and ore transporting. For millers and ore transporters (but not miners), the Act specifies two additional compensable diseases: primary renal cancer and chronic renal disease including nephritis and kidney tubal tissue injury. In cases involving these two illnesses, the Act's exposure criteria can be satisfied by combining periods of employment that include only milling and ore transporting.

CONTACT THE RADIATION EXPOSURE COMPENSATION PROGRAM

Contact the RECA Program by telephone:
Telephone: 1-800-729-RECP (1-800-729-7327)

Contact the RECA Program by U.S. Postal Service:
U.S. Department of Justice
Radiation Exposure Compensation Program
P.O. Box 146
Ben Franklin Station
Washington, DC 20044-0146

Contact RECA by e-mail:
Civil.RECA@usdoj.gov

DOCUMENT 9.2 DOE TOUR GUIDE BOOK, 1980S SOURCE: NATIONAL
ATOMIC TESTING MUSEUM, EPHEMERA COLLECTIONS

VEGETATION

Joshua trees, a member of the Yucca family found in most of the southwestern states, are numerous in this area and are present on the Test Site at
lower-middle elevations. The Joshua tree is the largest of the Yuccas and is
characteristic of the Mohave Desert. Mormon pioneers named this species
Joshua because its shape mimics a person praying with uplifted arms, referring to the biblical leader pointing the way to a promised land. Other
vegetation includes: grasses and numerous flowering desert plants, tumbleweed, sagebrush, and creosote bush. Juniper and pinion grow at the higher
elevations, especially on Rainier and Pahute Mesas on the NTS above
4,000 feet. Tumbleweed grows in abundance in areas where the soil has
been disturbed by our activities.

WILDLIFE ON THE TEST SITE

Wildlife on the NTS ranges from kangaroo rats to mule deer, from centi-
pedes to rattlesnakes, and from bats to turkey vultures. It is not uncom-
mon to see an occasional coyote, bobcat, wild horse, or rabbit during your
tour. All of these live on the NTS and thrive, largely because it is a job
dismissal offense to molest them and hunting is not permitted on the NTS.
More than 30 different birds have been identified on the Test Site, including robins, eagles, hawks, gambel quail, and chukars.

EARLY INHABITANTS OF NTS AREA

The first white man believed to have traveled any portion of the present test
site was Peter Ogden who may have crossed the northern portion of the site
in 1826. However, evidence of early cultures dating back some 5,000 to
10,000 years have been found. The Paiute Indians lived in the area and
numerous campsites have been found around natural springs. The Paiutes
and Shoshonean Indians lived off the land and subsisted on pinion nuts,
acorns, cactus fruits, or any animals they could kill. Life was hard and it
has been said that these Indians would eat anything which did not eat
them first.

HISTORICAL MINING SUMMARY
The Nevada Test Site was occupied by Paiute Indians at the time of their first known outside contact in 1849. More recent historical use of the NTS area primarily consisted of mining, grazing, and hunting. Two inactive mining districts, Oak Spring and Wahmonie, lie in or partially within the NTS. The Oak Spring Mining area was in the northeast corner of the test site, and included at least two on-site properties: the Climax Mine and the Crystal Mine.

HISTORY OF NEVADA TEST SITE

President Truman established the NTS in December 1950 as the nation's on-continent nuclear weapons testing area. Prior to 1950, most weapons tests were conducted in the Pacific This was costly, time-consuming, and logistically difficult. The NTS was originally called the Nevada Proving Grounds and consisted of 680 square miles, about half the present size. Additional land was added to the site in 1958, 1961, and 1964 and, with the acquisition of Pahute Mesa through a memorandum of agreement with the U.S. Department of Defense in 1967, the test site reached its present size of about 1,350 square miles, larger than the state of Rhode Island (1,250 square miles). The site was chosen because of its climate, low surrounding population density, and minimal risk to public safety and security because of the buffer zones consisting of the Nellis AFB bombing and gunnery range to the west, north, and east of NTS. The Nellis AFB range consists of 4,120 square miles. The 30 by 50-mile NTS is too large to be fenced. However, it is protected by roving security patrols, electronic detection equipment, and guardposts in classified areas. The first test shot was conducted on January 27, 1951.

TREATIES AND TEST FACTS

Since July 1962, all NTS weapons tests have been conducted underground. This is a result of the Limited Test Ban Treaty signed in Moscow on August 5, 1963. One hundred atmospheric tests were conducted at the NTS. Under terms of the 1974 Threshold Test Ban Agreement with Russia, tests are limited to a maximum yield of 150 kilotons. Total announced tests conducted at the NTS since the signing of the treaty is 454 as of December 13, 1986.

The largest atmospheric test conducted at the NTS was the 74-kiloton HOOD shot, fired in 1957 at Yucca Flat from a balloon at an altitude of 1,500 feet.

The 44-kiloton test, named SMOKY, was fired from a 700-foot tower on August 31, 1957.

The first nuclear test, named ABLE, was fired January 27, 1951. It was a one-kiloton device dropped from an Air Force plane at Frenchman Flat.

FORWARD AREAS

A mountain range separates Mercury from the main testing areas to the north. Just north of the mountain range lies Frenchman Flat, used extensively in the early days of testing and is now home for the liquified gaseous fuels spill test facility. Farther north are the underground testing areas Yucca Flat and Pahute Mesa. The NTS is not fenced. However, roving security guards, often using four-wheel vehicles, patrol the test site. Security areas are fenced and protected with armed guards and electronic security measures.

THE NUCLEAR DETERRENCE

Nuclear weapons have deterred war. We have not gone to war in Europe since 1945. Nuclear weapons *have* been the cornerstone of our national defense policy. That policy has been supported by every President since Truman and has had the backing of Congress continuously since 1945. Nevertheless, arms control and reduction—both conventional and nuclear—are desirable because any imbalance in strengths can lead to war. The cost of maintaining a strong nuclear deterrent and conducting the nuclear weapons testing program is substantially cheaper than the cost of maintaining a large standing military force. Were it not for the nuclear deterrent, this country probably would have to resort to mandatory military service to meet manpower needs.

AREA 3 WEAPONS EFFECTS TEST ON RESIDENCES
ITEM: Two Frame Two-Story Houses
EVENT: Annie, Upshot-Knothole Series
DATE: March 17, 1953; KILOTONS: 16
GROUND ZERO: 3,500 feet and 7,500 feet
OVERPRESSURE: Five lbs. per sq. inch and 1.7 lbs. per sq. inch
TYPE SHOT: Tower, 300 feet
RESULTS: The house 3,500 feet from ground zero was demolished. The first story disintegrated and the badly damaged second story crashed down on the remains of the first story. The house 7,500 feet from ground zero

was badly damaged inside; windows and doors were broken; exterior walls slightly damaged.

AREA 12 CAMP

The Area 12 camp can house approximately 600 people overnight. Many persons working at the northwestern end of NTS choose to live here during the week rather than commute the 220-mile round trip each day to Las Vegas.

The area has a cafeteria seating 280 persons, recreation hall, theater, heavy-duty equipment repair shop, and other support facilities.

EPA EXPERIMENTAL FARM (AREA 15)

The bioenvironmental experimental farm, operated about 16 years for DOE through an agreement with the U.S. Environmental Protection Agency (EPA), was used to conduct radionuclide uptake studies on various farm animals and crops. Cowboys herded beef cattle in areas contaminated by atmospheric nuclear detonations. The herd grazed those ranges for more than two decades without detrimental effect. In cooperation with the Nevada Department of Fish and Game, deer and other desert wildlife were periodically sampled. No adverse effects have been found. The farm was closed on December 30, 1981, because no more useful data was being obtained.

RADIATION COMPENSATION

There is documented evidence that certain elements of the population living in downwind sectors from the Nevada Test Site were exposed to elevated levels of radiation as the result of fallout. There is no evidence that any of the affected individuals were exposed to high levels of radiation.

The Task Force on Compensation for Radiation-Related Illnesses concluded that in the downwind population of 172,000, the total number of cancers which might be related to radioactive fallout is in the order of 9 to 96, of which 3 to 32 might be fatal. Some 35,000 to 45,000 cancer cases would be expected in this population without the added radiation exposure. Of these, some 25,000 to 30,000 would be fatal. The uncertainties in the number of radiation-related cancers were due to uncertainties such as the population dose and the risk coefficients of cancer induction by radiation. The basic point, however, is that the incidence of cancer in the downwind population that may be due to atmospheric testing is very small.

The basic problem boils down to finding some scientific way to establish that low levels of radiation cause cancers and that fallout was the source of the exposure to the radiation. The decision will always be subjective and will likely be designed to err in favor of the individual. If, from the estimated population of 172,000, a few tens of people were judged to be eligible for compensation, that would be an equitable solution.

DOE has taken the position that people who were indeed "injured" as a result of testing are entitled to and should be compensated. We believe that our work in Nevada (the Off-site Radiation Exposure Review Project) will provide, within a year or so, sufficient scientific evidence to arrive at a just solution.

Another DOE project is assembling in one location all the nonclassified documents dealing with off-site fallout. This collection is available to independent researchers, potential legal adversaries, or members of the public who may wish to review the records to make their own evaluations. Over 90,000 documents have been cataloged and are available for public review at the Coordination and Information Center at 3084 South Highland Drive, Las Vegas, Nevada.

DOCUMENT 9.3 GLADWIN HILL, "LAS VEGAS IS MORE THAN 'THE STRIP'" SOURCE: *THE NEW YORK TIMES*, MARCH 15, 1958

Blinded by the casinos' neon glitter, many a tourist fails to see the important industrial, scientific and other aspects of the Nevada resort.
By GLADWIN HILL

GLADWIN HILL, head of The Times Los Angeles bureau, covers a wide territory, in one part of which the palms, neons and industries of Las Vegas recently have sprouted.

LAS VEGAS, Nevada—MOST of the 8,000,000 people who annually stream through this neon-lighted oasis in the Nevada desert to gamble, gourmandize and gawk leave with just one mental picture: garish architecture, palm trees, dazzling electric signs, heaps of chips and silver dollars, bursts of applause punctuating a never-ending cavalcade of entertainment—a gewgaw setting for the world's largest, permanent non-floating crap game.

Actually, this is a reasonably fair impression of Las Vegas' most famous feature—the two-mile stretch of U.S. 91 known as the "Strip," almost solidly lined with casino-hotels and other centers of amusement. One in a thousand visitors may know other aspects of the community; the rest would, in fact, be surprised that Las Vegas has other faces.

That it has is attested in a number of ways, not necessarily meaningful to the tourist eye. A light blinks all night atop a downtown office building—sometimes blue, sometimes red—and that has significance for hundreds of residents. Jet planes roar overhead and certain people are interested. A local newspaper carries a headline with seemingly cryptic initials in it, but they are well recognized. In a supermarket a surprisingly large number of pretty legs perambulate the aisles. A smog that can only betoken important industry blankets a near-by valley.

These are all clues to the other facets of Las Vegas, so ramified and so spread out geographically that the Chamber of Commerce in recent years has felt moved to talk not in terms of "Las Vegas" or "Greater Las Vegas" or even "Clark County" but "Southern Nevada Valley" or, better yet, "Southern Nevada."

***

THE light that blinks—red or blue—is on a flagpole on a one-story building downtown. On the door of the building is written "Atomic Energy Commission" and the light signals whether within a few hours there will be another nuclear explosion at the A. E. C.'s desert proving ground north of the city. Its message is for newspaper men, interested citizenry and the thousands of A. E. C. personnel who become part of the Las Vegas community for several months during atomic tests.

The tests seldom impinge physically on the city, even to the extent of vibrations. But atoms have become a big business for Las Vegas. Mercury, as the test base is called—sixty-five miles away across mostly uninhabited desert—now represents a taxpayers' investment of more than $20,000,000 in permanent facilities. More millions are being spent on the development, at adjacent Jackass Flats, of facilities for testing nuclear-propelled rockets. Each atomic explosion in itself represents an outlay of a million dollars or so, much of it in quickly "expended" construction.

When the atomic tests started here, seven years and sixty-nine explosions ago, the top test personnel lived in town. Even such an august figure as Dr. Henry DeWolf Smyth, the academic "elder statesman" of atomic fission, could be seen on occasion around the gaming tables. Now, with the Mercury base in operation, and Las Vegas' resort area nearly doubled in size, the atomic folk are less conspicuous. But their presence is felt no less. A good deal of the multi-million-dollar payrolls from the test activity pours into Las Vegas. During test projects, the highway between Las Vegas and Mercury becomes a round-the-clock breakneck speedway of trucks and commuting workmen.

In addition to the A. E. C. facilities, involving upward of 5,000 people at test peaks, in North Las Vegas is Nellis Air Force Base, a jet training center with some 6,500 in its personnel and an annual payroll of about $21,000,000.

***

THE eight-column banner headline on the afternoon Review Journal says: "Las Vegas L. D. S. Woman Killed in Texas Crash." Not just "Las Vegas Woman"—but "Las Vegas L. D. S. Woman."

This is a reminder that Las Vegas began a century ago as a water stop on the Mormon trail from Utah to California, and that the Mormons—the Latter Day Saints—are still a major element in the community.

From a wagon-trail and railroad water stop, Las Vegas became in the Nineteen Thirties the railhead for the construction of Hoover Dam on the Colorado, some twenty-five miles away. The construction boom merged into a World War II boom of military training and defense industry, and then into the gambling resort boom. But, amid it all, Las Vegas has not lost its identity as a Mormon center.

In Clark County, the L. D. S. Church has fifteen congregations with 13,400 members. The president of the Las Vegas "stake," or church subdivision, is Reed Whipple, a city commissioner and vice president of the First National Bank of Nevada. The church membership, by time-honored practice, maintains with donated labor two local dairy and feed farms, covering some 200 acres, whose proceeds go to the church welfare fund.

All told, Greater Las Vegas has sixty-eight congregations of various sects, apart from the multitude of wedding chapels which account for most of its 30,000 marriages annually.

***

LAS VEGAS' most eye-filling show of female charm is not at one of the casinos. It unfolds every afternoon at Market Town, the shopping center at the end of the "Strip."
To Market Town come girls from not one but all the shows, in shorts and halters, prosaically shopping for groceries. There are several hundred of them, working in the town's dozen major cathedrals of chance. They get from $125 to $250 a week. But living costs are high, so as a general thing the girls live plainly in housekeeping apartments.

Along with them to market come waitresses, bellhops, croupiers and other functionaries of the resorts. Of Clark County's 100,000 inhabitants, and Las Vegas' 50,000, around 10,000 are employed in hotels.

In their off-hours from Las Vegas' massive midway, most of them lead surprisingly conventional lives, well integrated with the Las Vegas majority whose relationship to the bright lights is only peripheral.

At a between-shows gathering at the Sands Hotel it develops that everybody around the table has a niche in local affairs. The hotel's musical director, Antonio Morelli, is likewise the spark plug of city musical activities and director of its Community Chorus. Al Freeman, the press agent, who attends a local synagogue, has been spending his spare time for a couple of years promoting the sale of a special bread for the benefit of a Catholic hospital. A winsome blonde girl named Carol Hoffman devotes three afternoons a week to a downtown school for children with cerebral palsy. At night she is one of the "Copa Girls," dancing in the chorus line.

And, at another resort, the cigarette girl in the cocktail lounge was identified this way: "That girl has the sharpest eyes in town. She's the star of our Ground Observer Corps."

* * *

ONLY a few miles south of the "Strip," but worlds beyond the notice of the all-night gamblers, dawn finds a gently sloping desert valley frequently shrouded in a pall reminiscent of Germany's Ruhr. Beneath the pall lies a community of thousands of homes. Thrusting up through the pall are the smokestacks which are its source. This is the suburb of Henderson, thirteen miles southeast of Las Vegas.

Henderson sprang from barren desert in World War II—a site, handy to the power of Hoover Dam, for the production of vital magnesium. Some $140,000,000 was spent building the plant and auxiliary facilities of the huge Government-owned enterprise. With the war's end, production stopped. The plant became a white elephant, reduced at one point to the production in one of its crannies of handicrafted Indian jewelry.

But local and state promotional agencies pitched in to keep Henderson alive. Today it is producing on a bigger scale than ever, with amplified facilities shared by such concerns as American Potash and Chemical. Titanium Metals Corporation, Stauffer Chemical Company, United States Lime Products and Manganese, Inc. Henderson's population has passed its wartime peak to reach a total of more than 15,000. About 2,500 of its citizens work in Henderson industry. Many others commute to Las Vegas—part of the flux of people whose lives are obscured by the plaster-and-neon brilliance of the Las Vegas midway.

Beyond Henderson lies Boulder City, a picture-book "model town" of neat white houses and green lawns. You can't gamble here, and you can't buy anything stronger than beer because it is a Government town—the construction and operating center for Hoover Dam, whose 4,000 residents, after two decades, still resist severing Federal ties. Boulder City is twenty-two miles southeast of Las Vegas (only a stone's throw in these open spaces) and the development of the two communities is tightly linked. It was the dam construction that sparked Las Vegas' emergence from sun-baked somnolence into a chronic boom town. Today the dam area is Las Vegas' multi-million-dollar equivalent of the old swimming hole—the place where people go to splash, boat and fish. Conversely, the dam's nation-wide allure for tourists serves as an important tributary of Las Vegas business.

* * *

THE dam, spanning Black Canyon just below Boulder City, and the environs of 100-mile-long Lake Mead behind the dam, comprise the Lake Mead National Recreation Area, visited by upward of 2,500,000 people a year. In the last two years, the lake has become the site of one of the nation's top speed-boat events, the Sahara Cup Races, sponsored by a Las Vegas hotel.

About 500,000 people every year go on the tour through the awesome innards of the huge dam, under the guidance of Park Service rangers. One former ranger. Arthur Olsen, used to spend his spare moments poring over law books. He passed the bar exam and a year ago became the Justice of the Peace of Las Vegas Township.

It is probably the most remunerative unsalaried job in the world. Of Las Vegas' 30,000 marriages a year (most of them involving people avoiding California's waiting period) about one-third of the couples prefer a civil ceremony. Except for a few district court judges, Olsen has a monopoly in the civil field. He performs as many as eighty marriages a day, at $5 each—with an annual income potential approaching $50,000.

***

PERHAPS the best wrap-up of the multiple community called Las Vegas may be obtained from statistics, which don't fall quite the way a casual visitor might expect. The tourist and gambling trade ranks only second among Las Vegas' sources of income. It yields a tidy $175,000,000 a year, but it is topped by retail trade, serving the general area, at $200,000,000. Third, producing $100,000,000 a year, is industry. And fourth come Federal expenditures, for both civilian and military purposes, at $50,000,000.

It is evident that the eager-eyed visitor with a hundred or two of throwaway money in his poke is by no means the most important citizen in Las Vegas.

DOCUMENT 9.4 NEVADA-SEMIPALATINSK MOVEMENT POSTER

SOURCE: *COLLECTION OF AUTHOR*

DOCUMENT 9.5 KAZAKH POET AND PROTEST LEADER OLZHAS SULEIMENOV MEETS WESTERN SHOSHONE PROTEST LEADER CORBIN HARNEY OUTSIDE NTS GATES SOURCE: NEVADA DESERT EXPERIENCE RECORDS, UNLV SPECIAL COLLECTIONS, MS2007-04

DOCUMENT 9.6 WESTERN SHOSHONE NATION PERMIT TO GATHER, GO AND COME SOURCE: GREENPEACE PACIFIC SOUTHWEST RECORDS, UNLV SPECIAL COLLECTIONS, MS00363

No   3091

WESTERN SHOSHONE NATION

Western Shoshone National Council
P.O. Box 68, Duckwater, NV. 89314

Application For Individual Non-Western
Shoshone Permit to Gather, Go And Come

Todays Date:_____ Issued By_____
                                       (authorizing signature)

This application for an individual exempt permit to gather, go and come
is by issue only from the Western Shoshone National Council. It is
good for the resource zone indicated on the adjacent map. A permit
must be carried at all times when within the resource zone to comply
with permitting requirements and to enjoy the priviledges unobstructed,
associated with the issuance of a permit to gather, go and come. Upon
request by a duly authorized officer of the Western Shoshone Nation,
the permit must be made available for inspection. The permit may be
revoke d by the officer at the officers discretion or by the Western
Shoshone National Council. The information gathered is for our records
and will not be released beyond the Western Shoshone Nation government.

(This application must be fully completed)

Name_____
        (Last, First, Middle)
Address_____

City_____State_____

Zip Code_____Country_____

Height_____Weight_____Hair_____Eyes_____

Sex_____Date of Birth____-____-____Age_____

Date & Length of Issuance From:_____

To:_____(length not to exceed 1 year)

WESTERN SHOSHONE NATION

I certify that I have read and agree to abide by all the terms for the
issuance of a permit to gather, go and come.....above all in a peaceful
nonviolent manner. Destruction of private property is prohibited and I
further understand that this permit does not allow for the use alchohol,
drugs or firearms for the resource area indicated, and that such use is
cause for revocation.

Applicant Signature:_____Date:_____

PART III
THE HISTORICAL CONTEXT

THE WORLD AT TRINITY

On the night of July 15, 1945, a group of ninety international scientists quietly boarded buses and headed out of the high desert town of Los Alamos, New Mexico, where they had spent the past two years working in total secrecy on the first atomic bomb. The men represented one of the greatest collections of scientific minds ever gathered in one place. They were "America's Athenian world," a melting pot of refugees from fascism and genocide.[1]

The group included experts from many scientific areas, but all were pioneers in the field of atomic physics. Many were Jews who had escaped Hitler's Europe in 1938 just as the last exits were closing, or refugees from fascist regimes in Italy and Hungary. Among the travelers that night were Nobel Prize winners such as Italy's Enrico Fermi and Denmark's Niels Bohr and his son Aage Bohr. Nearly every seat on the bus held a genius like Hungarian Edward Teller or Austrian Jon von Neumann, a man that Robert Oppenheimer, the head of the Manhattan Project, called the "brightest person [he] ever met." Most of the scientists shared some doubts about the goal of the trip to the remote New Mexico desert. They knew that if their experiment worked, they would change the course of history—and they were not all were sure it would be for the better.

The buses deposited the scientists twenty miles away from the test detonation point in a remote valley on the ancient Spanish Camino Real, locally known by the name explorer Oñate gave it in 1598, Jornado del Muerto (Journey of Death). Crews constructed the atomic bomb in a commandeered ranch-house kitchen. In the predawn hours of the following day, Monday, July 16, 1945, observers received pieces of dark welder's glass to cover their eyes and sunscreen to protect their faces.

---

[1] On Trinity, see Ferenc Morton Szasz, *The Day the Sun Rose Twice: The Story of the Trinity Site Nuclear Explosion, July 16, 1945* (Albuquerque: University of New Mexico Press, 1984); Richard Rhodes, *The Making of the Atomic Bomb* (New York: Simon & Schuster, 1986). For atomic science beautifully explained, see Jonathan Fetter-Vorm, *Trinity: A Graphic History of the First Atomic Bomb* (New York: Hill & Wang, 2013).

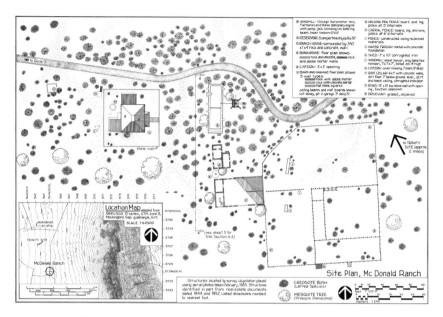

FIG. 1 McDonald Ranch Trinity Site.

Deciding where to test that first atomic device was a serious problem for the scientists and military leaders who had spent billions of dollars and millions of man hours learning how to turn energy from splitting atoms into weapons. Before Trinity, no one knew just how destructive an atomic weapon would be but all indications pointed to something tens of thousands of times more powerful than conventional explosives. How can you test such a thing? What places on Earth could host such an event? How would that environment be changed, and what might happen to the people who lived near that place? Could you find a place big enough, empty enough, worthless enough to be expendable in an all-out effort to end the horrors of WWII? The deserts of central New Mexico were chosen for the Trinity test because they were easily accessible from Los Alamos where the bomb was designed during the Manhattan Project, but also because of prevailing assumptions about the character of desert "wastelands" and the "marginal" peoples living in them. With the Trinity test these questions were not deeply considered. It was wartime and there was a desperate rush to see if the atomic bomb would work.

As illustrated in the graphic history, at 5:29 am, exactly as planned, a flash ten times brighter than the sun lit up the night in three states. An eerie, multicolored plasma ball formed within a millionth of a second before launching a 38,000-foot cloud of radioactive debris into the atmosphere. At "ground zero," where the bomb had sat seconds before, a half-mile-wide crater was covered by a sheet of gray-green glass—dubbed "trinitite" by the scientists—formed when the heat of the blast melted the desert sands. Far above New Mexico, radioactive isotopes floated into the atmosphere where they rained down on an area the size of Australia, showing up months later in straw grown in Maryland and in milk from cows outside of Chicago. Oppenheimer famously recalled the event by citing Hindu scripture: "Now I am become death, destroyer of worlds."

By the time of the Trinity blast, the United States was moving quickly toward the main island of Japan but at a terrible cost of lives. Fire bombings of Tokyo in March 1945 killed more than 100,000 civilians, while desperate fighting at Iwo Jima and Okinawa left tens of thousands of U.S. casualties. The Soviets stalled on promises to enter the war against Japan, leaving Truman with a choice: launch a full-scale invasion of the Japanese mainland with estimates of death tolls in the millions or use the new atomic bomb. Truman steadfastly maintained that the decision was a simple one. With some confidence about the stability of Europe, Truman prepared for the final assault on Japan.

U.S. leaders feared the cost of a full-scale invasion of Japan, since the militarists in Tokyo seemed unwilling to surrender on any terms acceptable to the Allies. At Yalta and Potsdam, Stalin agreed to attack Japanese forces in Northeast Asia three months after Germany surrendered. Most of Japan's army was stationed on the Asian mainland. Although Soviet military help would greatly reduce America's burden and casualties, Truman feared that if the Red Army joined the war against Japan it would support communist forces in China. Given this potential problem, Truman chose to use the atomic bomb: its use could shock Japanese hardliners into surrender, avoid U.S. casualties, and end the war before the Soviets could move into Japan. Furthermore, the use of the bombs would provide a graphic example of U.S. power in the Soviet's backyard.

As you now know, on August 6, 1945, a lone U.S. bomber, the B-29 Enola Gay, carrying only one bomb, named "Little Boy," flew unbothered through a cloudy early morning sky toward the Japanese city of Hiroshima. The plane was named for the mother of mission commander Paul Tibbits, who selected the plane himself for his historic mission. At 8:15 a.m. Japan time, the crew released their bomb. It detonated at 2,000 feet above the city, just as planned. The blast released energy equivalent to 16 kilotons of TNT in a millionth of a second. The power of the bomb was incredible. Thousands of people were vaporized, their shadows burned into the concrete where they stood. With the push of a button, a dozen men invisible to their enemy at 31,000 feet in the sky instantly obliterated almost five square miles of a city with a weapon that was merely ten feet long. Seventy to eighty thousand people, about 30 percent of the city's population, were killed instantly; another 70,000 were injured; and tens of thousands were contaminated by radiation in the days and weeks that followed.

The utter destruction of Hiroshima and Nagasaki, just weeks after that first Trinity test, shocked the world and raised immediate practical and ethical questions about the continued production of these unprecedented new weapons and especially about the idea of testing them on home turf during peacetime. The then mysterious effects of radiation—invisible, tasteless, odorless—increased the concern that a force of nature had been unleashed that was possibly beyond our control. Parts of this early history of atomic weapons science and use are well known and, perhaps because of their wartime context, easier to understand than what followed. The remarkable story of how the United States and Great Britain organized the largest science project in history during the war has been told in many ways, but most often the bombing of Japan is the conclusion of the story. The lengthy and complicated history of atomic weapons development and testing that continued for another half-century is not nearly as well understood.

For a brief moment following the bombing of Nagasaki there were no more bombs, and many influential people thought there never should be. Others embraced this new technology and quickly planned a regime of research, design, and testing of bigger and better nuclear weapons. The former gained influence in the coming decades, but the latter prevailed and atomic testing became a central feature of the emerging Cold War. To move forward with expanded nuclear testing, presidents, policymakers, scientists, and military leaders had to revisit questions about domestic testing sites and develop procedures and protocols that had been briefly considered only in the rush leading to that first Trinity test. Where and how could continued and expanded atomic testing happen? When, if ever, would it end? What could be done about the complicated radiation safety questions for those participating, and what protections could be offered to ensure the health of those living in the test regions? This last point is the crux of the testing story and the source of intense debate at the time; the controversy continues to this day. What was known about radiation, when was it known, and how was this information shared with the public? As you've seen, these questions of the day are the lasting questions that framed the graphic history you just read.

Few events in history have generated as much controversy as the decision to use the atomic bomb on human targets. Unlike the clarity of purpose and shared sense of sacrifice of World War II, the dawning Cold War and its nuclear escalation divided opinion and forced Americans to rethink the relationship of the nation to the world. Atomic power brought heavy responsibility. The history of atomic weapons development and testing after Hiroshima and Nagasaki was inexorably tied to the complex domestic culture and foreign policies of the Cold War.

WHAT IS A COLD WAR?

Harry S. Truman, the man who made the decision to use those first two atomic weapons, was still a mystery to most Americans when he became president after the sudden death of Franklin Roosevelt, on April 12, 1945. Truman inherited the moral responsibility for the atomic bomb, the job of ending WWII, the management of a faltering alliance with the Soviet Union, and the drafting of American foreign and domestic policy in the dawning postwar world.

Soon after assuming the presidency, Truman worried about a growing rift between the United States and its wartime ally, the communist Soviet Union.

In April 1945 British and American troops closed in on Berlin from the west, while the Soviets slugged their way toward the city in the face of dogged resistance from the east. Hours after assuming the presidency, Truman learned that Stalin was pushing his troops to capture the city ahead of the Americans. With big shoes to fill on the world stage, Truman worked to understand the complicated relationship with the Soviets. Roosevelt had left the Yalta Conference convinced that his hard-won alliance with Stalin would help ensure that the Soviets would live up to their agreements in Eastern Europe. In his first months in office, Truman shared his predecessor's optimism. In his diaries he described Stalin as "honest" and "smart as hell."

Briefings with Roosevelt's top military advisers tempered Truman's optimism and raised his distrust of Stalin and the Soviets. They now cautioned Truman to avoid appeasing Stalin as he gained control of Eastern Europe. Truman sent top diplomat W. Averell Harriman to Moscow. Harriman's dispatches decried Stalin's "barbarian invasion of Europe." He warned the Soviets that Truman would not stand for communist expansion. Forced to formulate a foreign policy strategy in less than a week, Truman latched on to the strong anticommunist position of Harriman. The growing rivalry between the members of the Grand Alliance heated up as the final battle of the war in Europe took shape around Berlin.

By April 1945 the German army was reduced to young boys and old men and Berlin was in ruins. Still, the fight for the city remained brutal to the end. When the Soviets reached the city first, they symbolically hosted their red flag on the roof of the ruined Reichstag while Hitler lay dead of a self-inflicted gunshot in his underground bunker.

Germany formally surrendered on May 8, 1945. Even as the German guns finally fell silent, it was clear that the peace would be complicated and contested. While citizens and soldiers rejoiced, political and military leaders remained deeply concerned by news of deteriorating relations with

FIG. 2 Cold War Europe, 1950.

Stalin. The Soviets occupied Berlin and controlled a vast territory stretching from the Black Sea in Romania to Poland's Baltic shores. They also controlled a large swath of eastern Germany past Berlin and up the Elbe River. The Allies had agreed at Yalta to partition Germany into occupation zones, but no formal mechanism existed for cooperation between the Soviets, the United States, and Great Britain. Tensions grew when the Soviets annexed a huge swath of eastern Poland, confirming the Poles' worst fears.

In Washington, only eleven days after taking office, Truman faced off with Soviet foreign minister Vyachslav Molotov and accused the Soviets of breaking their agreement to give Poland independence. Stalin responded by firmly maintaining they were only establishing a "security zone" in Poland and that Soviet interests in Eastern Europe were more important than good relations with America's new president. The leaders of the Alliance met for the last time in Potsdam, a suburb of Berlin. On July 15, Truman and secretary of state James F. Byrnes arrived at Potsdam without a clear understanding of the extent of Stalin's expansionist ambitions and with the war in Japan entering a pivotal moment. Still hoping for Soviet assistance in subduing the millions of Japanese troops on the Asian mainland, Truman tempered his position on Poland and agreed to the Soviet occupation of Eastern Europe.

The debate about Poland symbolized the brewing ideological Cold War to come. Two years earlier, at a critical meeting of the Alliance at Tehran, Iran, Roosevelt and Churchill had secretly agreed to Stalin's demand that the allies accept Soviet control of eastern Poland. Unaware of this agreement, Polish resistance leaders organized a massive uprising against the Germans in Warsaw with the assumption that the nearby Red Army would join the fight. In one of the bloodiest events of the war, German troops, crushing the uprising, slaughtered a quarter-million civilians, reducing Warsaw to ruins. The Soviets stayed away and allowed Warsaw to fall. Months later Truman agreed to let the Soviets formally redraw the map of Poland—a crushing blow to the Poles. From the perspective of Central Europe the battle lines of the coming Cold War were clear. The ideological battle between the emerging superpowers would be fought on other people's territory with profound and lasting consequences for those nations. It was at Potsdam that Truman received coded word from New Mexico of the successful TRINITY explosion. The news, he confided to advisers, was "a great load off [his] mind." Truman knew the atomic bomb would change the situation in the Pacific and mentioned the news of a "new weapon of great power" to Stalin. Stalin simply nodded, having known of the Manhattan Project through an elaborate espionage operation linking New Mexico to Moscow. The nuclear arms race was underway before the first bombs were used.

DIVIDING THE GLOBE

The United States emerged from the cataclysmic war stronger and wealthier than before. Between 1940 and 1945, while U.S. enemies and allies alike endured massive physical and financial destruction, the U.S. gross domestic national product (GDP) increased by over 170 percent. Aside from the attack on Pearl Harbor and a few Japanese incendiary bombs carried by balloon over the Pacific Northwest, the U.S. homeland remained unscathed. Its industrial complex had dramatically expanded, its navy and air force were unmatched, and its president and military leaders had sole possession of the atomic bomb. Meanwhile, the Soviet Union was devastated, with entire cities leveled and an estimated 28 million citizens dead.

FIG. 3 Cold War world map.

Despite the relative strength of the United States compared to the USSR, concerns about the spread of communism in the aftermath of war escalated. American leaders framed the contest as a struggle between Western democracy and a global communist conspiracy led by the Soviet Union.

The war unleashed dramatic forces of global change and created conditions for a transnational ideological power struggle. The war irreparably altered the colonial empires of European nations and enabled the rise of revolutionary nationalism in Asia, Africa, the Middle East, and Latin America. All over the world, in countries like India and French Indochina (soon to be known as Vietnam), crumbling colonial control fueled nationalist desires and demands for independence, modernization, and higher quality of life. Even before the war ended, boundaries shifted as diverse peoples searched for ideologies and leadership to enable a new phase of their history. U.S. policymakers pejoratively labeled these mostly nonwhite developing nations and contested regions the "Third World" in contrast to the presumed civility and superiority of the "First" and "Second" nations. The assumed lack of sophistication, cultural development, and national cohesiveness in former colonies prejudiced critical Cold War decision making in the coming years, often with disastrous results.

At the end of the war America had a clear military and economic advantage over the Soviets. To succeed in the growing Cold War, however, Truman needed another resource: an appealing ideology to counter communist promises that had gained popularity among those disillusioned by the democratic capitalist model. Many people in former colonies of Western powers viewed the capitalism of their colonizers as the cause of depression, war, and fascism. In the coming decades the selling of American culture and ideology became an important weapon in the Cold War. Spreading American ideals through international marketing of everything from jeans and cars to music and movies provided the "soft power" behind hard-edged Cold War foreign policy.

There were very real reasons to fear the expansion of communism. By 1947 alarming statistics about the growing popularity of communism across Europe raised concerns that the Soviets would have the balance of power handed to them by nations reeling from the aftermath of war. Between 1935 and 1945, communist party membership increased from 17,000 to 70,000 in Greece, from 28,000 to 750,000 in Czechoslovakia, and from 5,000 to 1,700,000 in Italy. Much of this rapid growth stemmed from the key anti-Nazi role played by local communists during the war rather than from admiration for Stalin's policies. Still, there seemed to be evidence that communism was a powerful force in the postcolonial world.

In the summer of 1946 a quick series of events solidified U.S. atomic policy. In July Truman signed the Atomic Energy Act, creating the Atomic Energy Commission (AEC). Truman supported the creation of this new agency as a compromise between two opposing factions: those who supported the scientist movement for international control of atomic energy and only peaceful development of atomic energy, and those who wanted American control and rapid development of more and better atomic weapons. The civilian AEC eased the minds of some scientists but permanently ended the dream of international control of atomic energy proposed by Bernard Baruch only a month before the formal creation of the AEC. As shown in the graphic history, the dramatic demonstrations of the atomic bomb's destructive power in the Bikini Atoll during Operation Crossroads in 1946 showed how quickly the science and technology of atomic weapons was progressing while raising new concerns about the need to continue full-scale nuclear tests. The August 1946 publication and serialization of John Hersey's best-selling *Hiroshima* brought home the reality of nuclear

FIG. 4 Crossroads aerial shot with clock.

war to readers shocked by Hersey's bleak descriptions of utter destruction and lingering death from radiation. Wide media coverage of atomic developments and frightening doomsday scenarios like those described with brutal simplicity by Hersey and others made the consequences of atomic warfare more real for the American public even before the Soviets got the bomb.

CONTAINMENT

In 1946 Truman needed a clear policy to respond to both real and perceived changes in the global balance of power in the nuclear age. Inspiration for a critical foreign policy plan came from Soviet expert George F. Kennan. In 1946 he sent his analysis of the postwar Soviet Union from his post in Moscow to Washington in a widely circulated 8,000-word "Long Telegram." In July 1947 Kennan published an even longer version of his pessimistic assessment of the Soviets in the influential journal *Foreign Affairs*. Kennan argued that Soviet communism was "impervious to the logic of reason," inherently expansionist, and controllable only through "long-term, patient but firm and vigilant containment." Kennan's idea, containment, became the foundation of U.S. foreign policy for the next four decades.

Although Kennan's assessment was alarming, he assured policymakers that the Soviets did not want war. Instead, they hoped that economic desperation in Western Europe and Japan would drive these key regions into the Soviet camp. Kennan believed that if U.S. reconstruction programs stabilized Western Europe, Japan, and the Middle East and Third World, the Soviets would be contained and ultimately destroyed without actual war.

Faced with the need to garner support for massive funding efforts to fight communists across the globe, Truman stepped up his anticommunist rhetoric in a stark March 12, 1947, speech to Congress. Truman told Congress and the American people that "it must be the policy of the United States to support free peoples who are resisting attempted subjugation by armed minorities or by outside pressures." This bold new commitment to fight "communist tyranny" wherever it might appear became known as the Truman Doctrine. Michigan Republican senator Arthur Vandenberg advised Truman to "scare hell out of the American people," so they would understand the seriousness of the threat. In several speeches, Truman painted a dramatic picture of a world communist conspiracy that could be contained only through aggressive force. These warnings secured $400 million from Congress to fight communism in Greece and elsewhere while creating a high level of anxiety about communism in America. These fears fed a growing "Red scare" that contributed to the debate about nuclear weapons in the years to come. Those who opposed nuclear proliferation and the testing regimes that support it found themselves at odds with the politics of the Red scare. During the height of the Red scare, dissent—no matter how reasoned—was easily dismissed as naïve or subversive and anti-American. Patriotism was expected and part of being patriotic in mid-century America was unquestioning support for military might.

The acceptance of the Truman Doctrine required not just unified public support for an ideological war against communism but a significant reorganization of the government in preparation for a protracted Cold War. With the creation of the Department of Defense, the National Security Act of 1947 consolidated the U.S. military command; a representative from each military branch would now advise a newly created secretary of defense and the president through the Joint Chiefs of Staff office. The act also created a National Security Council to advise the president and the Central Intelligence Agency (CIA) to gather intelligence about hostile, mostly communist, activities throughout the world.

TIPPING POINTS AND ATOMIC ESCALATION

A series of events between 1948 and 1950 accomplished Harry Truman's goal to "scare the hell" out of the American public. First, the Soviets caused an international crisis when they blockaded Berlin in hopes of gaining control of the divided city and thwarting U.S. efforts to rebuild a powerful West Germany. Between June 1948 and May 1949, the Soviets, locking down all roads leading to the city, forced the first showdown of the Cold War. The United States responded with the most remarkable air supply effort in history. For almost a year U.S. transport planes carried food and coal into the city twenty-four hours a day. The Berlin Airlift won the hearts of Berliners and humiliated the Soviets, who reopened the city on May 11, 1949. By then the United States had realized its goal of unifying the western zones of Germany into a pro-western state in opposition to the Soviet-controlled eastern zones. Policymakers had only a few months to enjoy the success in Berlin as the shocking news arrived on August 29, 1949, that the Soviets had successfully tested an atomic bomb. The Soviet's ability to catch up with American technology so rapidly revealed what U.S. leaders had suspected, that communist spies had successfully infiltrated the Manhattan Project. America's monopoly on atomic power was over.

Throughout the Cold War the Soviet atomic program was shrouded in mystery. After Hiroshima and Nagasaki, Stalin ordered a crash program to build a Soviet bomb. The Soviet and American political systems were completely different, but in both cases brilliant scientists had to work with industrial managers, military leaders, and politicians who were almost completely ignorant about the science behind the splitting of the atom.[2] In both cases the collision of science and policy caused tension and confusion. In the case of the Soviets, the speed of their program was extraordinary and the consequences of failure for those tasked with catching the Americans stark. Even at the highest level of the Soviet program, death or imprisonments were real possibilities for scientists. Just as in the United States, Soviet scientists chafed at the level of control policymakers and military leaders placed on their scientific research and worried about the decline of the international fraternity of shared scientific knowledge as Cold War tensions escalated. During and after the creation of the Soviet bomb, the scientists argued for more command and control of atomic energy. Just as in

---

2   The best study of the Soviet atomic program is David Holloway, *Stalin and the Bomb: The Soviet Union and Atomic Energy, 1939–1956* (New Haven, CT: Yale University Press, 1994), 1.

the United States, the most vocal scientists had their loyalty to the state questioned and were removed from their positions of authority.

In October 1949, only one month after the stunning news about the Soviet atomic bomb, China fell to the communists under the leadership of Mao Zedong. The formation of the communist People's Republic of China especially disheartened Americans because of their longstanding charitable and missionary aid to the nation and significant diplomatic efforts by general George Marshall to ensure that China would remain free. Marshall had spent most of 1946 in China arranging a coalition between the Chinese nationalists, led by Chiang Kai-shek, and his communist rivals, led by Mao. Despite Marshall's efforts, the coalition faltered. Chiang's incompetence contrasted with the communists' rising popularity and superior organization. Full-scale civil war broke out in 1947, and by 1949 Mao led a unified China that allied itself with the Soviet Union.

Americans worried that the new alliance between Stalin and Mao threatened to spread communism more widely in Asia. All of these events in 1949 raised U.S. fears and seemed to confirm the basic premise of the Truman Doctrine that communist revolutionaries threatened freedom around the globe. Any doubts about a world communist conspiracy faded with the news of a communist North Korean invasion of South Korea on June 25, 1950.

A top secret National Security Council document known as NSC-68 supported Truman's decisive military response in Korea. Early Cold War containment policy focused on building allies through economic programs like the Marshall Plan. By 1950, escalating tensions led State Department officials like Paul H. Nitze to suggest that economic diplomacy was not enough and that countering Soviet and Chinese actions in places such as Korea required direct use of U.S. military force. Though never fully implemented, NSC-68 painted a graphic picture of a fanatically expansionist USSR bent on world domination and demonstrated a willingness to consider radical options to combat communism. The document concluded with a strong recommendation for massive military spending and decisive military response to any and all Soviet actions around the globe.

NSC-68 called for expanded annual military spending to accomplish these goals. Part of the increase would fund more and bigger nuclear weapons. Expanding and improving the nuclear arsenal required much more extensive testing. Testing in the Pacific would be expanded and new, more convenient continental testing sites were proposed in PROJECT NUTMEG. From reading the graphic history you know that PROJECT NUTMEG ultimately resulted in the selection of Nevada as the home for the primary U.S. atomic proving ground. By this point the American atomic test sites had Soviet twins and all the other emerging atomic nations had constructed

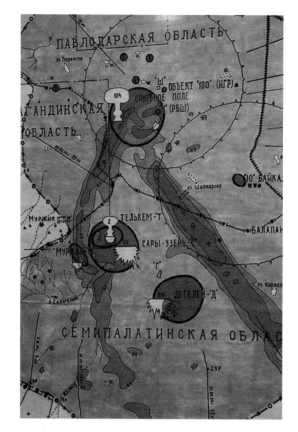

FIG. 5 Soviet "Polygon" test site map.

networks of testing sites around the globe. All of these testing regions and their peoples shared key characteristics: the places had been deemed "wastelands" by the nations that controlled them and the residents were considered—when considered at all—unimportant, expendable, suitably compliant, or simply expendable. Widespread assumptions about the exceptional nature of nuclear science and nuclear testing during the Cold War allowed for exceptional scientific and governmental command and control of information, environments, and people, even in democratic nations. It is easy to see these developments as inevitable outcomes of the Cold War but at each stage the escalation of atomic testing was hotly contested. Even the atomic scientists working on these projects disagreed throughout the testing era and conflicting scientific information challenged policy responses. This was particularly true during Eisenhower's presidency.[3]

---

[3]   Benjamin Greene, *Eisenhower, Science Advice, and the Nuclear Test-Ban Debate, 1945–1963* (Stanford, CA: Stanford University Press, 2007).

EISENHOWER'S NEW LOOK

Eisenhower inherited the nuclear arms race from president Harry Truman but brought his own philosophy on how to maintain technological dominance, cut military costs, and improve fighting efficiency. Working closely with his stridently anticommunist secretary of state John Foster Dulles, Eisenhower launched a military reorganization dubbed the "New Look." The central philosophy of the New Look was Dulles's pronouncement of the doctrine of "massive retaliation" in January 1954. Simply put, massive retaliation meant that if the United States or its NATO and Japanese allies were attacked by the USSR, the United States would respond with enough nuclear strikes to completely destroy Soviet society. The plan was backed later by a "triad system" that kept some of the U.S. nuclear arsenal constantly on the move on trains, eternally patrolling aircraft, and eventually submarines, to ensure a rapid response to a Soviet first strike.

Under the New Look, the U.S. atomic arsenal increased from 1,000 to over 18,000 weapons. Additions to the military included the giant B-52 bomber, capable of carrying nuclear payloads 7,000 miles from the United States to the heart of the USSR and the high-flying U-2 spy plane. Eisenhower and Dulles believed the New Look had at least two advantages over Truman's containment policy: it would deter the Soviets from directly challenging U.S. interests, and it would be cost-effective, since atomic weapons ultimately cost less than large conventional armed forces. Testing new warheads to match the new policy was the primary focus of the atomic weapons tests in Nevada between 1954 and 1957.

In 1954, Eisenhower appointed mathematician and physicist John von Neumann to the AEC. Von Neumann contributed critical mathematical research to the Manhattan Project and brought "game theory" and computational analysis and expertise to the AEC. Most famously, von Neumann explained the aggressive expansion of nuclear weapons with the phrase "mutually assured destruction" (MAD). The successful Bravo tests and rapid development of highly accurate intercontinental missiles (ICBMs) provided the technological basis for the MAD philosophy that argued that assured destruction would force the two sides in the Cold War to maintain peace. These ideas meshed perfectly with the New Look and supported a dramatic expansion of atomic weapons development and testing between 1954 and 1958. Von Neumann's intentional dark humor (calling this policy MAD for short) was not lost on the growing numbers of opponents of atomic weapons who believed that expansion and testing were simply crazy, with no hidden logic and no obvious exit strategy. As illustrated in the graphic history, Eisenhower was doubtful about the role of atomic weapons in his policies. Still, throughout his two terms as

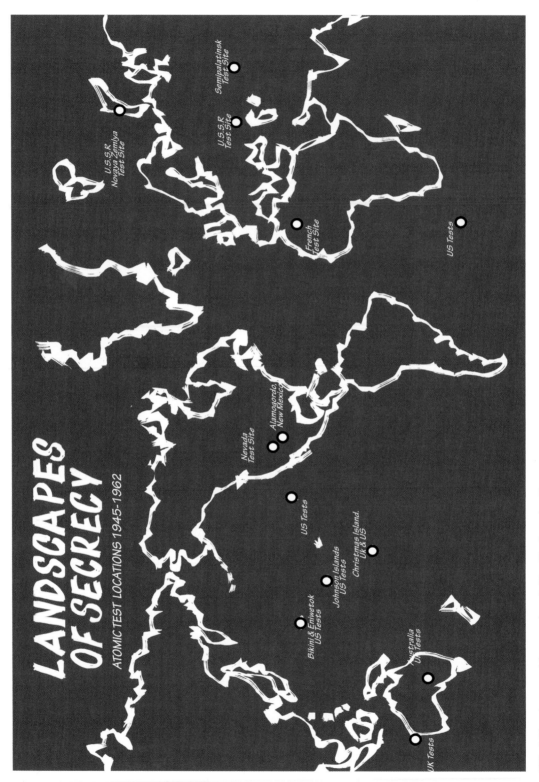

FIG. 6 "Landscapes of Secrecy: Atomic Test Site Locations" map.

president, the atomic testing regimes expanded dramatically. No region was more affected by these evolving nuclear policies and programs than the American West.

ATOMIC WEST

The entire United States experienced significant change during and after World War II, but the newly industrialized American West was transformed. The West benefited from the war mobilization that redistributed tens of millions of soldiers and support staff and billions of dollars to massive new military installations constructed or expanded throughout the region. Military leaders favored the West for wartime mobilization because of warm weather, clear skies, and wide-open spaces. The demographic and economic impact in areas surrounding military bases was immediate and dramatic. During the Manhattan Project perceptions of the arid and desert southwest and the people who lived throughout the region shaped decisions about where to locate facilities, how to dispose of waste, and ultimately where to test the first device.

Cold War imperatives ensured the continued growth of the atomic industrial complex in the West after WWII. For America's Cold War nuclear-industrial complex, the West afforded vast tracts of remote lands where large military bases could be hidden. Only one major atomic installation was built outside the region, at Oak Ridge, Tennessee. The rest of America's atomic complex was scattered across the West in New Mexico, Washington, California, and Nevada. In California both the California Institute of Technology and, starting in 1952, Lawrence Livermore National Laboratory became important centers of atomic research.

The military-driven industrialization of the West dramatically expanded the political and cultural importance of the region. Between 1910 and 1950 migrations to the West led to significant congressional reapportionments resulting in a net gain of twenty-eight new seats in Congress. California alone gained nineteen new seats during this time. In the coming decades, California produced two presidents, completing the shift in the West from a frontier periphery to a vital center of American culture and politics. The Cold War completed the long process of incorporating the desert regions of the West into the nation but also required a continuation of longstanding perceptions of the area as an empty wasteland suitable for activities that would be impossible in the more populated and presumed productive regions of the nation.

Throughout much of the early Cold War most westerners welcomed the expanded military presence and the economic development and positive

FIG. 7 Atomic West map.

attention this presence brought to their region. The military complexes
that industrialized the West during WWII paved the way for the "nuclear
frontier" of the Cold War. New Mexico had Los Alamos and Sandia, California had atomic programs throughout its university systems and the
Livermore Labs, Washington State had the massive Hanford reactor facilities, and Arizona and Utah had extensive uranium mining operations. For
those who knew the history of the region, this atomic enthusiasm, followed
by controversy and fear about loss of regional control and despoliation of
western lands, conformed to a familiar pattern. As western historian Patricia Limerick said, "Western American history was offering another course

in its standard curriculum . . . another case study in the conquest of nature and the unforeseen, maddening, and persistent side effects of that conquest."[4]

This pattern held true for Nevada. In 1951, when Nevada was chosen as the location for the new continental nuclear test site, the state's governor Charles H. Russell told reporters that it was "exciting that the sub-marginal land of the proving ground was furthering science and helping national defense." "We had long ago written off that terrain as wasteland," he continued, "and today it's blooming with atoms." Those living for generations in the "wasteland" sections of Nevada and Utah disagreed with these blunt assessments of their natural environment from the beginning, but widespread concern about desert environments and peoples took decades to develop.

Political and business leaders in Nevada and Las Vegas immediately recognized the economic benefits of locating the atomic test site in their state and the new political power and cultural legitimacy that atomic testing would bring to the region. Boosters of atomic testing tapped a rich vein of enthusiasm and support for federal projects in the area; Hoover Dam in the 1930s, Basic Magnesium in the 1940s, and atomic testing in the 1950s brought money, power, and influence to a region that would have had much less otherwise. Hailed as wonders of the world and keystones to national development and defense, these massive federal projects provided a sense of importance to a region and its people, who knew the sting of living on the margins. Westerners were master promoters by the 1950s, and Las Vegas had some of the best. They marketed atomic testing as a spectacle and cashed in on the legions of official visitors and observers like Gladwin Hill and William Geagley who passed through during the years of atmospheric testing. But questions about safety and long-term environmental health tempered this enthusiasm quickly. The West was changing, and clashing perspectives about the nature of the region contributed to changing views about atomic programs leading to extended debates about fallout and later nuclear waste storage.

PICTURING WASTELANDS

Las Vegas was a small town in 1940 and a city of over two million only fifty years later. The once scorned and fearsome "great American desert" was recast during this period as the benign "sunbelt," a place welcoming

---

[4] Patricia Limerick, *The Legacy of Conquest: The Unbroken Past of the American West* (New York: W. W. Norton, 1987), 163.

FIG. 8 TEAPOT/WASP PRIME comparison.

to baby-boom families and warmth-seeking seniors. Regional magazines like *Sunset* promoted the southwest to a national audience and helped foster a new appreciation for desert landscapes. At the same time the AEC and FCDA needed to convince Americans that the southwest was also suitably empty and worthless to justify continued continental nuclear testing. How could the West be both a sunbelt paradise for life and leisure and an empty wasteland suitable for nuclear testing? Balancing these dueling regional images required subtle national propaganda throughout the Cold War. The American people needed reassurance that atomic testing on home soil was acceptable and being conducted in a suitably contained environment. The entire U.S. continental testing program was predicated on the assumption that testing at the NTS was somehow "contained." Borders between the testing zone and surrounding areas were drawn sharply on official maps with thick black ink, and government documentary photographic images were carefully constructed to support assertions that the valleys of the NTS were somehow compartmentalized from surrounding ecosystems, safely removed from human settlement and shielded by nature and science from the regional culture and economy.

This version of Cold War *containment* was circulated to the nation through carefully produced government films and publications. During the height of atmospheric nuclear testing, between 1951 and 1958, the FCDA and AEC used extensive visual imagery to shape public opinion about the environment of the NTS and the nature of nature in the atomic testing zones in order to explain and justify continental nuclear testing. The graphic

FIG. 9 NTS map with thick black lines.

documentation of the natural setting of atomic testing intentionally and unintentionally influenced attitudes about the regional environment and perceptions of nature in the nuclear age, resulting in widespread misunderstandings about the ecological consequences of testing. Of particular importance were the extensively documented and widely publicized civil effects tests between 1953 and 1957.[5]

Pictures and visual imagery were central to civil defense information programs. Civil defense publications were widely distributed and played an important role in shaping perceptions of global testing regions and their environments and forming lasting opinions about ecological health and safety in the atomic age. Simple articles casually explained the extensive testing programs at the Nevada Test Site (NTS) and the South Pacific locations. The "Doom Town" series pictured in the graphic history was the focus of photo essays and commentary on the environmental conditions of the testing zones. The Mojave and Great Basin Deserts that comprised the 5,000-square-mile continental atomic testing bioregion were described variously as a "landscape almost as barren as the moon," a "wasteland," and a "sub-marginal" place sparsely populated by "insignificant" populations.

The NTS was the atomic Comstock of the postwar West, and the history of this migration and its engineers, miners, workers, cooks, prostitutes, bar keeps, sheriffs, and ranchers is every bit as interesting as those of the Virginia City silver-lode communities a century earlier that so captivated Mark Twain and other chroniclers of the nineteenth-century West. But like

---

[5] The classic study of atomic culture is Paul Boyer, *By the Bomb's Early Light: American Thought and Culture at the Dawn of the Atomic Age* (New York: Pantheon, 1985).

that earlier Comstock, the NTS was less a place of exceptional or exotic experience than one might assume. The activity of atomic testing was mysterious to many, but the testing landscape was populated by a diverse group of people with familiar motives for migration, work, home, and quality of life. It was a place of racial, religious, and ethnic tensions and reconciliations familiar to the West. Like earlier migrants, atomic laborers came to appreciate misunderstood western environments through their work and lives.

Unlike their atomic counterparts in more familiar places like Los Alamos and Livermore, the Nevada testing communities were not planned utopias or exclusive enclaves for science and scientists. NTS workers lived with equally intense secrecy, surveillance, and restrictions at work but ranged more freely across the region and surrounding towns without the benefits of the exclusive community. The tens of thousands of men and women who worked or lived in and around the NTS enjoyed little of the national status or patriotic celebration that attended the elite scientists and the families of the lab cities around the West.

Researchers spending time with these people or reviewing the extensive historic photo collections online will notice a marked difference between the images and descriptions chosen by the FCDA and AEC for publication and the unpublished environmental images and cultural memories of the testing region. The published images usually zoom in on the experiments and experimental landscapes with no landscape and no people. Unpublished images tend to zoom out and show the environmental context more clearly and often include workers and technicians going about their jobs. The unpublished photos show the Mojave Desert of the NTS region as a richly complex and beautiful landscape that could just as easily grace the cover of *Sunset* as a civil defense booklet.

When considered from most vantage points the NTS was hardly the desolate wasteland or dead lunar landscape the AEC and the mass media often described. Iconic images like those of the Doom Town houses obliterated in super slow motion are part of the reason. Vernon Jones, pictured in the graphic history, was one of the photographers who captured the famous sequence of the houses with a special high-speed gunsight camera shooting 1,000 feet of film per second. The film footage of the Doom Town events was truly mesmerizing. The best-known sequence shows a house obliterated in super slow motion during the first two seconds of a nuclear blast. The house lights up for a split second before first the heat and then the blast slam into the structure. The blinding light illuminates the house and the desert fades to black.

A record television audience of fifteen million watched the Doom Town events live. Six hundred invited representatives from all fifty states saw

FIG. 10 Complete destruction of House No. 1.

these events in person from surrounding hillsides. The footage captured by Jones and a corps of atomic photographers is so mesmerizing, the "atomic sublime" so morbidly captivating, that many Americans only knew the Mojave Desert as seconds or less of unnatural light and destruction, mushroom clouds and human artifacts obliterated in eerie predawn flashes. Official government press releases said the televised events of the Doom Towns were "for the purpose of impressing Americans with the deadly seriousness of nuclear device detonations and the need for arousing a keener interest in civilian defense." It was a strategy that worked. All those present remembered the destruction of civilian artifacts as disturbing and frightening. Especially disconcerting were striking images of child mannequins clutched by mothers huddled in basement corners waiting for the end and then "after" photos showing them blown into scattered chunks. Regardless of how viewers on site or at home interpreted the action it was all as dramatic and unforgettable as the AEC hoped.

For downwinders and others protesting testing in the decades between the signing of the 1963 Limited Test Ban Treaty and the adoption of the Comprehensive Nuclear-Test-Ban Treaty by the United Nations General

FIG. 11 Witnesses.

Assembly on September 10, 1996, perceptions of environmental containment and desert desolation supported in part by Doom Town images and other public information about testing regions proved difficult to overturn. Misunderstanding and misrepresentation of testing environments and indigenous and regional peoples played a role in all the global testing regions. In the U.S., misperceptions of desert ecosystems and peoples had far-reaching impacts, influencing decisions to create the Yucca Mountain high-level radioactive waste facility and shaping protracted political and legal debates about a wide range of radiological health and safety issues.

Protest and legal action ultimately brought recognition of testing-region citizen health with the passage of the Radiation Exposure Compensation Act (RECA) on October 5, 1990. RECA was expanded in the year 2000 to include a formal apology to those who lived in the testing region and those who served or were employed in service of the creation of the nation's nuclear weapons programs during the era of atmospheric nuclear testing. The act was officially described as an "expeditious, low-cost alternative to litigation." RECA did not require claimants to establish causation of their disease, only proof that they had one of twenty-seven covered illnesses and that they resided in certain regions or worked in certain occupational settings related to the development and testing of nuclear weapons.[6]

---

[6]   On-site testing participants were eligible to receive $75,000 in compensation, uranium miners $100,000, and downwinders $50,000. The complete details of RECA are available on the U.S. Department of Justice website, http://www.justice.gov/civil/common/reca.

RECA COVERED AREAS

Uranium Worker States
Downwind Counties
Overlapping Uranium Worker States
and Downwind Counties

FIG. 12 Radiation Exposure Compensation Act (RECA) map.

For most in the protest community RECA was too little too late. Others inside and outside the testing regions saw the legislation as a capitulation to "deluded" protesters who, they believed, had never fully understood the science of radiation safety or the requirements for sacrifice necessary to wage a global Cold War. In other words, opinions on this issue after RECA and today remain sharply divided. Both camps do agree on one thing: the history of atomic testing, the nature of the testing regions, and the stories of the hundreds of thousands of people who participated or protested need to be more widely known.

The legacies of testing and protest in other parts of the world are, for the most part, more unsettled. Kazakhstan achieved its independence from the former Soviet Union on December 16, 1991, in part because of the unifying effect of the antinuclear protest movement that sparked massive national demonstrations following aborted Soviet discussions of resumed testing in the waning years of the union. Upon achieving independence, the newly autonomous modern state of Kazakhstan rapidly divested itself of the thousand-plus nuclear warheads left in the nation in the wake of the collapse of the Soviet Union and dismantled the nuclear testing infrastructure at Semipalatinsk. Anti-nuclear testing remains a core value for the nation after a quarter-century. There was no RECA for those who lived throughout the former Soviet testing zone where health and environmental effects were far more devastating than anywhere else. Across the other global testing regions international recognition of dislocation and health effects raised awareness of the role these places and peoples played in the atomic Cold War but fell short of restoring lost homelands or resolving persistent health and environmental concerns.

In Las Vegas and the American West, not everyone lamented the Doom Towns or worried about misperceptions of deserts or even their own personal health from participation in atomic testing. Many of the people who worked in the testing world or lived in the effected regions left the experience proud of their accomplishments and secure in the knowledge that their effort was part of a larger fight for freedom against tyranny at a critical juncture of modern global history. Retired test site workers serve as docents in atomic testing museums in New Mexico and Nevada that celebrate the scientific and technological achievements of this era. Others, indicated by a substantial number of oral histories, were simply glad to have had good-paying jobs, a working environment where their labor and expertise were generally valued, and interesting places to make a home. As with all histories, there was no typical experience of atomic testing. Individual actors were motivated for their own reasons and understood the events they were living in their own ways. The British novelist L. P. Hartley famous wrote, "The past is a foreign county: they do things differently there."[7] I hope this graphic introduction to atomic history sparks your interest in this "foreign country" of the recent past and encourages you to read further and explore some of the remarkable primary and secondary sources on this subject, enabling you to reach your own informed conclusions. You can start with the questions that follow.

---

[7]   L. P. Hartley, *The Go-Between* (New York: New York Review Books, 2002), 17. For a wide-ranging analysis of this concept, see David Lowenthal, *The Past Is a Foreign Country* (Cambridge: Cambridge University Press, 1985). For a more detailed version of this Cold War history in the broader context of American and global perspective, see Michael Schaller et al., *American Horizons: U.S. History in a Global Context* (New York: Oxford, 2015).

PART IV
THE QUESTIONS

CONTINGENCY

1. What were the possible futures for development and control of atomic energy in 1946? Can you identify one specific plan and its leading advocates? Which plan ultimately prevailed? Was it possible one of the other plans could have prevailed?

2. Why was OPERATION CROSSROADS organized so quickly after the end of the WWII? What factors contributed to continued nuclear testing during peacetime? Was there another option?

3. PROJECT NUTMEG explored the location options for continental nuclear test sites explaining strengths and weaknesses of each. The plan was initially rejected but shortly after the plan was reexamined and Nevada was quickly chosen. What caused this rapid change in opinion about the viability of a continental test site? Why did Nevada emerge as the sole choice? (See Primary Document 3.1; also, full version can be found on OpenNet.)

ORAL HISTORY

(http://digital.library.unlv.edu/ntsohp/)
(http://www.oralhistory.org)

1. The era of atomic weapons testing is recent history, and millions of people remember some of the events in this book. Find someone you know who lived part of the Cold War and do a brief oral history interview. The Oral History Association has all the resources you need to learn about method, best practices, and interview protocols.

2. Choose an interview from the Nevada Test Site Oral History Project. Read and listen to the interview, and create a concise report identifying

your subject, explaining their role in atomic history, and summarizing your conclusions about this topic based on the actual experience of your historical actor. Name something we learn from oral history that we would not have known otherwise.

3. Read and listen to the Native American Forum on Nuclear Issues http:// digital.library.unlv.edu/objects/nts/1339. How does oral history work in a group setting? What does this specific forum reveal about the perceptions and concerns of a group of people who lived in the testing region much longer than anyone else?

DOE OPENNET

(https://www.osti.gov/opennet/)

1. Choose a subject covered in the graphic history and search for related documents on the OpenNet. Pick one document to explore in detail. Explain how this source expands your understanding of the topic. Identify the author/authors and discuss their reliability.

2. Search for a topic, event, or person you thought was missing from the graphic history. Can you find sources that would enable you to fill in the gaps?

3. Search the word *radiation* on OpenNet. How many hits did you get? What types of documents are included? Could these documents help answer lingering questions about radiation exposure and human health effects? How might you direct your search to reveal important historical sources?

4. Search the word *Indians* on OpenNet. What types of documents appear, and what can they tell you about the relationship between the atomic agencies and indigenous peoples?

PRIMARY DOCUMENTS

1. In preparation for the Trinity test, Kenneth Bainbridge was the first to tackle the questions of where and how an atomic device should be tested. Based on his report to "All Concerned with Project TR" (Primary

Document 1.2), what were the primary concerns and criteria, and how were they addressed? Why do you think the map and weather information was highlighted as "secret"? Can you conclude anything about concerns about human safety from this document?

2. Use the excerpts from the DOE official guide for tour leaders (Primary Document 9.2) to create your own virtual tour of the NTS. Imagine you are leading a bus tour based on your new knowledge of the history of atomic testing. Would you stick to the DOE script or add other perspectives? Is there information in the official guide that you disagree with? What would you add to the story you are telling visitors? What, if anything, would you change about the guide descriptions?

3. What was the meaning of the "Size of the Risk"? Review the meeting notes compiled by Frederick Reines, "Discussion of Radiological Hazards Associated with a Continental Test Site for Atomic Bombs," Los Alamos, New Mexico, August 1, 1950 (Primary Document 3.2). What exactly was decided at that critical meeting? How did the scientists quantify risk? How certain were they about these conclusions?

4. What do you learn about the cultural and environmental setting of the Nevada Test Site from reading Frederick Worman's "Anatomy of the NTS" (Primary Document 3.3)? How does Worman's depiction of the area differ from the descriptions circulated by the AEC?

5. The warning poster (Primary Document 3.6) circulated on January 11, 1951, was the only information most Las Vegans had about atomic testing as it began sixty-five miles north of the city. Based only on this one source, what would a citizen have known about what was about to happen? Based on your reading of the graphic history, what might they have also learned by reading or listening to media coverage from previous atomic tests held elsewhere?

6. Compare Gladwin Hill's articles, "Atomic Boom Town in the Desert," 1951 (Primary Document 4.1), and "Las Vegas Is More Than the Strip," 1958 (Primary Document 9.3). In what ways had Hill's understanding of the city and its place in America changed in the eight years he spent covering atomic testing for the *New York Times*?

7. Examine the two Camp Desert Rock documents (Primary Documents 5.2 and 5.3). What were the goals of this program that brought tens of thousands of soldiers to the NTS to experience atomic warfare? In what ways did the Army believe these elaborate exercises would be useful?

8. In 1953, Los Alamos Scientific Laboratory Director Norris Bradbury wrote a memo on "How to Explain Atomic Testing" (Primary Document 5.4). What were his main points in this memo? What challenges of the process did he note? Why did he discourage including details of experiments?

9. Review Dr. Charles W. Mays's "Estimated Thyroid Doses & Predicted Thyroid Cancers in Utah Infants Exposed to Fallout" (Primary Document 6.2). What is the author's goal in this paper? What was his central conclusion, and what were his recommendations?

10. Examine President Eisenhower's "Atoms for Peace" speech draft, 1953 (Primary Document 6.6). How does Eisenhower explain the state of the world eight years after the first successful nuclear tests? What is his position on atomic weapons moving forward? What is the tone of this speech?

11. In his pre-series "PLUMBBOB Briefing" (Primary Document 7.4), James E. Reeves was asked about the names of the operations and the names of the bombs. What was his response? Is his answer convincing? What other explanation is there for the interesting names that run through the history of atomic testing?

12. Examine William Geagley's security documents prepared for his visit to Nevada in 1957 (Primary Document 8.2). What aspects of broader trends in American politics and culture are revealed in this process and these types of documents? What struck you as most interesting about a 1957 "Q" clearance?

13. Read the "Little Green Book: Atomic Tests in Nevada," 1957, distributed to residents of the testing region by the AEC (Primary Document 8.1). The book was designed to calm fears about nuclear fallout and inform testing region residents about precautions. What is the central message? What is the tone? How might readers of the time have reacted to this booklet? How does it read today?

14. What was "Project Gabriel"? Search the DOE OpenNet for documents related to "Gabriel" and the follow-up study "Project Sunshine." What do these two studies reveal about the state of radiologic safety research in the middle period of atmospheric atomic testing?

15. Read the "Check List of Actions to Reduce World Antagonisms to U.S. Nuclear Weapons Tests," 1954 (Primary Document 6.5). What does the existence of this little document indicate about U.S. testing policy in 1954? What was the plan to change the tide of world opinion?

IMAGES AS EVIDENCE

1. Watch the 1954 short film *The House in the Middle* (https://www.you tube.com/watch?v=pGJcwaUWNZg). What is the message of this little film? Why would a group like the "National Clean Up—Paint Up—Fix Up Bureau" produce a film about nuclear weapons? In what ways does this film address issues in 1950s American history and culture beyond nuclear testing?

2. Visit the DOE/NNSA Nevada Field Site Image Library OPERATION DOORSTEP collection and choose an image you find compelling to analyze and "read" (http://www.nv.energy.gov/library/photos/doorstep .aspx). Write a paragraph carefully describing this image. Can you conclude anything about the intent of the photographer? Is this simply an image of a scene, or is it an interpretation of a scene with a discernable goal in mind for viewers?

3. Take a close look at the image "ATOM BOMB—TESTS—NEVADA— 1951" (Primary Document 3.7). What questions does this image raise about the beginning of continental atomic testing in Nevada? What did the photographer have to say about capturing this image (Primary Document 5.5)? Can a simple image like this convey meaningful information about the cultural context for an historic moment? Explain.

4. Study the image "Graveyard on Bikini Island" (Primary Document 2.5). How do the documentary photos of the Smithsonian archive from 1946 contrast with the official explanation for the choice of Bikini for Crossroads? How can you explain this contrast?

5. Analyze the OPERATION PLUMBBOB certificate awarded to participants (Primary Document 8.8). What events from the graphic history can you identify in this artwork? What is the tone of this atomic folk art example? What does this certificate reveal about the culture of life and labor at the Nevada Test Site in 1957?

MAKING GRAPHIC HISTORY

1. Using the primary documents, oral histories, and historic images, create a one-page spread of a graphic history of your own. You can take one test series, an individual shot, or a person. Start with a graphic sheet, as shown in the introduction, and then create a draft of the final illustrated page. Use footnotes to support what you show and say.

2. Find a page or section of the graphic history where you wished for more detail or a better answer to the historic questions covered. Can you find primary source evidence that would allow the historian and artist to expand? Can you find a more complete answer in the sources? How would you include those answers or insights in graphic form or dialogue?

3. This graphic history relied heavily on actual photographic evidence as the basis for the illustrations whereas traditional graphic novels invent the graphics in service of the story. Which method would you choose? In your opinion what is the best way to balance historical accuracy with compelling graphic narrative?

BIBLIOGRAPHY

PRIMARY SOURCES

ORAL HISTORIES

Listed below are only the interviews that directly informed the historic interpretation and the interviews of those individuals specifically featured in the graphic history.

Interview with Harold M. Agnew, October 10, 2005, Mary Palevsky, Nevada Test Site Oral History Project, University of Nevada Las Vegas, Special Collections.

Interview with Robert Agonia, June 29, 2005, Charlie Deitrich, Nevada Test Site Oral History Project, University of Nevada Las Vegas, Special Collections.

Interview with Philip Allen, August 26, 2004, Mary Palevsky, Nevada Test Site Oral History Project, University of Nevada Las Vegas, Special Collections.

Interview with Zenna Mae and Eugene Bridges, November 19, 2004, Mary Palevsky, Nevada Test Site Oral History Project, University of Nevada Las Vegas, Special Collections.

Interview with Robert Brownlee, September 10, 2006, Mary Palevsky, Nevada Test Site Oral History Project, University of Nevada Las Vegas, Special Collections.

Interview with John F. Campbell, January 31, 2006, Charlie Deitrich, Nevada Test Site Oral History Project, University of Nevada Las Vegas, Special Collections.

Interview with Robert "Doc" Campbell Jr., March 12, 2005, Suzanne Becker, Nevada Test Site Oral History Project, University of Nevada Las Vegas, Special Collections.

Interview with Bruce Church, April 27, 2004, Jeffrey Richardson, Nevada Test Site Oral History Project, University of Nevada Las Vegas, Special Collections.

Interview with Charles Costa, February 13, 2009, Leisl Carr Childers, Nevada Test Site Oral History Project, University of Nevada Las Vegas, Special Collections.

Interview with Norma Cox, June 8, 2004, Shannon Applegate, Nevada Test Site Oral History Project, University of Nevada Las Vegas, Special Collections.

Interview with Donald E. English, March 25, 2004, Michael Childers, Nevada Test Site Oral History Project, University of Nevada Las Vegas, Special Collections.

Interview with William Flangas, November 12, 2004, Mary Palevsky, Nevada Test Site Oral History Project, University of Nevada Las Vegas, Special Collections.

Interview with Robert Friedrichs, February 25, 2005, Mary Palevsky, Nevada Test Site Oral History Project, University of Nevada Las Vegas, Special Collections.

Interview with Dorothy Grier, January 3, 2005, Mary Palevsky, Nevada Test Site Oral History Project, University of Nevada Las Vegas, Special Collections.

Interview with Raymond Harbert, July 14, 2005, Mary Palevsky, Nevada Test Site Oral History Project, University of Nevada Las Vegas, Special Collections.

Interview with Corbin Harney, July 24 and 25, 2006, Mary Palevsky, Nevada Test Site Oral History Project, University of Nevada Las Vegas, Special Collections.

Interview with Gladwin Hill, October 22, November 25, and December 21, 1987, Carlos Vasquez, Oral History Program University of California Los Angeles, Department of Special Collections.

Interview with Vernon Jones, October 4, 2005, Mary Palevsky, Nevada Test Site Oral History Project, University of Nevada Las Vegas, Special Collections.

Interview with Lawrence Krenzien, September 8, 2005, Suzanne Becker, Nevada Test Site Oral History Project, University of Nevada Las Vegas, Special Collections.

Interview with George and Theresa Maynard, January 26, 2004, Mary Palevsky, Nevada Test Site Oral History Project, University of Nevada Las Vegas, Special Collections.

Interview with Robert Mackenzie and Kari Chipman, January 5, 2005, Mary Palevsky, Nevada Test Site Oral History Project, University of Nevada Las Vegas, Special Collections.

Interview with Marie McMillian, February 2, 2004, Mary Palevsky, Nevada Test Site Oral History Project, University of Nevada Las Vegas, Special Collections.

Interview with James Merlino, November 7, 2004, Suzanne Becker, Nevada Test Site Oral History Project, University of Nevada Las Vegas, Special Collections.

Interview with Lewis Miller, September 14, 2005, Suzanne Becker, Nevada Test Site Oral History Project, University of Nevada Las Vegas, Special Collections.

Native American Forum on Nuclear Issues, April 10, 2008, Native Community Action Council, Nevada Test Site Oral History Project, University of Nevada Las Vegas, Special Collections.

Interview with Megan Rice, June 22, 2005, Suzanne Becker, Nevada Test Site Oral History Project, University of Nevada Las Vegas, Special Collections.

Interview with Elmer Sowder, July 29, 2005, Mary Palevsky, Nevada Test Site Oral History Project, University of Nevada Las Vegas, Special Collections.

Interview with Gracian N. Uhalde, December 1, 2006, Leisl Carr Childers, Nevada Test Site Oral History Project, University of Nevada Las Vegas, Special Collections.

Interview with Navor Valdez, June 20, 2005, Charlie Deitrich, Nevada Test Site Oral History Project, University of Nevada Las Vegas, Special Collections.

Interview with Charles E. Violet, May 22, 2004, Mary Palevsky, Nevada Test Site Oral History Project, University of Nevada Las Vegas, Special Collections.

Interview with Louis Vitale, May 19, 2004, Mary Palevsky, Nevada Test Site Oral History Project, University of Nevada Las Vegas, Special Collections.

Interview with Troy Wade, June 16, 2004, Joan Leavitt, Nevada Test Site Oral History Project, University of Nevada Las Vegas, Special Collections.

Interview with Ernest Williams, October 27, 2004, Joan Leavitt, Nevada Test Site Oral History Project, University of Nevada Las Vegas, Special Collections.

Interview with Herbert York, January 16 and July 18, 2004, Mary Palevsky, Nevada Test Site Oral History Project, University of Nevada Las Vegas, Special Collections.

All of the 200-plus interviews in Nevada Test Site Oral History Project (http://digital.library.unlv.edu/ntsohp/) collection directly pertain to this history. See also the Manhattan Project Oral History Collection, Atomic Heritage Foundation, and Los Alamos Historical Society (http://manhat tanprojectvoices.org).

NNSA/DOE OpenNet
Kenneth Bainbridge, To All Concerned with Project TR (ALLA0000919).
Dear Dr. Shields Warren (NV04087743).
Project Nutmeg Report (NV0411323).
Camp Desert Rock 1: A Psychological Study of Troop Reactions to an Atomic Explosion (NV0006252).
Desert Rock 1 Sketch Map (NV0767719).
Buster-Jangle Fallout Plan (NV0404739).
Mike Report (NV0029277).
Operation Doorstep Report (NV0014434).
Operation Upshot-Knothole Directive for Exercise Desert Rock V (NV0767909)
Norris Bradbury Memo to C. L. Tyler on How to Explain Atomic Testing, 1953 (NV0124371).
Los Alamos Conference on Livestock Losses (NV 0404967).
Estimated Thyroid Doses and Predicted Thyroid Cancers in Utah Infants Exposed to Fallout (NV 0403156).
Project Gabriel Report (NV0404830).
Checklist to Reduce World Antagonisms to U.S. Nuclear Weapons Tests (NV0304906).
AEC 141/33—Radiological Criteria for the Nevada Test Site (NV0408756).
Defense Technical Information Center, *Camp Desert Rock I* (NV0767823)
National Security Resources Board, "Civil Defense Planning Advisory Bulletin" (NV0720057).
U.S. Atomic Energy Commission, *Atomic Test Effects in the Nevada Proving Ground Region* (NV0057724).
U.S. Atomic Energy Commission, *Atomic Tests in Nevada*, Nuclear Testing Archive (NV0006327).
U.S. Atomic Energy Commission, *Continental Weapons Tests . . . Public Safety* (NV0049175).
U.S. Atomic Energy Commission, *Nevada Test Site Information Handbook* (NV0130410).
U.S. Atomic Energy Commission, "Radiological Defense in the Civilian Defense Program" (NV0404928).
U.S. Atomic Energy Commission, *REECO Continues as Support Contractor to AEC* (NV0324407).
U.S. Atomic Energy Commission Department of Defense, *Background Information on Continental Nuclear Tests, Nevada Proving Grounds and Military Installations* (NV0016359).
U.S. Atomic Energy Commission Department of Defense, *History of Camp Desert Rock* (NV0322977).
U.S. Atomic Energy Commission (Los Alamos, W-7405-ENG. 36, March 10, 1969).

LIBRARY OF CONGRESS
Nevada Test Site Historic Photo Collections, Library of Congress Prints and Photographs Division Washington, DC 20540 USA, http://hdl.loc.gov/loc.pnp/pp.print, http://www.loc.gov/pictures/search/?q=nevada%20test%20site.

NATIONAL ATOMIC TESTING MUSEUM
Historic Photography Collections.
Atomic Art Collections.
Archival Collections.

SMITHSONIAN INSTITUTION NATIONAL MUSEUM OF NATURAL HISTORY
Leonard P. Schultz Diary from Able Day July 1, 1946, Schultz Papers.

OREGON STATE UNIVERSITY SPECIAL COLLECTIONS
Ava Helen and Linus Pauling Papers, 1873–2013.
Linus Pauling to Barry Commoner, June 11, 1957, box #5.002, folder 2.1.

HARRY S. TRUMAN LIBRARY
Miscellaneous Historical Documents Collection.
Albert Einstein to President Franklin Delano Roosevelt, August 2, 1939.
U.S. Atomic Energy Commission, "An Interim Report of British Work on Joe,"
   September 22, 1949. President's Secretary's Files, box 199, NSC-Atomic.

DWIGHT D. EISENHOWER PRESIDENTIAL LIBRARY
Atoms for Peace Address Draft, C.D. Jackson Papers, box 30.

UNIVERSITY OF CALIFORNIA, LOS ANGELES CHARLES E. YOUNG RESEARCH LIBRARY
Gladwin Hill Papers.
Speech on Atomic Test Coverage (1706), box 50.
Field Notebook, May, 1957 (1706), box 50.

UNIVERSITY OF NEVADA, LAS VAGAS SPECIAL COLLECTIONS
Marie McMillian Papers.
Duke Daly materials.
William Geagley Papers.
Hugh D. Ivey to William C. Geagley, April 25, 1957.
Operation Plumbbob: Civil Effects Group, Project 36.1 Field Radiological De-
   fense Technical Operations, WT-1482 FCDA (March 1958).
Plumbbob Pre-Series Briefing, Nevada Test Organization Office of Test Informa-
   tion, Las Vegas, NV, May 1957.
Atomic Tests in Nevada, U.S. Atomic Energy Commission, March 1957.
Q Clearance form with Executive Order no. 10450 Restrictions.
NTS Bulletins PlumbBob.
Notes from Radiation Training.
Civil Effects Test Group Projects 36.1 and 36.2, Operational Plan, Monday June
   17, 1957.
Glyn G. Caldwell, MD, to Mrs. William C. Geagley, July 19, 1977.

LOS ALAMOS NATIONAL LABORATORY RESEARCH LIBRARY
Frederick Reines, Discussion of Radiological Hazards Associated with a Continental Test Site for Atomic Bombs, LAMS-1173.

GOVERNMENT DOCUMENTS
There are thousands of published government reports. The following specifically
   informed the graphic interpretations.

DNA 6004F, *Shot Smoky: A Test of the Plumbbob Series*, August 31, 1957, U.S. Atmospheric Nuclear Weapons Tests Nuclear Test Personnel Review.

FCDA, Operation Doorstep, 1953.

For the Record—A History of the Nuclear Test Personnel Review Program, 1978–1993, Defense Nuclear Agency, DNA 001-91-C-0022, March 1996.

National Academy of Sciences, *A Report to the Public on the Biological Effects of Atomic Radiation*, 1960.

Operation Cue: The Atomic Test Program, Federal Civil Defense Administration Nevada Test Site, Spring 1955.

Radiation Exposure Compensation Act (RECA), 1990, U.S. Department of Justice http://www.justice.gov/civil/common/reca.html, last accessed 10/24/14.

Summary of Upshot-Knothole Tests, June 4 1953, U.S. Atomic Energy Commission, "Health Aspects of Nuclear Weapons Testing," June 1964.

U.S. Defense Nuclear Agency, *For the Record—A History of the Nuclear Test Personnel Review Program, 1978–1993* (DNA 6041F, March 1996).

U.S. Department of Defense, Defense Nuclear Agency: *PlumbBob Series 1957* (DNA 6005F, September 15, 1981); *Shot Priscilla: A Test of the PlumbBob Series, June 24, 1957* (DNA 6003F, September 15, 1981); *Shot Smokey: A Test of the PlumbBob Series, August 31, 1957* (DNA 6004F, September 15, 1981); *Shots Boltzmann to Wilson: The First Four Tests of the PlumbBob Series, May 28–June 18, 1957* (DNA 6008F, September 15, 1981); *Shots Diablo to Franklin Prime: The Mid-Series Tests of the PlumbBob Series, July 15–30, 1957* (DNA 6006F, September 15, 1981); *Shots Wheeler to Morgan: The Final Eight Tests of the PlumbBob Series, June 24, 1957* (DNA 6007F, September 15, 1981).

U.S. Department of Energy, United States Nuclear Tests, July 1945 through September 1992.

COURT CASES

Allen v. United States, 816 F.2d 1417 (10th Cir. 1987), Irene H. Allen, et al., Plaintiffs-Appellees, v. United States of America, Defendant-Appellant.

NEWSPAPERS

U.S. and global newspapers covered the activities at the Nevada Test Site extensively. The DOE Archive has extensive clipping portfolios covering the years of atmospheric testing that show the extent and evolving character of this coverage. Of special importance to students of atomic testing history are the following: *Deseret News, Las Vegas Sun, Las Vegas Review-Journal, Los Angeles Times, New York Times, Washington County News*.

SECONDARY SOURCES

BOOKS AND ARTICLES

Abazov, Rafis, ed. *Green Desert: The Life and Poetry of Olzhas Suleimenov*. San Diego: Cognella, 2011.

Anders, Roger M. *Forging the Atomic Shield: Excerpts from the Office Diary of Gordon E. Dean*. Chapel Hill: University of North Carolina Press, 1987.

Arnold, Lorna, and Mark Smith. *Britain, Australia and the Bomb: The Nuclear Tests and their Aftermath*. New York: Palgrave Macmillan, 2006.

Ball, Howard. *Justice Downwind: America's Atomic Testing Program in the 1950s*. New York: Oxford University Press, 1986.

Blackhawk, Ned, *Violence Over the Land: Indians and Empires in the Early American West*. Cambridge, MA: Harvard University Press, 2006.

Boyer, Paul. *Fallout: A Historian Reflects on America's Half-Century Encounter with Nuclear Weapons.* Columbus: University of Ohio Press, 1998.

Bradley, David. *No Place to Hide.* New York: Little, Brown & Co., 1948.

Brown, Kate. *Plutopia: Nuclear Families, Atomic Cities, and the Great Soviet and American Plutonium Disasters.* New York: Oxford University Press, 2013.

Brunn, Stanley D. "Fifty Years of Soviet Nuclear Testing in Semipalatinsk, Kazakhstan." In *Engineering Earth: The Impacts of Megaengineering Projects, 1789–1820.* New York: Springer, 2011.

Butigan, Ken. *Pilgrimage Through a Burning World, Spiritual Practice and Non-Violent Protest at the Nevada Test Site.* Albany: University of New York Press, 1999.

Cantelon, Philip L., Richard G. Hewlett, and Robert C. Williams. *The American Atom: A Documentary History of Nuclear Policies.* Philadelphia: University of Pennsylvania Press, 1991.

Carothers, James, et al. *Caging the Dragon: The Containment of Underground Explosions.* Technical Report DOE NV-388, 1995.

Childers, Leisl. *The Size of the Risk: Histories of Multiple Use in the Great Basin.* Norman: University of Oklahoma Press, 2015.

Cohen, Michael P. *A Garden of Bristlecones: Tales of Change in the Great Basin.* Reno: University of Nevada Press, 1998.

Comer, C.L. *Fallout from Nuclear Tests.* Washington, DC: U.S. Atomic Energy Commission, 1963.

Commoner, Barry. *The Closing Circle: Nature, Man, and Technology.* New York: Alfred A. Knopf, 1971.

Coolidge, Mathew. *The Nevada Test Site: A Guide to America's Nuclear Proving Ground.* Los Angeles: Center for Land Use Interpretation, 1996.

Darlington, David. *The Mojave: A Portrait of the Definitive American Desert.* New York: Henry Holt, 1996.

Davis, Mike. "Dead West: Ecocide in Marlboro Country." In *Over the Edge: Remapping the American West,* edited by Valerie J. Matsumoto and Blake Almendinger, 339–369. Berkeley: University of California Press, 1999.

Del Tredici, Robert. *At Work in the Fields of the Bomb.* New York: Harper & Row, 1987.

Dennis, Jack, ed. *The Nuclear Almanac: Confronting the Atom in War and Peace.* Reading: Addison-Wesley, 1984.

Divine, Robert A. *Blowing on the Wind: The Nuclear Test Ban Debate, 1954–1960.* New York: Oxford University Press, 1978.

Dunaway, Finis. *Seeing Green: The Use and Abuse of American Environmental Images.* Chicago: University of Chicago Press, 2015.

Fehner, Terrence R., and F. G. Gosling. *Battlefield of the Cold War: The Nevada Test Site.* Vol. 1, *Atmospheric Nuclear Weapons Testing 1951–1963.* Washington, DC: U.S. Department of Energy, 2006.

Fermi, Rachel, and Esther Samra. *Picturing the Bomb: Photographs from the Secret World of the Manhattan Project.* New York: Harry Abrams, 1995.

Fernlund, Kevin J. *The Cold War American West, 1945–1989.* Albuquerque: University of New Mexico Press, 1998.

Fiege, Mark. "The Atomic Scientists, the Sense of Wonder, and the Bomb." *Environmental History* 12, no. 3 (July 2007): 578–580.

Findlay, John M., and Bruce Hevly. *Atomic Frontier Days, Hanford and the American West.* Seattle: University of Washington Press, 2011.

Fox, William L. *Playa Works: The Myth of the Empty.* Reno: University of Nevada Press, 2002.

Fradkin, Philip L. *Fallout: An American Nuclear Tragedy.* Tucson: University of Arizona Press, 1989.

Gallagher, Carole. *American Ground Zero: The Secret Nuclear War.* Cambridge, MA: MIT Press, 1993.

Glasstone, Samuel, ed. *The Effects of Nuclear Weapons.* Washington, DC: U.S. Atomic Energy Commission, 1962.

Goin, Peter. *Nuclear Landscapes.* Baltimore: Johns Hopkins University Press, 1991.

Greene, Benjamin P. *Eisenhower, Science Advice, and the Nuclear Test-Ban Debate, 1945–1963.* Stanford, CA: Stanford University Press, 2007.

Grodzins, Morton, and Eugene Rabinowitch, eds. *The Atomic Age: Scientists in National and World Affairs.* New York: Basic Books, 1963.

Guibert, Emmanuel. *Alan's War: The Memories of G.I. Alan Cope.* New York: First Second, 2000.

Hacker, Barton C. *The Dragon's Tail: Radiation Safety in the Manhattan Project, 1942–1946.* Berkeley: University of California Press, 1987.

Hacker, Barton C. *Elements of Controversy, the Atomic Energy Commission and Radiation Safety in Nuclear Weapons Testing, 1947–1974.* Berkeley: University of California Press, 1994.

Hales, Peter Bacon. *Atomic Spaces: Living on the Manhattan Project.* Urbana: University of Illinois Press, 1997.

Hales, Peter Bacon. "Atomic Sublime." *American Studies* 32 (Spring 1991): 5–31.

Hales, Peter Bacon. *Outside the Gates of Eden: The Dream of America from Hiroshima to Now.* Chicago: University of Chicago Press, 2014.

Hecht, Gabrielle. *Being Nuclear: Africans and the Global Uranium Trade.* Cambridge, MA: MIT Press, 2012.

Heefer, Gretchen. *The Missile Next Door: The Minuteman in the American Heartland.* Cambridge, MA: Harvard University Press, 2012.

Henriksen, Margot A. *Dr. Strangelove's America: Society and Culture in the Atomic Age.* Berkeley: University of California Press, 1997.

Hersey, John. *Hiroshima.* New York: Penguin Books, 1946.

Hevly, Bruce, and John M. Findlay. *The Atomic West.* Seattle: University of Washington Press, 1998.

Hewlett, Richard G., and Jack M. Holl. *Atoms for Peace and War: Eisenhower and the Atomic Energy Commission.* Berkeley: University of California Press, 1989.

Hill, Gladwin. *Madman in a Lifeboat: Issues of the Environmental Crisis.* New York: John Day Co., 1973.

Holloway, David. *Stalin and the Bomb: The Soviet Union and Atomic Energy, 1939–1956.* New Haven, CT: Yale University Press, 1994.

Jacobs, Paul. "Clouds from Nevada: A Special Report on the AEC's Weapons-Testing Program." *The Reporter,* May 16, 1957, 10–29.

Jacobs, Robert. "Nuclear Conquistadors: Military Colonialism in Nuclear Test Site Selection During the Cold War." *Asian Journal of Peacebuilding* 1, no. 2 (November 2013): 157–177.

Jacobs, Robert, ed. *Filling the Hole in the Nuclear Future: Art and Popular Culture Respond to the Bomb.* Lanham, MD: Lexington Books, 2010.

Jungk, Robert. *Brighter Than a Thousands Suns: A Personal History of the Atomic Scientists.* New York: Harcourt, Brace & Co., 1956.

Katz, Milton S. *Ban the Bomb, A History of SANE, the Committee for a Sane Nuclear Policy, 1957–1985.* New York: Greenwood Press, 1986.

Kirk, Andrew. "Rereading the Nature of Atomic Doom Towns." *Environmental History* 17, no. 3 (July 2012): 635–647.

Kuletz, Valerie L. *The Tainted Desert: Environmental and Social Ruin in the American West.* London: Routledge Press, 1998.

Kuran, Peter. *How to Photograph an Atomic Bomb.* Santa Clara, CA: VCE, 2006.

Lapp, Ralph E. *Voyage of the Lucky Dragon.* New York: Harper & Brothers, 1957.

Lear, John. "Hiroshima, U.S.A.: Can Anything Be Done About It?" *Colliers Magazine,* August 5, 1950, 11–15.

Leopold, Ellen. *Under the Radar: Cancer and the Cold War.* New Brunswick, NJ: Rutgers University Press, 2008.

Light, Michael. *100 Suns, 1945–1962.* New York: Alfred A. Knopf, 2003.

Limerick, Patricia Nelson. *Desert Passages: Encounters with the American Deserts.* Boulder: University of Colorado Press, 1989.

Limerick, Patricia Nelson. *The Legacy of Conquest: The Unbroken Past of the American West.* New York: W. W. Norton & Company, 1987.

Mackedon, Michon. *Bombast, Spinning Atoms in the Desert.* Reno, NV: Black Rock Institute Press, 2010.

Masco, Joseph. "Fantastic City," *Cabinet* 20 (Winter 2005/2006): 1–6.

Masco, Joseph. *The Nuclear Borderlands: The Manhattan Project in Post-Cold War New Mexico.* Princeton, NJ: Princeton University Press, 2006.

Masters, Dexter, ed. *One World or None,* 2nd ed. New York: New Press, 2007.

Matsumoto, Valerie J., and Blake Allmendinger. *Over the Edge: Remapping the American West.* Los Angeles: University of California Press, 1999.

Mazuzan, George T., and Samuel J. Walker. *Controlling the Atom: The Beginnings of Nuclear Regulation, 1946–1962.* Berkeley: University of California Press, 1984.

McCloud, Scott. *Understanding Comics: The Invisible Art.* New York: Harper-Collins, 1993.

McPhee, John. *Basin and Range.* New York: Farrar, Straus & Giroux, 1980.

Miller, Richard L. *Under the Cloud: The Decades of Nuclear Testing.* New York: Free Press, 1986.

Moehring, Eugene P. *Resort City in the Sunbelt, Las Vegas, 1930–2000.* Reno: University of Nevada Press, 2000.

Montoya, Maria. "Landscapes of the Cold War West." In *The Cold War American West,* edited by Kevin Fernlund, 9–28. Albuquerque: University of New Mexico Press, 1998.

Nye, David. *American Technological Sublime* and *America as Second Creation: Technology and Narratives of New Beginnings.* Baltimore: MIT Press, 2004.

Oakes, Guy. *The Imaginary War, Civil Defense and American Cold War Culture.* Oxford: Oxford University Press, 1994.

Palevsky, Mary. *Atomic Fragments: A Daughter's Questions.* Berkeley: University of California Press, 2000.

Portelli, Alisandro. *The Order Has Been Carried Out: History, Memory and Meaning of a Nazi Massacre in Rome.* New York: Palgrave Macmillan, 2003.

Rabinowitch, Eugene. "The First Pugwash Conference: History and Outlook." In *The Atomic Age: Scientists in National and World Affairs Articles from the Bulletin of the Atomic Scientists, 1945–1962,* 334–441. New York: Basic Books, 1963.

Rhodes, Richard. *The Making of the Atomic Bomb.* New York: Simon & Schuster, 1986.

Rhodes, Richard. *Dark Sun: The Making of the Hydrogen Bomb.* New York: Simon & Schuster, 1995.

Rogers, Harry. "The Bomb from the Bottom Up: How Site Workers and Southwestern Civil Society Interacted with the Nevada Test Site Between 1951 and 1963." M.A. thesis, Cambridge University, 2014.

Rosenberg, Howard L. *Atomic Soldiers: American Victims of Nuclear Experiments*. Boston: Beacon Press, 1980.

Saffer, Thomas H., and Orville E. Kelly. *Countdown Zero*. New York: Putnam's Sons, 1982.

Schlosser, Eric. *Command and Control: Nuclear Weapons, the Damascus Accident, and the Illusion of Safety*. New York: Penguin Press, 2013.

Schurcliff, W. A. *Bombs at Bikini: The Official Report of Operation Crossroads*. New York: Wm. H. Wise & Co., 1947.

Scott, Emily Eliza. "Desert Ends." In *Ends of the Earth: Land Art to 1974*, edited by Phillip Kaiser and Miwon Kwon, 67–92. Munich: Prestel, 2012.

Solnit, Rebecca. *Savage Dreams: A Journey into the Landscape Wars of the American West*. Berkeley: University of California Press, 1999.

Szasz, Ferenc Morton. *The Day the Sun Rose Twice: The Story of the Trinity Site Nuclear Explosion July 16, 1945*. Albuquerque: University of New Mexico Press, 1984.

Szasz, Ferenc Morton. *Atomic Comics: Cartoonists Confront the Nuclear World*. Reno: University of Nevada Press, 2012.

Szilard, Leo. "To Test or Not to Test." In *The Atomic Age: Scientists in National and World Affairs Articles from the Bulletin of the Atomic Scientists, 1945–1962*, 342–348. New York: Basic Books, 1963.

Taylor, Bryan C. "Nuclear Pictures and Metapictures." *American Literary History* 9, no. 3 (Autumn 1997): 567–597.

Titus, Alice Costandina. *Bombs in the Backyard: Atomic Testing and American Politics*, 2nd ed. Las Vegas: University of Nevada Press, 2001.

Udall, Steward, *The Myths of August: A Personal Exploration of Our Tragic Cold War Affair with the Atom*. New York: Pantheon, 1994.

Wammack, Mary. "Atomic Governance: Militarism, Secrecy, and Science in Post-War America, 1945–1958." Ph.D. dissertation, UNLV Department of History, 2010.

Wasserman, Harvey, and Norman Solomon. *Killing our Own: The Disaster of America's Experience with Atomic Radiation*. New York: Delacorte Press, 1982.

Weart, Spencer R. *The Rise of Nuclear Fear*. Cambridge: Harvard University Press, 2012.

Williams, Terry Tempest. *Refuge: An Unnatural History of Family and Place*. New York: Vintage, 2001.

Wills, Cathy A., and Kent W. Ostler. *Ecology of the Nevada Test Site: An Annotated Bibliography*. Las Vegas: U.S. DOE National Nuclear Security Administration, 2001.

Winkler, Alan M. *Life Under a Cloud: American Anxiety About the Atom*. New York: Oxford University Press, 1993.

Wittner, Lawrence S. *The Struggle Against the Bomb: One World or None, A History of the World Nuclear Disarmament Movement Through 1953*, Vol. 1. Stanford, CA: University of Stanford Press, 1993.

Worman, Frederick C. V. *Anatomy of the Nevada Test Site*. Los Alamos, NM: University of California Los Alamos Scientific Laboratories, 1965.

Worman, Frederick C. V. *Archeological Investigations at the U.S. Atomic Energy Commission's Nevada Test Site and Nuclear Rocket Development Station*. Los Alamos, NM: University of California Los Alamos Scientific Laboratories, 1969.

Wooster, Donald, *Nature's Economy: A History of Ecological Ideas*, 2nd ed. Cambridge: Cambridge University Press, 1997.

Zeman, Scott C., and Michael A. Amundson. *Atomic Culture: How We Learned to Stop Worrying and Love the Bomb*. Boulder: University Press of Colorado, 2004.

TIMELINE OF ATMOSPHERIC NUCLEAR TESTING

1940

1941

1942 ——— **1942** Creation of Manhattan Project

First nuclear chain reaction, University of Chicago

1943 ——— **1943** Los Alamos Laboratory established

1944

1945 ——— **1945** TRINITY, first nuclear explosion (21 kt)

Atomic bombings of Hiroshima (15 kt) and Nagasaki (21 kt), Japan

W W II ends

Federation of Atomic Scientists established

1946 ——— **1946** OPERATION CROSSROADS begins U.S. postwar atomic testing in Pacific

John Hersey, *Hiroshima*

One World Or None

1947 ——— **1947** Atomic Energy Commission established

Doomsday Clock announced

SANDSTONE—Pacific tests

1948 ——— 1948 David Bradley, *No Place to Hide*

Project NUTMEG

1949 ——— 1949 Joe 1—First Soviet atomic test

People's Republic of China established

1950 ——— 1950 North Korea invades South Korea

Klaus Fuchs confesses

1951 ——— 1951 Nevada Proving Grounds selected as continental atomic test site

OPERATION RANGER

OPERATION GREEN HOUSE

OPERATION BUSTER-JANGLE

1952 ——— 1952 Livermore Laboratory established

OPERATION TUMBLER-SNAPPER

OPERATION IVY

MIKE—first full-scale thermonuclear test (10.4 mt)

OPERATION HURRICANE—first U.K. atomic test

1953 ——— 1953 OPERATION UPSHOT-KNOTHOLE

1954 ——— 1954 OPERATION CASTLE-BRAVO (15 mt)

Fortunate Dragon contaminated

1955 ——— 1955 OPERATION TEAPOT

OPERATION WIGWAM

OPERATION PROJECT 56

1956 ——— 1956 REDWING

1957 ——— 1957 OPERATION PLUMBBOB

SANE founded

RAINIER—first contained underground test

HOOD—highest yield U.S. atmospheric test at NTS (74kt)

1958 ——— 1958 OPERATION HARDTACK

OPERATION ARGUS

OPERATION HARDTACK II

Temporary testing moratorium

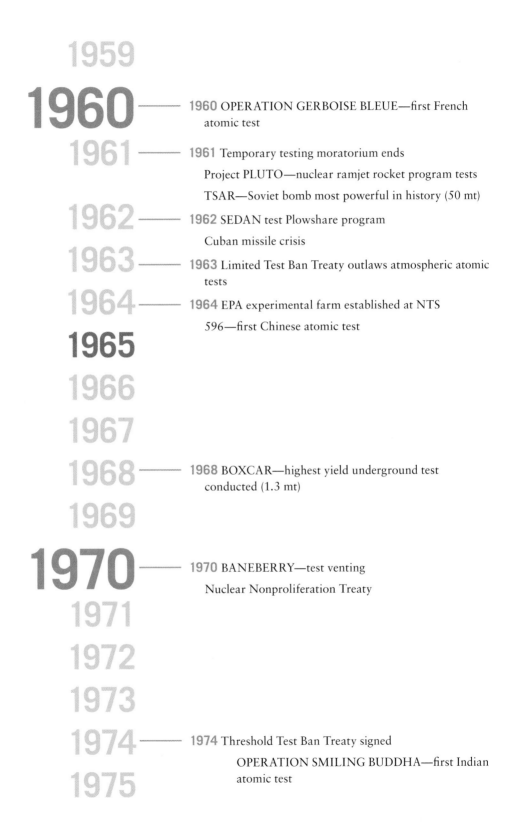

1959

1960 —— 1960 OPERATION GERBOISE BLEUE—first French atomic test

1961 —— 1961 Temporary testing moratorium ends
Project PLUTO—nuclear ramjet rocket program tests
TSAR—Soviet bomb most powerful in history (50 mt)

1962 —— 1962 SEDAN test Plowshare program
Cuban missile crisis

1963 —— 1963 Limited Test Ban Treaty outlaws atmospheric atomic tests

1964 —— 1964 EPA experimental farm established at NTS
596—first Chinese atomic test

1965

1966

1967

1968 —— 1968 BOXCAR—highest yield underground test conducted (1.3 mt)

1969

1970 —— 1970 BANEBERRY—test venting
Nuclear Nonproliferation Treaty

1971

1972

1973

1974 —— 1974 Threshold Test Ban Treaty signed
OPERATION SMILING BUDDHA—first Indian atomic test

1975

1976 ——— 1976 Peaceful Nuclear Explosions treaty signed

1977 ——— 1977 U.S. Department of Energy established

1978 ——— 1978 MX Missile program begins

1979 ——— 1979 Strategic Arms Limitation Treaty signed

1980

1981

1982 ——— 1982 Nevada Desert Experience begins annual protest program

1983 ——— 1983 KIRANA-I—first Pakistan atom test

1984

1985

1986

1987 ——— 1987 *Allen v. United States of America*

1988 ——— 1988 Largest antinuclear protests at NTS

1989 ——— 1989 Closure of Semipalatinsk Test Site

1990

1991 ——— 1991 Russian unilateral test moratorium announced
Kazakhstan independence

1992 ——— 1992 1,030th U.S. nuclear test conducted at NTS
United States approves nuclear weapons testing moratorium

1993
1994
1995
1996 ——— **1996** President Clinton signs Comprehensive Test Ban
Treaty (CTBT)

For dates and statistics on every U.S. atmospheric nuclear test, see *United States Nuclear Tests July 1945 through September 1992*, DOE/NV-209-REV 15 (December 2000).

GLOSSARY

Detailed explanations of atomic science and testing procedures, and nuclear effects may be found in Samuel Glasstone, ed., *The Effects of Nuclear Weapons* (Washington, DC: U.S. Department of Defense and U.S. AEC, April 1962).

ABSORBED DOSE: The amount of energy imparted by nuclear (or ionizing) radiation to unit mass of absorbing material. The unit is the rad. See also *dose; rad*.

AFTERWINDS: Wind currents set up in the vicinity of a nuclear explosion directed toward the burst center, resulting from the updraft accompanying the rise of the fireball.

AIR BURST: The explosion of a nuclear weapon at such a height that the expanding fireball does not touch the earth's surface when the luminosity is a maximum (in the second pulse).

ALPHA PARTICLE: A particle emitted spontaneously from the nuclei of some radioactive elements. It is identical with a helium nucleus, having a mass of four units and an electric charge of two positive units. See also *radioactivity*.

ANTHROPOCENE: A proposed term for the current geological age, from the Industrial Revolution forward, during which humanity became the dominant force of environmental change.

ATOM: The smallest (or ultimate) particle of an element that still retains the characteristics of that element. Every atom consists of a positively charged central nucleus, which carries nearly all the mass of the atom, surrounded by a number of negatively charged electrons, so that the whole system is electrically neutral.

ATOMIC BOMB (OR ATOMIC WEAPON): A term sometimes applied to a nuclear weapon utilizing fission energy only.

BACKGROUND RADIATION: Nuclear (or ionizing) radiations arising from within the body and from the surroundings to which individuals are always exposed. The main sources of the natural background radiation are potassium-40 in the body, potassium-40 and thorium, uranium, and their decay products (including radium) present in rocks and soil, and cosmic rays.

BASE SURGE: A cloud that rolls outward from the bottom of the column produced by a subsurface explosion. For underwater bursts the visible surge is, in effect, a cloud of liquid (water) droplets with the property of flowing almost as if it were a homogeneous fluid. After the water evaporates, an invisible base surge of small radioactive particles may persist. For subsurface land bursts the surge is made up of small solid particles but it still behaves like a fluid. A soft earth medium favors base surge formation in an underground burst.

BETA PARTICLE: A charged particle of very small mass emitted spontaneously from the nuclei of certain radioactive elements. Most (if not all) of the direct fission products emit (negative) beta particles. Physically, the beta particle is identical with an electron moving at high velocity.

BIOLOGICAL HALF-LIFE: The time required for the amount of a specified element that has entered the body (or a particular organ) to be decreased to half of its initial value as a result of natural, biological elimination processes.

BLAST LOADING: The loading (or force) on an object caused by the air blast from an explosion striking and flowing around the object. It is a combination of overpressure (or diffraction) and dynamic pressure (or drag) loading.

BLAST WAVE: A pulse of air in which the pressure increases sharply at the front, accompanied by winds, propagated from an explosion. See also *shock wave.*

BOOSTED FISSION WEAPON: A weapon in which neutrons produced by thermonuclear reactions serve to enhance the fission process. The thermonuclear energy represents only a small fraction of the total explosion energy. See also *fission; thermonuclear.*

BURST: Explosion or detonation.

CLEAN WEAPON: One in which measures have been taken to reduce the amount of residual radioactivity relative to a "normal" weapon of the same energy yield.

CLOUD COLUMN: The visible column of weapon debris (and possibly dust and water droplets) extending upward from the point of burst of a nuclear (or atomic) weapon. See also *radioactive cloud.*

CONTAINED UNDERGROUND BURST: An underground detonation at such a depth that none of the radioactive residues escape through the surface of the ground.

CONTAMINATION: The deposit of radioactive material on the surfaces of structures, areas, objects, or personnel, following a nuclear (or atomic) explosion. This material generally consists of fallout in which fission products and other weapon debris have become incorporated with particles of dirt, and so on. Contamination can also arise from the radioactivity induced in certain substances by the action of neutrons from a nuclear explosion. See also *decontamination; fallout.*

CONTINGENCY: A future event or circumstance that is possible but cannot be predicted with certainty.

CRATER: The pit, depression, or cavity formed in the surface of the earth by a surface or underground explosion. Crater formation can occur by vaporization of the surface material, by the scouring effect of air blast, by throw-out of disturbed material, or by subsidence. In general, the major mechanism changes from one to the next with increasing depth of burst. The apparent crater is the depression which is seen after the burst; it is smaller than the true crater (i.e., the cavity actually formed by the explosion), because it is covered with a layer of loose earth, rock, and so on.

CURIE: A unit of radioactivity; it is the activity of a quantity of any radioactive species in which 3.700×10^{10} nuclear disintegrations occur per second. The *gamma curie* is sometimes defined correspondingly as the activity of material in which this number of gamma-ray photons are emitted per second.

DECAY (OR RADIOACTIVE DECAY): The decrease in activity of any radioactive material with the passage of time due to the spontaneous emission from the atomic nuclei of either alpha or beta particles, sometimes accompanied by gamma radiation. See also *radioactivity.*

DECONTAMINATION: The reduction or removal of contaminating radioactive material from a structure, area, object, or person. Decontamination may be accomplished by (1) treating the surface so as to remove or decrease the contamination; (2) letting the material stand so that the radioactivity is decreased as a result of natural decay; or (3) covering the contamination so as to attenuate the radiation emitted. Radioactive material removed in process (1) must be disposed of by burial on land or at sea, or in other suitable ways.

DESERT: A dry, barren area of land, especially one covered with sand, that is characteristically desolate, waterless, and without vegetation. Also called *wasteland.*

DOSE: A (total or accumulated) quantity of ionizing (or nuclear) radiation. The *absorbed dose* in rads represents the amount of energy absorbed from the radiation per gram of specified absorbing material. In soft body tissue the absorbed dose in rads is essentially equal to the exposure in roentgens. The biological dose (also called the *RBE dose*) in rems is a measure of biological effectiveness of the absorbed radiation. See also *exposure; rad; rem; roentgen.*

DOSE RATE: As a general rule, the amount of ionizing (or nuclear) radiation that an individual or material would receive per unit of time. It is usually expressed as rads (or rems) per hour or in multiples or submultiples of these units, such as millirads per hour. The dose rate is commonly used to indicate the level of radioactivity in a contaminated area.

DOSIMETER: An instrument for measuring and registering the total accumulated dose of (or exposure to) ionizing radiations. Instruments worn or carried by individuals are called *personnel dosimeters.*

DOSIMETRY: The theory and application of the principles and techniques involved in the measurement and recording of radiation doses and dose rates. Its practical aspect is concerned with the use of various types of radiation instruments with which measurements are made. See also *dosimeter.*

DYNAMIC PRESSURE: The air pressure that results from the mass air flow (or wind) behind the shock front of a blast wave. It is equal to the product of half the density of the air through which the blast wave passes and the square of the particle (or wind) velocity behind the shock front as it impinges on the object or structure.

ELEMENT: One of the distinct, basic varieties of matter occurring in nature that, individually or in combination, compose substances of all kinds. Approximately ninety different elements are known to exist in nature, and several others, including plutonium, have been obtained as a result of nuclear reactions with these elements.

EXPOSURE: A measure expressed in roentgens of the ionization produced by gamma (or X-) rays in air. The *exposure rate* is the exposure per unit time (e.g., roentgens per hour). See also *dose, dose rate; roentgen.*

FALLOUT: The process or phenomenon of the descent to the earth's surface of particles contaminated with radioactive material from the radioactive cloud. The term is also applied in a collective sense to the contaminated particulate matter itself. The *early (or local) fallout* is defined, somewhat arbitrarily, as those particles which reach the earth within twenty-four hours after a nuclear explosion. The *delayed (or worldwide) fallout* consists of the smaller particles that ascend into the upper troposphere and into the stratosphere and are carried by winds to all parts of the earth. The delayed fallout is brought to Earth, mainly by rain and snow, over extended periods ranging from months to years.

FIREBALL: The luminous sphere of hot gases that forms a few millionths of a second after a nuclear (or atomic) explosion as the result of the absorption by the surrounding medium of the thermal X-rays emitted by the extremely hot (several tens of million degrees) weapon residues. The exterior of the fireball in air is initially sharply defined by the luminous shock front and later by the limits of the hot gases themselves (radiation front).

FISSION: The process whereby the nucleus of a particular heavy element splits into (generally) two nuclei of lighter elements, with the release of substantial amounts of energy. The most important *fissionable materials* are uranium-235 and plutonium 239; fission is caused by the absorption of neutrons.

FISSION PRODUCTS: A general term for the complex mixture of substances produced as a result of nuclear fission. A distinction should be made between these and the *direct fission products* or *fission fragments*, which are formed by the actual splitting of the heavy-element nuclei. Something like eighty different fission fragments result from roughly forty different modes of fission of a given nuclear species (e.g., uranium-235 or plutonium-239). The fission fragments, being radioactive, immediately begin to decay, forming additional (daughter) products, with the result that the complex mixture of fission products so formed contains over 300 different isotopes of thirty-six elements.

FLASH BURN: A burn caused by excessive exposure (of bare skin) to thermal radiation. See also *thermal radiation.*

FUSION: The process whereby the nuclei of light elements, especially those of the isotopes of hydrogen—namely, deuterium and tritium—combine to form the nucleus of a heavier element with the release of substantial amounts of energy. See also *thermonuclear.*

GAMMA RAYS (OR RADIATIONS): Electromagnetic radiations of high photon energy originating in atomic nuclei and accompanying many nuclear reactions (e.g., fission, radioactivity, and neutron capture). Physically, gamma rays are identical with X-rays of high energy, the only essential difference being that X-rays do not originate from atomic nuclei, but are produced in other ways (e.g., by slowing down [fast] electrons of high energy).

GENETIC EFFECT: The effect of various agents (including nuclear radiation) in producing changes (mutations) in the hereditary components (genes) of the germ cells present in the reproductive organs (gonads). A mutant gene causes changes in the next generation that may or may not be apparent.

GROUND ZERO: The point on the surface of land vertically below or above the center of a burst of a nuclear (or atomic) weapon; frequently abbreviated to GZ. For a burst over or under water, the corresponding term is *surface zero* (SZ). Surface zero is also commonly used for ground surface and underground bursts.

HALF-LIFE: See *biological half-life.*

H-BOMB: See *hydrogen bomb.*

HEIGHT OF BURST: The height above the earth's surface at which a bomb is detonated in the air. The *optimum height* of burst for a particular target (or area) is that at which it is estimated a weapon of a specified energy yield will produce a certain desired effect over the maximum possible area.

HOT SPOT: Region in a contaminated area in which the level of radioactive contamination is somewhat greater than in neighboring regions in the area. See also *contamination.*

HYDROGEN BOMB (OR HYDROGEN WEAPON): A term sometimes applied to nuclear weapons in which part of the explosive energy is obtained from nuclear fusion (or thermonuclear) reactions. See also *fusion; thermonuclear.*

INITIAL NUCLEAR RADIATION: Nuclear radiation (essentially neutrons and gamma rays) emitted from the fireball and the cloud column during the first minute after a nuclear (or atomic) explosion. The time limit of one minute is set, somewhat arbitrarily, as that required for the source of part of the radiations (fission products, etc., in the radioactive cloud) to attain such a height that only insignificant amounts of radiation reach the earth's surface. See also *residual nuclear radiation.*

INTENSITY: The amount or energy of any radiation incident upon (or flowing through) unit area, perpendicular to the radiation beam, in unit time. The intensity of thermal radiation is generally expressed in calories per square centimeter per second falling on a given surface at any specified instant. As applied to nuclear radiation, the term *intensity* is sometimes used, rather loosely, to express the exposure (or dose) rate at a given location.

INTERNAL RADIATION: Nuclear radiation (alpha and beta particles and gamma radiation) resulting from radioactive substances in the body. Important sources are iodine-131 in the thyroid gland, and strontium-90 and plutonium-239 in bone.

ISOTOPES: Forms of the same element having identical chemical properties but differing in their atomic masses (due to different numbers of neutrons in their respective nuclei) and in their nuclear properties (e.g., radioactivity, fission). For example, hydrogen has three isotopes, with masses of 1 (hydrogen), 2 (deuterim), and 3 (tritium) units, respectively. The first two of these are stable (nonradioactive), but the third (tritium) is a radioactive isotope. Both of the common isotopes of uranium, with masses of 235 and 238 units, respectively, are radioactive, emitting alpha particles, but their half-lives are different. Furthermore, uranium-235 is fissionable by neutrons of all energies, but uranium-238 will undergo fission only with neutrons of high energy.

KILOTON ENERGY: Defined strictly as 10^{12} calories (or 4.2×10^{19} ergs). This is approximately the amount of energy that would be released by the explosion of 1 kiloton (1,000 tons) of TNT. See also *TNT equivalent.*

MEGATON ENERGY: Defined strictly as 10^{15} calories (or 4.2×10^{22} ergs). This is approximately the amount of energy that would be released by the explosion of 1,000 kilotons (1,000,000 tons) of TNT. See also *TNT equivalent.*

MONITORING: The procedure or operation of locating and measuring radioactive contamination by means of survey instruments which can detect and measure (as dose rates) ionizing radiations. The individual performing the operation is called a *monitor.*

NEUTRON: A neutral particle (i.e., with no electrical charge) of approximately unit mass, present in all atomic nuclei, except those of ordinary (light) hydrogen. Neutrons are required to initiate the fission process, and large numbers of neutrons are produced by both fission and fusion reactions in nuclear (or atomic) explosions.

NUCLEAR RADIATION: Particulate and electromagnetic radiation emitted from atomic nuclei in various nuclear processes. The important nuclear radiations, from a weapons standpoint, are alpha and beta particles, gamma rays, and neutrons. All nuclear radiations are ionizing radiations, but the reverse is not true: X-rays, for example, are included among ionizing radiations, but they are not nuclear radiations since they do not originate from atomic nuclei

RAD: A unit of absorbed dose of radiation; it represents the absorption of 100 ergs of nuclear (or ionizing) radiation per gram of absorbing material, such as body tissue.

RADIOACTIVE (OR NUCLEAR) CLOUD: An all-inclusive term for the cloud of hot gases, smoke, dust, and other particulate matter from the weapon itself and from the environment, which is carried aloft in conjunction with the rising fireball produced by the detonation of a nuclear (or atomic) weapon.

RADIOACTIVITY: The spontaneous emission of radiation, generally alpha or beta particles, often accompanied by gamma rays, from the nuclei of an (unstable) isotope. As a result of this emission the radioactive isotope is converted (or decays) into the isotope of a different (daughter) element that may (or may not) also be radioactive. Ultimately, as a result of one or more stages of radioactive decay, a stable (nonradioactive) end product is formed. See also *isotopes*.

REM: A unit of biological dose of radiation; the name is derived from the initial letters of the term "roentgen equivalent man (or mammal)." The number of rems of radiation is equal to the number of rads absorbed multiplied by the RBE of the given radiation (for a specified effect). The rem is also the unit of dose equivalent, which is equal to the product of the number of rads absorbed and the "quality factor" of the radiation. See also *dose, rad*.

RESIDUAL NUCLEAR RADIATION: Nuclear radiation, chiefly beta particles and gamma rays, which persists for some time following a nuclear (or atomic) explosion. The radiation is emitted mainly by the fission products and other bomb residues in the fallout, and to some extent by earth and water constituents, and other materials, in which radioactivity has been induced by the capture of neutrons. See also *fallout, initial nuclear radiation*.

ROENTGEN: A unit of exposure to gamma (or X-) radiation. It is defined precisely as the quantity of gamma (or X-) rays that will produce electrons (in ion pairs) with a total charge of 2.58×10^{-4} coulomb in 1 kilogram of dry air. An exposure of 1 roentgen results in the deposition of about 94 ergs of energy in 1 gram of soft body tissue. Hence, an exposure of 1 roentgen is approximately equivalent to an absorbed dose of 1 rad in soft tissue. See also *dose; rad*.

SHOCK WAVE: A continuously propagated pressure pulse (or wave) in the surrounding medium that may be air, water, or earth, initiated by the expansion of the hot gases produced in an explosion. A shock wave in air is generally referred to as a *blast wave*, because it resembles and is accompanied by strong, but transient, winds. The duration of a shock (or blast) wave is distinguished by two phases. First there is the *positive (compression) phase* during which the pressure rises very sharply to a value that is higher than ambient and then decreases rapidly to the ambient pressure. The positive phase for the dynamic pressure is somewhat longer than for overpressure, due to the momentum of the moving air behind the shock front. The duration of the positive phase increases and the maximum (peak) pressure decreases with increasing distance from an explosion of given energy yield. In the second phase, the *negative (suction, rarefaction, or tension) phase*, the pressure falls below ambient and then returns to the ambient value. The duration of the negative phase may be several times the duration of the positive phase. Deviations from the ambient pressure during the negative phase are never large and they decrease with increasing distance from the explosion. See also *dynamic pressure*.

SURFACE BURST: The explosion of a nuclear (or atomic) weapon at the surface of the land or water at a height above the surface less than the radius of the fireball at maximum luminosity (in the second thermal pulse). An explosion in which the weapon is detonated actually on the surface (or within $5 W^{0.3}$ feet, where W is the explosion yield in kilotons, above or below the surface) is called a *contact surface burst* or a *true surface burst*. See also *air burst*.

SYNDROME, RADIATION: The complex of symptoms characterizing the disease known as *radiation injury*, resulting from excessive exposure of the whole (or a large part) of the body to ionizing radiation. The earliest of these symptoms are nausea, vomiting, and diarrhea, which may be followed by loss of hair (epilation), hemorrhage, inflammation of the mouth and throat, and general loss of energy. In severe cases, where the radiation exposure has been relatively large, death may occur within two to four weeks. Those who survive six weeks after the receipt of a single dose of radiation may generally be expected to recover.

THERMAL RADIATION: Electromagnetic radiation emitted (in two pulses from an air burst) from a fireball as a consequence of its very high temperature; it consists essentially of ultraviolet, visible, and infrared radiations. In the early stages (first pulse of an air burst), when the temperature of the fireball is extremely high, the ultraviolet radiation predominates; in the second pulse, the temperatures are lower and most of the thermal radiation lies in the visible and infrared regions of the spectrum. For high-altitude bursts (above 100,000 feet), the thermal radiation is emitted as a single pulse, which is of short duration below about 270,000 feet but increases at greater burst heights.

THERMONUCLEAR: An adjective referring to the process (or processes) in which very high temperatures are used to bring about the fusion of light nuclei, such as those of the hydrogen isotopes (deuterium and tritium), with the accompanying liberation of energy. A *thermonuclear bomb* is a weapon in which part of the explosion energy results from thermonuclear fusion reactions. The high temperatures required are obtained by means of a fission explosion. See also *fusion*.

TNT EQUIVALENT: A measure of the energy released in the detonation of a nuclear (or atomic) weapon, or in the explosion of a given quantity of fissionable material, expressed in terms of the mass of TNT that would release the same amount of energy when exploded. The TNT equivalent is usually stated in kilotons or megatons. The basis of the TNT equivalence is that the explosion of 1 ton of TNT is assumed to release 10^9 calories of energy. See also *kiloton energy; megaton energy; yield.*

UNDERGROUND BURST: The explosion of a nuclear (or atomic) weapon with its center more than 5 $W^{0.3}$ feet, where W is the explosion yield in kilotons, beneath the surface of the ground. See also *contained underground burst.*

UNDERWATER BURST: The explosion of a nuclear (or atomic) weapon with its center beneath the surface of the water.

YIELD (OR ENERGY YIELD): The total effective energy released in a nuclear (or atomic) explosion. It is usually expressed in terms of the equivalent tonnage of TNT required to produce the same energy release in an explosion. The total energy yield is manifested as nuclear radiation, thermal radiation, and shock (or blast) energy, the actual distribution being dependent upon the medium in which the explosion occurs (primarily) and also upon the type of weapon and the time after detonation. See also *TNT equivalent.*